2.00

P9-EEC-523

Natural Foods Cookbook

Natural Foods Cookbook

Vegetarian Dairy-Free Cuisine

by

Mary Estella

Japan Publications, Inc.

Tokyo · New York

©1985 by Mary Estella
Photographs by Eric Roth
Cover design by Susan Ragsdale

Published by
JAPAN PUBLICATIONS, INC., Tokyo and New York

Distributors:
UNITED STATES: *Kodansha America, Inc. through Farrar, Straus & Giroux, 19 Union Square West, New York 10003.* CANADA: *Fitzhenry & Whiteside Ltd., 91 Granton Drive, Richmond Hill, Ontario, L4B 2N5.* BRITISH ISLES AND EUROPEAN CONTINENT: *Premier Book Marketing Ltd., 1 Gower Street, London WC1E 6HA.* AUSTRALIA AND NEW ZEALAND: *Bookwise International, 54 Critenden Road, Findon, South Australia 5023.* THE FAR EAST AND JAPAN: *Japan Publications Trading Co., Ltd., 1–2–1, Sarugaku-cho, Chiyoda-ku, Tokyo 101.*

First edition: April 1985
Seventh printing: August 1992

LCCC 84–080647
ISBN 0–87040–583–7
Printed in U.S.A.

Foreword

I began teaching cooking in New York in 1960, and after we moved to Boston in 1964, I taught macrobiotic cooking classes regularly. Later my husband, Michio, and I established the Kushi Institute as a place for the education of future leaders of macrobiotics.

Soon after we established the Kushi Institute, Mary Estella came to study. She was a unique student. Some of the students had professional cooking experience, but her devotion was exceptional. I frequently asked her to speak to the class about her cooking experience, techniques and skills.

In the early days, whenever there was a party in the community I would stay up all night to prepare food for it. Of course, I enjoyed it but my cooking is really day-to-day family cooking. Mary, along with her friends, took over the party preparations, especially when guests came to town. She made beautiful presentations and party dishes of delicious macrobiotic meals. It was a great joy to see our many friends appreciate her talents and how gracefully she prepared food.

After graduating from the Kushi Institute, she started to cook at the staff cafeteria at Erewhon, our natural foods company, which had approximately 160 employees. Of course, the staff enjoyed the food, but I think this was also an important time in which Mary really developed her understanding of whole natural foods. Many of our friends tried her wonderful recipes and commented on how much they enjoyed her food.

I am very happy to see that her book has materialized and that many friends can benefit. I hope that all the readers will feel the tremendous energy and devotion that she has.

AVELINE KUSHI
Brookline, MA
May 3, 1984

Acknowledgments————————

I wish to express my gratitude to my mother whose joy and adventurous, creative flair in the kitchen inspired me to cook, and to my father, whose dedicated career as a musician instilled faith in me to express and pursue my dream.

Thanks to all my teachers who influenced my thinking and cooking through classes or books, beginning with the great chefs of Europe—whose traditions have been passed down and adapted. Thanks to Annemarie Colbin, William Dufty, Michio and Aveline Kushi, Helen and Scott Nearing, William and Akiko Shurtleff, Peter Matthiessen, Saul Miller, Masanobu Fukuoka, Karin Stephan and Francis Moore Lappé.

My thanks goes out to Ilana Wagner, who cheerfully typed and retyped the entire manuscript, Lorraine Estella, my sister-in-law, for endless hours typing and retesting recipes, Rhoda Schalmm and Muriel Mannos for careful editing of recipes, Beverly Klayman and Anne-Marie Zwierzyna for tireless editing and help in reorganizing material, Ann Rawley for loving advice and support during the final stages, Eric Roth for the beautiful photographs and to Susan Ragsdale for designing the book cover.

Thanks to all my friends from around the world who shared their delicious regional recipes with me while cooking together—giving this book an international flavor. My dear friends Joan and Tom were always there to share meals and take short holidays to the mountains and ocean, away from the stove and the typewriter.

A special thanks to Lynne Paterson Davis for our years of cooking, teaching and writing together. Her energy, enthusiasm, insight, advice and support were integral in planning this book and seeing it to completion.

Thanks to the farmers, distributors and retailers who bring healthful whole foods to the stores. To the publishers and editors of magazines and books that provide us with information and articles to make conscious choices in food selection and preparation. Finally, a sincere thanks to my family, relatives and neighbors for their prayers and constant encouragement. Thanks to you all, I hope you enjoy this book.

M. E.

1   2   3   4

5   6   7   8   9   10   11

12   13   14   15

16

17

18

19   20   21

22   23

24   25   26   27   28

29

30   31   32

33

34

35
—
36

37

38

39

40   41   42

Contents

12

6. Vegetables, 113

Introduction

The kitchen was the heart of our home. During my New England childhood, Mom delighted us with country-style cooking from her French-Canadian background. She greeted us with spicy, hot muffins and warming cereals in the mornings, brightened with her smile and a bustle of activity. Hearty vegetable soups and homemade breads were among our staples. Weekend trips in the station wagon to nearby farms were treasured experiences. We'd pick luscious strawberries in the spring, golden corn and blueberries in summer, apples and pumpkins in the fall. At home with our bounty, my mother would transform the bushels of ripe fruits and vegetables into shortcakes, pies, crisps and jack-o'-lanterns.

While other kids on the block were making mud pies, I was turning out the real thing, with a little help from my mom. With her patience and encouragement I was kneading bread dough and mixing cake batters. Before long we were a team, baking thousands of cookies for Christmas presents and catering get-togethers. These cooking experiences were magical, enhancing the special feelings of family reunions.

High school years are a time for experimenting and fitting in with the crowd. My friends, budding artists who fancied themselves vegetarians, persuaded me to try yoghurt and alfalfa sprouts, which I found unappealing at the time. In an attempt to expand my culinary horizons, they lent me Frances Moore Lappé's *Diet for a Small Planet* and other natural food cookbooks. My repertoire grew to include broccoli quiche, mushroom pizza and cheesecakes, which I served at our teenage parties.

When high school came to an end, I packed a bag and headed to Europe to visit museums, cathedrals and castles. Arriving in Paris, I wandered down cobblestone streets, passing pastry shops bursting with fruit-filled tarts and colorful confections. As I lingered in sidewalk cafés instead of the Louvre, I scribbled postcards home, describing in detail the delicacy of croissants and sweet tarts. On morning excursions to local markets I soon discovered that the joys of food crossed all barriers of language and nationality.

In Athens, black olives and juicy tomatoes were offered for sampling in shaded stalls, protected from blazing skies; on a drizzly Oslo morning, a smiling vendor handed me slivers of smoked salmon for approval. In every country I would buy local vegetables and, with instructions in sign language from shopkeepers, I'd attempt to recreate the regional specialties. After a year of food-related jobs in various countries, I headed home to apply my artistic interests to cooking—professionally.

Determined to benefit from its comprehensive curriculum, I enrolled at the Culinary Institute of America in New York, quietly planning to develop my own style of wholesome cuisine. Chefs from all over the world taught us their native fare—from Chinese stir-fry to fabulous French sauces. In daytime kitchen courses we sliced, sautéed and souffléed, learning techniques of traditional cooking as well as contemporary nouvelle cuisine. We covered the basics of bookkeeping and restaurant management as well. In this school it was popular to serve exotic, elaborately prepared food to an exclusive audience, at exorbitant prices, but I couldn't help asking, why not feed everyone simply and economically?

During the evenings I explored the Institute's famous library. Each aisle featured cookbooks from a different country and period. I was consistently drawn to the nutrition and natural foods section. Here I came across *The Findhorn Cookbook* by Barbara Friedlander, which describes the kitchen of a spiritual community in Scotland. Rodale's *Natural Foods Cookbook* and William Shurtleff's *Book of Tofu* also supplied me with plenty of food for thought.

After a morning baking class, *Sugar Blues* caught my eye in the library. William Dufty's statistics had the sobering effect of a cold shower. Acknowledging my own case of sugar blues, with its high-low energy cycles, I vowed to cut down and eventually cut out sugar from my diet. Eliminating it while in culinary school would have been a feat for *The Guinness Book of World Records*! Intent on shedding those few pounds that I had accepted as part of being a chef, I made my classes an exercise of willpower. I planned to make sugar-free variations of my favorite desserts.

Conscious of the prevalent overconsumption of sugar, I lamented the haphazardness of my vegetarian diet. Tropical fruits and salads left me shivering on the ski slopes. How much cottage cheese and omelettes could I eat? At this time, Nancy, a fellow student and vegetarian, suggested that I base my diet on whole grains, beans and vegetables, and avoid dairy foods altogether. Her suggestions made sense to me. From my study of food in history I knew that grains had adequately and healthfully fed civilizations for centuries. It wasn't until whole grains began to be milled and refined, losing much of their life-giving force, that they also lost their place as our central, primary foods.

Nancy lent me a copy of *East West Journal* that featured the article "Is Milk a Natural?" After whipping mountains of cream and beating thousands of eggs, it was a relief to eliminate these ingredients. I learned that dairy foods are not needed for protein or calcium—soy foods and green vegetables are just two of many sources of these essential nutrients. When I heard that dairy foods are believed to be a contributing factor in degenerative diseases and obesity, I had another incentive to change my diet.

My way of eating was transformed when I graduated from the culinary school and returned home to study at the Kushi Institute in Boston. During cooking classes taught by experienced teachers, the principles of eating in harmony with nature were presented. Intriguing international foods—miso, tamari, and adzuki beans from Japan; tempeh from Indonesia; tahini from the Middle East—all sparked my imagination. Here was a wealth of color, taste and texture I had never experienced. I found these foods to be not only health-supporting—many have medicinal properties—but also delicious. Umeboshi plums, a condiment from the Orient, soon became my favorite seasoning. Kuzu, a starch similar to arrowroot, makes velvety sauces in minutes—no more time-consuming butter and flour thickeners for me! Agar-agar, a sea vegetable, could create exquisite gelatins without products of animal origin.

Gradually I learned to appreciate the unique benefits and delicate flavors of many healthful foods. I continued my training with experienced macrobiotic chefs and was given the chance to cook for the employees of Erewhon Natural Foods. Supervising the employees' cafeteria was the perfect opportunity to combine my culinary background with macrobiotic principles.

This conscious change in diet has blessed my family and myself with good health and boundless energy. Our lifestyle allows time for yoga, swimming and outdoor sports, as food is not the only key to health. I find the ritual of sharing meals with friends or family—especially wholesome natural foods—nourishes the spirit as well as the body.

A smooth transition to whole foods is possible when one gratefully accepts successes and failures in the kitchen, freely blending available ingredients with basic skills. Good humor, and appealing artful presentations, have also helped me to introduce unusual foods to hundreds of people.

The crossroads in my cooking career came during my training to be a gourmet chef. I began to choose and prepare whole foods that enable everyone to enjoy variety and good health. This cookbook is a result of my desire to blend the sensual qualities of food with a sensible approach to well-being.

1. Getting Started

My kitchen shelves are lined with international cookbooks, ranging from those specializing in the vegetarian dishes of yoga teachers to the ultimate gourmet cuisine of the chef of chefs, Escoffier. When I chose to center my diet on whole foods, the staples in my pantry changed, but my cookbooks continued to offer sources of inspiration. You don't have to throw out your cookbooks with the sugar bowl. Learn to read your cookbooks with new eyes, looking for ideas and techniques, not just ingredients. Most of your favorite recipes are adaptable to whole foods cookery.

The recipes in this book were gleaned from my years as cook at the employees' cafeteria at Erewhon. There we had high-quality whole foods, and a crew of hungry enthusiastic workers who were eager to be part of our culinary creations and experiments. We learned from trial and error which dishes were crowd pleasers and which weren't. An international group of employees encouraged us to cook their traditional foods: red beans and rice Caribbean style, Indonesian tempeh dishes and everyone's favorite—pizza!

In Boston, I catered with the best natural foods chefs and taught many cooking classes. My recipe file overflowed with a wealth of material, enough for several books. Over the past year these recipes were retested on my family, who all have healthy New England appetites. After sampling the day's recipes, everyone would offer comments and support, all of which were invaluable.

The additional information included with each recipe is intended both to help novice cooks become familiar with basic skills and to inspire seasoned chefs to adapt recipes to their repertoire. When starting out, most cooks have questions about timing and substitution of ingredients. I hope the comments, variations and menu suggestions with each recipe will benefit your meal planning.

How to Use the Recipes

The *time* stated is an average for completing each dish, from start to finish. Many grain and bean dishes need only a few moments of preparation time, and one hour or more unattended cooking. Some dishes, such as polenta or French-style onion soup, need to be stirred often.

The *quantity* each recipe makes is indicated in serving sizes for a family of four to six, or in terms of what the recipe yields: 2 cups, or a dozen muffins.

The *equipment* list provided is a suggested guide. What's important here is for you to use flexibility and imagination. For example, when a recipe calls for puréeing a sauce in a blender, you may use a food mill or a suribachi, a Japanese mixing bowl. The consistency will be different, but such differences often create new dishes. If you don't have a cookie tray, a large baking pan will work. Bread or loaf pans can stand in for muffin tins, making muffin "bread." My favorite way to bake corn bread is in a black cast-iron skillet, to be served warm at the table.

The *variations* are included merely to inspire your own. No two cooks will follow a recipe without interpreting it their own way. Don't feel you have to run out to buy certain ingredients, unless a recipe calls for something that has no substitute, such as baking powder to make a cake. It's a good idea to record any changes you make in a new recipe for future reference. Keep a notebook in the kitchen for this purpose.

Salt, spices and herbs are a matter of personal choice. Some may find these recipes need more salt, others may omit any spices. Please, season to your own taste!

The *menu suggestions* offer my ideas for combining recipes. They are not necessarily meant as complete, unchangeable menus, but serve to illustrate balance. For example, a bean soup is paired with a grain entrée. A golden corn chowder may be served with a lentil casserole or tofu sandwich. A vegetable-miso soup is a suitable prelude to any meal. Pickles and desserts are not always included in menu ideas. I generally serve a light fruit kanten with a filling meal, or a rich raisin and rice pudding with a main course salad or light noodle dinner. I do mention greens or salad with most menus. Since they are seasonal foods, you will vary them, choosing what is fresh and local. So please, use the menus as a flexible guide.

Cooking for one or two people. To cook for yourself or just one other person can be frustrating at times. The recipes in most cookbooks, including this one, are written for 4 to 6 persons. Fortunately, whole foods cookery lends itself to cooking in either small or large amounts, so equip your kitchen with a collection of 1 quart pots that are small enough to cook 1 or 2 cups of grain. You will also need another 2-quart pot for soup or beans, and a 4-quart pot for steaming or boiling vegetables. A steamer basket and skillet or wok complete your kitchen.

Look for containers for storing cooked food that are made of glass, ceramic or stainless steel; never store food in aluminum. Cooked grains and beans can be stored for two to three days in the refrigerator, if covered tightly. I store meal-sized portions in Corningware dishes that go from the refrigerator to the stove to the table; they save a lot of time and dishwashing.

Some people, like me, are content to make a large pot of soup or stew and enjoy it for two or three meals. If you like more variety in your meals, cook grains and beans separately and make infinite variations with portions of each. You can make salads, stir-frys, croquettes or burgers, to name a few variations.

When cooking for small groups, shop three to four times a week. Buy small amounts of perishables for that day's meals. It's discouraging to throw away good food because there wasn't time to cook it.

Meals taste better when shared. So invite friends over and share the cooking and conversation. It's interesting to eat other people's food on occasion. It provides inspiration and contrast with your own home-cooked meals.

Whole Foods ──────────────────

My grandfather used to say, "To cook corn, boil a pot of water, and then run to the field to pick it." Swift of foot, my mother and her long-legged sisters were given the chore to run and pick corn while the big black kettle came to a boil on the stove.

On many occasions, my mother has recounted to me with relish the abundant meals that nourished her large family. Platters were piled high with corn, juicy tomatoes still warm from the vine, and some pan-fried fish if one of her brothers shirked his farm work to go fishing. Dinner was completed with glass bowls of sliced peaches and blackberries topped with fresh cream.

On their farm, my grandmother canned tomatoes, made sweet jams, pressed apples for cider and filled ceramic crocks with shredded cabbage sprinkled with salt for sauerkraut. Each morning my grandmother baked six loaves of bread. My aunts rotated the chore of churning butter from the sweet milk of Buttercup, the family's cow.

Throughout history people have transformed their harvests into meals using the elements of salt, fire or sunlight. Native Americans dried corn, then ground it into meal for bread or tortillas. In the fall they dried fruit, vegetables and fish. European settlers arrived with their methods of preservation, and pickles, yoghurt, cheese, beer and wine were among their favorite foods. For centuries in Asia, soybeans and grains were skillfully made into miso, shoyu, vinegar and saké. These original natural foods were made from home grown, whole foods.

Today, many natural foods are made commercially, the food companies following with integrity the recipes and techniques passed down from generation to generation. This book emphasizes whole grains and beans, along with many foods naturally produced from these ingredients, such as tofu, tahini and kuzu. You won't find here an elaborate nutritional analysis of these foods or specific dietary recommendations. Many excellent books on these subjects are readily available; bibliographical references are provided at the end of this book.

The whole foods described here were not only familiar to our grandparents but sustained civilizations for millenia. The art of preparing simple food offers us a return to health and vitality. Vegetarian cuisine draws on, and incorporates, the best of all traditional fare from around the world.

Whole Grains ──────────────────

Rice: The principal food of India, Japan, Indonesia, parts of the Caribbean and elsewhere. Rice is also one of America's largest food crops, grown in California, Louisiana and Arkansas. Most rice eaten today is polished, thus lacking the fiber, protein and vitamins found in the bran. Natural brown rice is unpolished and comes complete with the bran and germ. There are hundreds of varieties of rice—five types are described below.

Short Grain Brown Rice: A small, oval-shaped grain. This hearty rice is best for a temperate or cool climate.

Medium Grain Brown Rice: An excellent year round grain. It's not as hearty as short grain, but very substantial and readily available.

Long Grain Brown Rice: The lightest and fluffiest brown rice. Closest to white rice in texture, it is a good choice for people just beginning to make the switch to whole foods. It is a perfect grain for warmer weather. Short, medium and long grain brown rice can be interchanged in these recipes.

Glutinous Brown Rice: Also known as "sweet rice," this variety of brown rice is delicious cooked with other grains or beans. Popular in Japanese cuisine, its natural sweetness lends itself to desserts, rice pudding and two Japanese "sweet rice" foods: amasake and mochi.

Wild Rice: This is actually a cereal, native to the Great Lakes region in the United States. It is still hand-harvested by Native Americans. Wild rice has been a gourmet item because of its exquisite, nutty flavor and unusual dark brown color. Due to its expense, I recommend you use it in combination with other grains. For example, add 1/4 cup wild rice to 1 cup brown rice.

Barley: The most ancient of all grains, it is said to have been the choice of the Greek gods. Readily available in most supermarkets, it is good in stews and soups, or as a hot cereal sweetened with dried fruits.

Buckwheat: This hearty "grass" from Russia is also known as kasha. It can be bought as roasted or unroasted groats. If unroasted, it is tastier dry-roasted before cooking. A quick-cooking grain with an earthy flavor, buckwheat has been traditionally prepared as a hot cereal, shaped into croquettes and deep-fried, or wrapped in dough as knishes.

Corn: A grain native to North and South America. In ancient times, corn grew in many varieties: red, blue, white and, of course, popcorn. This is one grain that is usually eaten fresh picked in the fall. Dried corn, the staple of Native Americans, is most often ground into flour for tortillas, corn bread, polenta or corn muffins.

Millet: A tiny, round, golden grain that feeds millions in China and India. Millet is a versatile grain. It cooks up fluffy and can be seasoned and fried as croquettes or simmered long and slow with vegetables and spices.

Oats: The indigenous grain of the British Isles. We know it best in its quick-cooking variations, as rolled oats (oatmeal) or cracked (steel-cut) oats. Whole oats are a warming winter grain, or can be enjoyed all year. The outer bran of whole oats requires 2 to 3 hours of cooking to soften and turn into creamy porridges and soups.

Rye: The northern grain of Scandinavia and Europe. Rye is usually ground into flour and combined with other more glutinous grains in baking crisp, flat bread and other whole grain breads. Whole rye berries can be soaked overnight and cooked either alone or as a chewy addition to rice pilafs.

Wheat: Probably the most versatile of all grains, it is primarily ground into flour for breads or noodles. Whole wheat berries can be soaked and cooked as a whole grain. In the Middle East, whole wheat is cracked for quicker cooking or made into bulghur or couscous. Wheat is also sprouted and used in bread baking.

Noodles: A quick-cooking, easily digestible form of grain. Traditionally, they were made from wheat. Today they are also available in buckwheat, corn or rice as well as artichoke, spinach and mung bean varieties.

Seitan: Wheat gluten, also known as "wheat meat" in America. This is a wheat product, developed long ago in the Orient. High in protein and used as a meat substitute, seitan has found a place in vegetarian cooking today. Making seitan at home is an easy but time-consuming process. It can, however, be purchased fresh or frozen at natural foods stores.

Beans

Adzuki Beans: A small, shiny, red bean favored in Japan and China for its flavor and strengthening qualities. This bean combines well with squash, onion and kombu. Cook it into a thick bean dish or use in "dahl" recipes. Adzuki beans are natural companions for rice and millet.

Black Turtle Beans: A staple of South American fare. Black beans are traditionally cooked with spices and garlic and served with rice or corn.

Black Soybeans: Distinct from our American black bean in shape, texture and taste, this is a type of soybean. They are available in Oriental markets or at natural food stores. Black soybeans cooked with sweet brown rice is a special treat.

Chickpeas: A rich, nutty bean featured in cooking from India to Africa and America, this renowned bean can be puréed into hummus, or added to soups, salads or stews. It requires presoaking and long cooking.

Kidney Beans: Native Americans depended on these large red beans as a source of fat and protein. They are ideally suited to use in chilis, stews or casseroles.

Lentils: Relished in Middle Eastern and Indian cuisine, they are the quickest-cooking of all beans. There are many types, but we are most familiar with red and brown lentils. Lentils lend themselves to velvety soups and creamy patés.

Lima Beans: A large white bean, native to America. It is commonly cooked along with fresh corn in succotash. It can also be served as a side dish or puréed as a spread or a dip.

Mung Beans: A small, pale-green bean savored in the Near East and India. This jewel of cuisine is usually sprouted and eaten as a fresh vegetable—as mung sprouts in salads or stir-fry dishes. Dried mung beans can be simmered with spices and served as "dahl," a thick bean sauce spooned over grain.

Navy Beans: Native to America, this small white bean is best known as Boston baked beans. Its flavor is best when slow-simmered, with time allowed to absorb seasoning and spice. Navy beans make rich, creamy soups with leeks and carrots.

Pinto Beans: Another American bean, a rose-colored relative of the kidney bean. Pintos are perfect for chilis or casseroles, or refried. They can be used interchangeably in red bean recipes.

Yellow or Green Split Peas: These lovely round peas are hulled, split, and ready for simmering into delectable soups. Split peas "melt" as they cook, creating a smooth base for your favorite seasoning.

Soy Foods

Soybeans, the king of beans, are ironically not often eaten as whole beans, but instead are processed into miso, shoyu, tofu, tamari, and tempeh. Soybeans are a low-fat, low-calorie source of digestible protein and various vitamins and minerals.

Miso: Famous in Asia, miso is a salty paste made from soybeans that are cooked, then aged with salt in large wooden tubs from two months to several years. Primarily used to flavor soups, miso is rich in enzymes and is known for its beneficial effect on digestion. Packed with nutrients and flavor, soybeans are also mixed with grains for distinctly different misos: barley is used in mugi miso; natto miso is a sweet miso combining barley, kombu and ginger; genmai miso mixes brown rice with soybeans; kome, a light, less salty miso also uses rice. Hatcho miso is a strong-flavored soy miso. As a general guideline, the longer the miso is aged, the darker its color and the stronger (saltier) its flavor.

Soy Sauce: Soy sauce is a generic term for all dark, salty seasonings made from soybeans, water and salt. There are three basic types of soy sauce, listed below, that are distinctly different from each other. Shoyu and tamari can be used interchangeably, but each has its own character.

   Shoyu: A naturally brewed soy sauce made from soybeans, wheat, water and sea salt. It is processed in the traditional Japanese way and aged for 2 to 3 years. No coloring or preservatives are used. Smooth, rich and dark, shoyu is delicious in vegetarian cooking.

   Tamari: Another natural soy sauce, tamari is primarily made from soybeans with up to 10% wheat. It is also available wheat-free, with a slightly stronger flavor than shoyu.

Commercial Soy Sauce: Similar in appearance to naturally brewed shoyu, commercial soy sauces are artificially colored and processed. They are not recommended for daily use.

Tofu: Known as "meat without the bone" in its Asian homeland, this humble white cake made from cooked soybeans is gaining an enthusiastic following in America. Low in fat, high in protein and easily digestible, tofu is the centerpiece of soy food cuisine. Mild tasting, it readily absorbs seasoning when baked, boiled, fried or marinated.

Tempeh: Indonesians developed this unique soy food. Tempeh is a sliceable cake of soybeans that have been cooked and split to remove the hull. A culture is added to the cooked soybeans, and they are allowed to age for 1 to 2 days. The culture covers the cake, holding it together. Tempeh has a distinct aroma and flavor. High in vitamin B_{12} and protein, tempeh can be sliced thin and deep-fried, braised, boiled or baked.

Cooking Condiments

Salt: Natural sea salt is sun-dried, washed and sun-dried again. This is preferable to commercial salt, which is "iodized" with potassium iodide and mixed with sugar and sodium bicarbonate to retain its white color. Silicon aluminate is also added to prevent sticking or caking. Sea salt, naturally processed, looks and feels different from commercial salt, and is complete with its natural mineral balance. Some of the recipes call for a pinch of sea salt or sea salt to taste. A little salt is helpful to bring out the delicious flavors of whole foods and to aid digestion. Sea salt is primarily used for cooking. I don't place it on the table, but rather offer a variety of condiments for seasoning.

Umeboshi: A pink, slightly sour salt plum from Japan. The umeboshi develops its flavor by being pickled in salt with beefsteak leaves for 1 to 2 years. It is available in many forms: as a whole salted plum, as paste or as vinegar. These forms can be interchanged in recipes. A delightful pink color, umeboshi adds zip to salad dressings, sauces or soups. Highly alkaline, umeboshi is known in Asia for its medicinal qualities.

Kuzu: A white, lumpy substance that resembles broken chalk, kuzu is a miraculous thickener that can help create smooth velvety sauces, soups and desserts. Extracted from the large root of the kuzu vine, this high-priced food is sold in natural food stores or Oriental markets. A tablespoon of kuzu will thicken one cup of liquid, so a little goes a long way. Kuzu is also noted for its medicinal properties.

Fresh Herbs: Fresh herbs from the store or from your garden enliven vegetarian cuisine. Parsley, basil, tarragon, dill, rosemary and thyme can be used liberally to season dishes, alone or in combination. Fresh herbs are usually added toward the end of cooking to preserve their delicate flavors. They may be chopped and added raw to salads and dressings or used as aromatic garnishes.

Dried Herbs: A sprinkle of dried herbs in soups, sauces and bean dishes adds variety to meals. Their concentrated flavors are released by slow simmering. Dried herbs will lose their rich flavors after a few months, so it's best to purchase them in small amounts and store in a cool dark place.

Spices and Seasonings: Spices are best bought whole and ground when ready to use. An electric grinder or a Japanese suribachi can be used. Store-bought spices do not compare with spices freshly ground at home. Cumin, coriander, turmeric, white pepper, chili and curry blends add an international flair to meals. Dill seed, caraway and anise are a few typical European seasonings. Dessert spices such as cinnamon, nutmeg, cloves and allspice fill the house with sweet smells. They can be bought whole, then ground or grated as needed. Garlic, ginger, prepared mustard and horseradish (Japanese wasabi) are additional seasonings to incorporate into your cooking, especially if you are trying to reduce salt and hot spices in your diet.

Vegetables and Fruits

Grains and beans may be the soul, but vegetables are the heart of this cuisine—they make cooking a joy. Grains keep for years; some ancient varieties were recently found in Tutankhamen's tomb in Egypt, and when they were planted, they grew! Vegetables and fruits are perishable and seasonal. They have their own cycles, appearing at a certain time each year to delight the natural foods cook. Each season brings special bounty: spring's first watercress and dandelions, summer's lettuce, strawberries and corn, and autumn's squash, pumpkins and apples. Vegetables constitute a large part of this cookery. Choose a wide selection and prepare them in a variety of ways: sprouted, raw, marinated, steamed, sautéed, fried, baked or pickled.

Vegetables: Choose from the greens: collards, kale, mustard greens, broccoli, dandelions, spinach and watercress. The lettuces include Bibb, Boston, chicory, escarole, curly or red leaf. The cabbage family is becoming popular; it includes bok choy, Chinese, savoy, red cabbage and nappa. Cauliflower, string beans and brussel sprouts, peppers, snow peas, parsley, leek and scallions make cooking an adventure. Sweet root vegetables, available most of the year are: onions, sweet potatoes, beets, parsnips, yams and carrots. Garlic, lotus root, daikon, radish, turnip and burdock are other roots to look for.

Sea Vegetables: A rich source of vitamins and minerals. They have long been overlooked in contemporary cuisine. Although used in traditional diets and present-day processed foods, sea vegetables are finally being recognized as fine foods in their own right. Agar-agar, a gelatin from the sea, and arame, hijiki, wakame, kombu and dulse are now used in vegetarian cooking from soups to salads to desserts.

Fruits: Fresh, seasonal fruits, dried fruits and juices add a light, sweet touch to this cuisine. Fruits grown locally or in a climate similiar to your own are preferable to imported, unseasonal and exotic delicacies. Tropical fruits are great to cool the body in hot climates. For North America's temperate climate, apples, pears, plums, peaches, blackberries, cranberries, watermelon, cantaloupe, grapes and other local fruit are more suitable than imported bananas and pineapples. Lemons and oranges can be used for flavoring in dressings and desserts.

Dried Fruits: Their natural, concentrated sweetness is excellent in chutneys, spreads, sauces and cooked desserts. Choose from dried apples, raisins, dates, peaches, prunes and figs.

Sweeteners: Maple syrup, barley malt and rice syrup are the liquid sweeteners I prefer to use. Honey, brown sugar, molasses and white sugar are not as desirable because they are more refined and break down in your system too quickly. The natural grain or maple syrups are generally less sweet and easier for our bodies to assimilate.

Nuts and Seeds

Nuts and seeds are an essential source of proteins, oil and minerals in a vegetarian dairy-free diet. They should be regarded as condiments, however, and be eaten in small quantities (by volume) in contrast to the grains and vegetables that they complement. They are concentrated protein and are not as easy to digest as grains and vegetables.

Sunflower and pumpkin seeds, walnuts, cashews and almonds can be roasted and seasoned with shoyu for a snack or crunchy condiment. Sesame seeds are roasted and ground with sea salt to make gomasio, a delicious "sesame salt" to sprinkle over grains. Use nuts and seeds in desserts, such as cookies, cakes or granola. Seeds and nuts are more digestible when ground into spreads such as tahini, a sesame paste popular in the Middle East.

Oils

Sesame oil and olive oil are the two basic oils used in this cookbook. Sesame oil, long used in Oriental cooking, is light, digestible and perfect for sautéing. Sesame oil can be purchased unroasted (light) or roasted (dark). The dark type has a stronger flavor and is used sparingly as a flavor in Oriental cooking. Olive oil, extra virgin if available, can be used to sauté vegetables or in salad dressing. When shopping for oils, look for pure, unrefined vegetable oil; safflower oil is suitable for deep-frying and desserts, corn oil is excellent for baking.

Fish

Fish is a good quality, concentrated protein, especially helpful when you are reducing or eliminating other animal foods from your diet. Fish should always be bought fresh and then cooked and served in proper balance with other foods for optimal flavor and sustenance.

Shopping for Whole Foods

At most supermarkets you can buy the basic whole foods, but you may have to supplement your supermarket's stock with occasional trips to a natural foods store, or mail order natural foods from a distributor. At large markets you can find brown or unpolished rice, steel-cut oats or oatmeal, barley, corn grits, cornmeal, wholewheat or unbleached white flour and popcorn. Kasha (buckwheat), bulghur or couscous are found in the gourmet sections of large supermakets or in Jewish markets. In the dried foods section look for split peas, lentils, navy beans, chickpeas and kidney beans. Often the prices of beans and other dried goods are considerably lower in supermarkets than in natural foods stores.

At supermarkets also look for pure olive oil, and cold-pressed or unrefined sesame oil. Maple syrup is usually available, but purchase only the 100% pure kind. Dried fruits, nuts and seeds are often good buys when offered on sale, as they keep well. Your condiment shelf can be filled with imported stone-ground mustard, pickles and sauerkraut (made with no preservatives), and spices and herbs. Fresh produce and fish are featured at all markets, and many stores have enlarged these areas due to growing demand. When choosing fruit and vegetables, buy those that are not sealed in plastic if possible. Unwrapped vegetables are usually fresher and you can examine them more easily.

When shopping, if you don't see what you want, ask for it. This holds true in restaurants, too. The management wants to please its customers, so ask for the items you want. It is helpful if you know the name of distributors who carry the products you want. When your grocers and local restaurants receive enough requests, you'll soon see your favorite whole foods on their shelves and menus.

Mail order shopping is helpful if you don't live near a natural foods store, are looking for specialty items, or would like to save money. Place large quantity orders and reduce the cost per pound. For example, purchasing a 25- or 50-pound bag of rice is less expensive than buying a few pounds each week at the store. Get together with a few friends and place a large order of grains, beans and goods by the case or tub. Miso can be purchased in 10- to 25-pound tubs and divided easily. Cases of noodles or juice can be shared, saving you shopping time and money.

If you are lucky and live near a good natural foods store, shopping can be an enjoyable and educational experience. Many stores have cooking demonstrations, free product samples and recipe handouts. Produce and other foods may be labeled as "organic," but there has been a history of abuse surrounding this term and you may want to ask to see the certification. Store managers are usually happy to answer your questions. It is an excellent opportunity to learn about the farmers, producers and distributors of your foods.

Your Kitchen, Tools and Skills

The kitchen is the heart of the home. It is from this heart—our modern day hearth—
that love pours forth in the form of wholesome foods. Kitchens come in all shapes
and sizes, just like the cooks that tend their fires. There are compact, efficiency apart-
ment kitchens with just enough room for a cutting board, and spacious country kitchens
centered around large wooden, butcher block tables. Bigger doesn't necessarily mean
better when it comes to kitchens. Organization and care can make even a tiny kitchen
happy and productive.

Whether you are just learning to cook or are a seasoned chef with gadgets galore,
you do need to make space in your kitchen to introduce whole foods cookery. The
first step in setting up a kitchen is doing a spring cleaning. Whatever the season, clean
out all cabinets and shelves; discard old food. Wash your stove and oven, clean the
refrigerator inside and out. Get rid of everything you don't use on a regular basis.
Store electrical appliances, large pots, pans, extra dishes and serving pieces under
the counters. As a final touch, fill a bucket with warm, soapy water and wipe down the
walls, all surfaces, floor and windows. Cleaning your kitchen is a ritual of respect
for the food being prepared and for yourself as a cook, to create not only wholesome
food, but also a pleasant environment in which to work.

The next step in setting up is to consider the quality of two essential elements of
cooking—heat and water.

Heat: Woodburning stoves are the first choice for cooking. However, few people
have the opportunity to use them on a regular basis. Practically speaking, gas is the
most convenient fuel for home cooking. It is quick-to-heat, easy to control and gives a
clean, calm feeling to your kitchen.

Electric: Electric stoves are popular appliances today, but they present problems
in whole foods cooking because they are not easy to control. When cooking grains
and beans, you may need to bring it to boil on one burner, and transfer it to another
burner on a lower heat setting for gentle cooking. There is more guesswork involved
until you become familiar with a particular stove.

Microwave ovens: Whole foods kitchens have no use for these appliances. I choose
to avoid foods cooked or heated in them. Microwaves are products with dubious safety
that clearly sacrifice quality and aesthetics for convenience and speed.

Toaster Ovens: Though electric, they are quicker and more economical than heating a
large stove. Toasting or heating small amounts of food is practical in a counter-top oven.

Water: Spring or well water is an important element in cooking whole foods. Most
city water has undesirable additives that not only are unhealthy, but impart an un-
pleasant taste and odor. It will take a little research to find out the quality of your
local water, but it's worth it. Some lucky areas have clean, pure water. I choose to
buy bottled spring water for cooking and drinking. All the washing of grains, beans
and vegetables can be done with tap water. Buying water may seem rather extreme
or expensive at first, but the taste and vitality of your food will be enhanced. If you
have family members on a healing diet, the quality of water you use is especially
important.

Essential Equipment

Vegetarian cuisine requires very few fancy items. Stainless steel, cast iron, clay or enameled cast iron are the best choices for cookware. Aluminum should be avoided because it is a toxic substance that can leach into your foods; the same thing goes for plastic coated, non-stick pans. Here's a suggested list of equipment to set up a kitchen for a family of four or more.

Washing and Cutting Vegetables:
  1 stainless steel or carbon steel vegetable knife
  1 paring knife
  sharpening stone or steel
  1 large cutting board
  1 small cutting board (optional for garlic or fish)
  brush to scrub vegetables
  colander to drain vegetables
  strainer to rinse grains

Pots and Pans:
  soup pot (1 gallon or more), stainless steel or cast iron
  heavy pot for grain
  stainless steel pressure cooker
  heavy pot to cook beans
  1 or 2 flame tamers (heat diffusers)
  skillet or fry pan (1 large, 1 small)
  large pot to boil noodles and blanch vegetables
  small pots, 2 or 3 with lids for sauces or for reheating foods

Utensils:
  wooden spoons
  spatula
  whisk
  large chopsticks
  vegetable peeler
  melon baller
  ginger grater
  juicer

Useful Equipment:
  bamboo vegetable steamer
  stainless steel steamer
  wok
  wooden bowl for grain
  clay bean pot
  tea pot and strainer
  mixing bowls
  towels
  sponges

Baking Needs:
  measuring cups
  measuring spoons
  large bowl
  cookie sheet
  muffin tray
  cake pan
  baker's paper
  pastry brush

Electric:
  blender
  food processor
  mixer
  food mill
  toaster oven
  juicer

Organizing Your Kitchen

Now that your kitchen is sparkling clean and equipped with all the right tools, there are a few other areas to consider.

Natural Lighting is Best: My favorite kitchens have a window over the sink and cutting area, so I can watch the seasons change. I feel more in harmony with nature than in a windowless room. Most kitchens have a bright, central, overhead light in order to reach all working areas. Such lights are tiring and not very pleasing for the eyes. Try installing a light over the stove, with a covered or "safety" bulb. A light over the sink and cutting area is helpful too.

Exhaust Fan: This rids the kitchen of the heat and smoke from deep-frying. I don't usually use a fan or timer while cooking because I prefer to rely on my senses to tell me when the food is done.

Organization for Work Flow: Work flows effortlessly in a kitchen arranged to minimize unnecessary motion. The ideal place for the cutting board is on a counter between the sink and the stove, or on a table with easy access to both areas. Keep a knife rack nearby, but out of children's reach. Colanders, strainers and graters can be hung near the stove ready to use. A wide-mouthed jar, full of wooden spoons and the utensils you use frequently, should be placed near the stove. However, grains, beans and oils should be stored in a cool, dry place. It's all right to leave a small jar of salt next to the stove, but nuts, herbs and spices should be kept away from the heat. Cooking condiments such as oils, vinegar, mustard and kuzu can be placed on shelves near the stove.

Baking Ingredients: Dried fruits, nuts, sweeteners and flavorings can be grouped together to inspire desserts and snacks.

Harvest Vegetables: Squash, pumpkins, onions, garlic, cabbage, apples and other harvest foods can be stored in a root cellar, in the basement, on an enclosed porch or in a cool pantry. The temperature must be steady and approximately 40 to 50 degrees F., not below freezing. To prevent moisture from accumulating under boxes of foods, keep vegetables in wooden crates or baskets placed on boards or shelves off the floor.

Organizing the Refrigerator: Place all jars, flours, oils and pickles on one shelf. Group vegetables together in the bottom drawers, the coldest part of a refrigerator. Keep the top shelf for storing cooked food in plain view, so it is easy to reach. A well-organized refrigerator will allow you easy access to all foods, and a quick visual assessment of your food inventory. Foods should be rotated for maximum freshness and minimal waste.

Kitchen Ecology: A final thought in arranging your kitchen: recycle or re-use the non-edible goods. You need a special storage place for bottles, jars, paper, plastic bags and containers. Empty milk crates are suitable; they can be filled and stacked while collecting enough to return to the store or recycling center. Paper shopping bags can be saved and used again. Don't throw out those plastic vegetable bags or containers from the natural foods store. Rinse them and hang them out to dry. Children often enjoy helping to recycle kitchen goods. It gives them a sense of responsibility; at the same time they have the benefit of using containers, boxes and other materials for their own creative projects.

The Knife: Selection and Skill

The most important tool I own is a Japanese vegetable knife. It's a relatively inexpensive knife, purchased at the local natural foods store. Lightweight and versatile, it is easy to care for. With one minute on the sharpening stone each day, it glides through vegetables effortlessly.

My collection of gourmet cutlery is scarcely used these days. I seldom need the heavy French knife, designed for cutting meat, although it is handy sometimes for cutting open squash or shredding cabbage for sauerkraut. My filleting or boning knife serves no purpose either, except for the occasional fish dinner. These unused tools are a clear reflection of the changes I've made in my diet.

A stainless or carbon steel vegetable knife of good quality can be found in most department stores, natural foods stores, or Asian markets. Look for brand-name Japanese or European knives that offer a guarantee. A stainless steel knife will not rust and can be used to cut all fruits and vegetables. It holds a good edge, but it can chip if used improperly. A carbon steel knife is easy to sharpen, but will rust if not washed and dried carefully. It also cannot be used to slice acid foods such as lemons, tomatoes and fruits. I recommend the first knife you purchase be of stainless steel, or a blend of the two metals, because of their greater versatility.

A paring knife comes in handy for peeling and cutting small fruits and vegetables. Look for full "tang"—solidly riveted blades with steel that extends the length of the handle.

"A sharp cook has a sharp knife" is an old kitchen saying. A knife is an extension of yourself. It is the first thing that comes in contact with your food. A sharp blade reflects clear thinking and respect for your cooking. If all of your knives become dull with use, cutting vegetables will be not only drudgery but dangerous. Sharpening your knife on a whetstone should be a daily practice.

To sharpen a knife, choose a whetstone or oilstone with both a coarse and fine grain texture. One side is rough; one side is fine. Place the stone, with the coarse side up, on a damp cloth to keep it from sliding. Sprinkle the stone with water or oil. Hold the handle with one hand; grip the back of the blade with the other. Draw the blade away from you at a 10 to 15 degree angle. You can draw the blade in a circular motion to sharpen on one side; then turn the blade around and sharpen the other side. After several sweeps, turn the stone over to its smooth surface and repeat the process to give the knife an extra sharp edge.

Apply moderate and steady pressure along the entire blade to insure an evenly sharpened knife. There are as many styles of knife sharpening as there are chefs. I

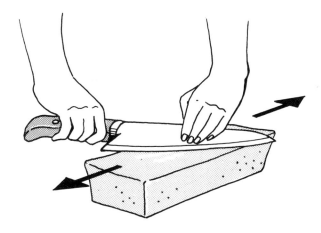

Fig. 1 Sharpening your knife.

have seen chefs sharpen knives on the bottom of a ceramic cup. The one aspect they all agree on is to keep your blade in excellent condition, so find a technique that works for you and use it. Wash the blade after sharpening, and clean the stone. Now you are ready to begin.

You will develop your cutting skill only through practice. Japanese chefs train for many years to cut vegetables into paper thin garnishes or slice fish into sushi. To slice food at home, an organized approach should be your goal. Here are a few tips for safety and skill.

Always follow an orderly work flow. Clear your work space of any unnecessary material; wash all foods to be cut beforehand, and allow them to drain. Slippery produce and wet hands can cause an accident. Trim the tops and ends of produce; cut the food into manageable 3- to 4-inch pieces. Set up your cutting board in the work flow arrangement.

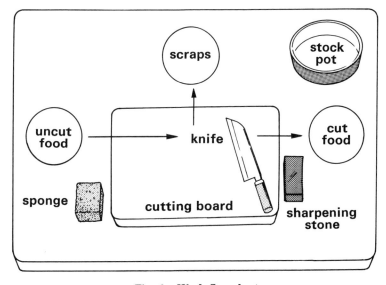

Fig. 2 Work flow chart.

If you are right-handed, work from left to right, and vice versa for lefties. Place all food to be cut in a bowl to one side of the board. Place one empty bowl for scraps in front and another empty bowl on the other side for cut food. Keep a towel or sponge on hand to clean your knife and board after slicing each food.

Maintain a balanced posture and work rhythmically as you slice. Face the work table squarely; do not rotate your hips or shoulders, but stand with your weight evenly distributed upon both feet. Your table should be neither too high or too low—about waist height is good. You should be able to rest your hands comfortably on the table without bending over or creating tension in your shoulders. Many counters are too high. If you have to keep your arm bent while cutting, you may tire quickly. You may find placing your cutting board on the kitchen table is more comfortable.

Hold your knife firmly, not tightly. With your hand, steady the vegetable on the cutting board. Curl your fingers under, tuck your thumb under your fingers. Your knuckles will act as a guide for the blade. Slide the knife through the vegetable, moving the blade down and forward. The entire length of the blade should be used. The difference between slicing and chopping is the long, forward motion used to slice, and the down, rough action used to chop. Let the sharpness of your blade and the weight of your arm do the work. If you have to apply much pressure, your blade is dull. Once you've gained some dexterity, you'll be able to slice in a continuous motion with grace and speed.

Washing Vegetables and Fruits

To wash and drain produce thoroughly, each item requires special care. Root vegetables such as carrots, daikon, radishes and unwaxed squashes can be placed in a large bowl or sink filled with cool water. Scrub each with a vegetable brush and rinse. To wash leafy greens, salad, parsley and watercress, fill a large bowl or your sink with water. Separate the leaves and wash each leaf by dunking and gently swirling to loosen sand. Place washed greens in a colander. Run your fingers over the bottom of the sink or bowl. If you feel a grainy, sandy texture chances are there is still sand in the greens. So empty the water, fill it again and wash for a second time. To wash leeks, slice off the root end just above the bottom and slice the leek in half lengthwise. Separate the inner layers and wash carefully. By submerging fruits and vegetables in water, rather than running water over them, you loosen any sand, wash off sprays and save water.

Vegetable Garnishes

If you have eaten in authentic Japanese restaurants, you have marveled at the amazing ability of the chefs to handle their knives, and enjoyed the artful presentations of the meals. These talented people have trained for many years with masters. "Mukimono," the art of Japanese vegetable garnishing, features simple, whimsical and usually edible garnishes. Their purpose is not only to be visually pleasing but to create a harmony of taste and texture throughout the entire meal.

The following vegetable garnishes are easy enough for new cooks to master. Try one or two at a time until you become skilled. Remember to sharpen your knife, and practice.

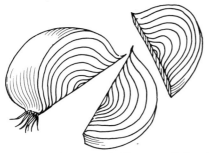

Fig. 3 Onion, sliced, or half-moon. Onion is peeled and sliced root to tip in thin slices.

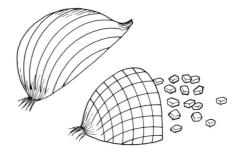

Fig. 4 Onion, diced. Onion is first sliced as 1/4 inch, leaving root end uncut (to hold onion together). Then dice across in 1/4-inch slices to make medium dice. The root end can be diced quickly. Onion can be large or small dice.

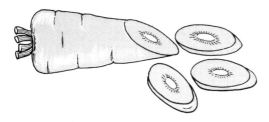

Fig. 5 Carrot, diagonal cut. One of the basic cutting techniques.

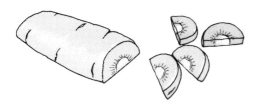

Fig. 7 Carrot, half-moon cut. A basic cut. Carrot is sliced in half lengthwise, then cut across in half circles.

Fig. 6 Carrot, matchstick cut. A basic cut, diagonal cuts of carrot are sliced into thin matchstick or "julienne" cuts. These can be 1/4-inch or smaller.

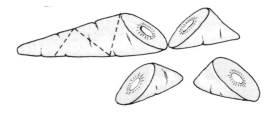

Fig. 8 Carrot, triangle cut. A basic cut. This triangle or "roll cut" is made by slicing carrot in diagonal and then rolling away from you to create triangle shape.

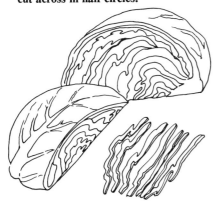

Fig. 9 Cabbage, sliced. A basic cut. Cabbage is cut into 2–3 inches wedges, then sliced thin or diagonal.

Fig. 10   Squash sliced into wedges for steaming or baking. A basic cut. Slice squash in half lengthwise, scoop out seeds, cut into wedges.

Fig. 11   Broccoli "spear." Broccoli is trimmed, sliced in half, ready for steaming or boiling.

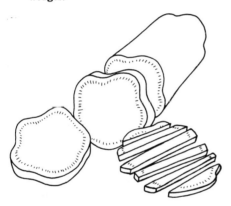

Fig. 13   Broccoli flowerettes. A basic cut. Broccoli is cut near the "flower."

Fig. 12   Broccoli stems, matchstick or "julienne" cut. A basic cut. Broccoli stems are peeled, sliced into thin rounds and cut into matchsticks.

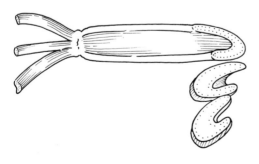

Fig. 14   Celery, diagonal cut. A basic cut for stir-fries or salads.

Fig. 15   Radish flower. A garnish cut. Trim ends of radish. Slice radish into thin cuts, leaving the bottom uncut to hold flower together. Turn radish, and make slices on diagonal of first cuts. Place radish in cold water, it will open.

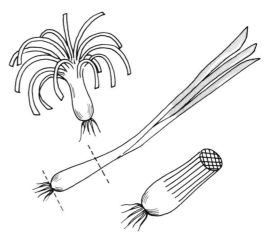

Fig. 16   Carrot flower. A garnish cut. Cut carrot into 4 inches lengths, make 4–5 "V" cuts into carrot, about 1/4 inch deep. Slice carrot across into thin flowers.

Fig. 17   Scallion flower. A garnish cut. A scallion is cut 3 inches above root. The roots of scallion are trimmed just below end of scallion. Holding the scallion by the root end, press tip of knife into scallion to the middle, draw the blade through the scallion. Continue to make 1/4 inch slices through scallion, leaving the root end together. Place scallion in cold water, the hard center piece of scallion may be removed as it opens in water.

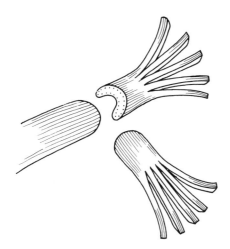

Fig. 18   Celery fan. A garnish cut. Celery is cut first into 2 inches pieces. Then make 5–6 cuts through celery, leaving one end uncut. Place in cold water, fan will open in 1 hour.

2. Planning Meals

Lorraine, my sister-in-law, lives in a large country home with two teenage boys and her husband. She works at the office every day, exercises regularly and still manages to cook whole meals from scratch. How does she do it? Organization is her secret.

On a typical day, Lorraine arrives home from work after running a few errands. She jogs a mile or so to keep in shape and then returns to the kitchen. She quickly sharpens her knife and starts to prepare dinner.

In the refrigerator, she finds a bowl of rice, a container of chickpeas (both cooked yesterday) and a pound of tofu. The vegetable drawer supplies some carrots, broccoli, cauliflower and a few salad greens. Lorraine first washes all the vegetables and then slices the broccoli, cauliflower and carrots to make a stew with the chickpeas. She places the rice in a steamer to heat and some sunflower seeds in a toaster oven to roast as a garnish.

As one of the boys sets the table, she puts out the salad dressings and condiments. She tosses a salad, seasons the stew with some herbs and miso and puts out the word that dinner's ready. In less than 30 minutes, Lorraine has prepared a delicious sit-down meal of chickpea stew, rice with sunflower seeds and salad.

For dessert, Lorraine might make a fresh fruit dish topped by a tasty sauce. She simply dissolves a tablespoon of kuzu in 2 cups of juice, stirs gently while it thickens, and adds sliced peaches or strawberries. It's light, refreshing and ready in minutes.

After dinner, Lorraine prepares a few dishes for tomorrow as she cleans the kitchen. She soaks a cup of barley and simmers a half pound of apricots for breakfast, and mixes up her favorite tofu sandwich filling with mayonnaise, mustard, chopped pickle, relish and scallion for lunch. If time allows, she'll stir up rolled oats, nuts, maple syrup and cinnamon for granola, and bake it while she washes dishes.

The next morning, Lorraine turns the flame on low under the soaking barley, which will cook quickly because it has soaked overnight. She places a cup of almonds in the oven to roast and then pops into the shower. A breakfast of barley with almonds, stewed apricots, tea and toast is soon ready. While the family is still bustling about getting ready to leave for the day, she makes some tofu and sprout sandwiches, heats the remaining chickpea stew for her husband's lunch and quickly plans dinner. She decides to wash a cup of split peas and soak them with a strip of kombu (a sea vegetable). She also rinses a cup of millet and covers it with 3 cups of water to soak. Breakfast, lunch and dinner preparations are thus completed just as the family is ready to leave for work and school.

After a smooth day fueled by slow-calorie-burning grains and protein-rich beans, Lorraine returns home. Today she attended an aerobics class at lunchtime, so no need to run tonight. She moves confidently about the kitchen, knowing that dinner will be ready soon. She turns on the flame under the split peas and millet, and sits down to talk with the boys about their day at school. A few minutes later, she takes some vegetables from the refrigerator and washes them. She chops an onion, some carrots and some celery for the soup. When the millet is cooked she forms it into balls and rolls them in a spicy walnut condiment. She slices a squash to steam along with the bright green kale and makes a quick basil dressing in the blender.

Tonight's supper is split pea soup with vegetables, millet balls, steamed squash and kale, basil dressing, and for dessert apple sauce and granola. Tomorrow there will be enough millet balls for lunch, and the leftover soup might serve as a nice topping for a grain. As the boys and her husband help Lorraine clean up, she lets the neatly lined jars of grains and beans that accent a kitchen wall, inspire tomorrow's meals.

Planning and Cooking Ahead

The "cooking ahead" rhythms described here are the foundation of a vegetarian, dairy-free cuisine. When you begin to include whole foods in your diet, a little more thought may be required than in a dairy-based or meat-and-potatoes diet, which tends to rely on processed or quick-cooking proteins.

How to plan weekly menus is a mystery to new cooks. *Balance* is the key. Balance the season, the weather, your health, your individual tastes, what's available at the grocery store, your cooking and working schedule and the dietary needs of your family. Don't worry, you won't need a food processing computer to handle all these factors. Just keep a few of these suggestions in mind.

To start with, whole foods have a greater versatility within a menu. The chickpeas, rice and vegetables Lorraine fixed for dinner can be prepared in endless combinations. The bowl of rice, for example, can be stir-fried with a few vegetables, or simmered in soup with the broccoli, carrots, and scallion, and seasoned with miso. A cup or two of rice can be mixed in a salad with sliced radish, cucumbers and celery and topped with a tahini-basil dressing.

A container of chickpeas is a gold mine of menu ideas. These nutty beans can be added to soup, marinated in an oil and umeboshi dressing to toss in a salad, or mashed with lemon juice, garlic, tahini and olive oil to make hummus, the Middle Eastern chickpea dip. Brown rice can even be simmered in apple juice with raisins and spice to make a sweet rice pudding.

Tofu, a star of vegetarian cuisine, exemplifies the versatility of natural foods. Cut into tiny cubes, tofu can garnish miso soups. Tofu can also be "wokked" with Oriental vegetables, deep-fried, sautéed with spices, blended into mayonnaise or whipped into a dessert.

To plan a menu for myself, first I think of what my activities will be and what sounds good. On snowy winter days, I crave hearty carbohydrates, and fix a pot of Boston baked beans and a batch of kasha knishes (buckwheat and potato filling wrapped in pastry dough) to warm me while skiing. After an intensive yoga session, I like whole grain noodles in a soothing broth, a light tofu salad or a delicate fruit kanten jelled with agar-agar, a sea vegetable.

Every once in a while, after a long swim, I find myself standing at the fish counter gazing at a pink, silver-skinned salmon from Alaska. Salmon is superb grilled, baked or sautéed with teriyaki sauce. But if I come home ravenous, I quickly pan-fry it.

Generally, I try to incorporate a whole grain, a protein such as nuts, beans or fish, and seasonal vegetables into my daily meals. I don't necessarily eat all of these in one meal, though. My breakfast may be a bowl of cornmeal (polenta), lunch is a lentil soup with croutons, and dinner is a Mediterranean-style salad with pita bread.

On a note pad, I may jot down headings such as "grain," "bean" and "green," a habit from my restaurant training. Then I'll fill in a few combinations: rice-adzuki-kale, black beans-corn-collard or noodles-fish-salad. Finally, I decide which food will become the soup, the salad or the entrée. Black beans could be simmered in a soup with garlic, added to a casserole with squash or mashed with hot sauce for a dip. Fresh corn-on-the-cob is juicy and sweet when baked, or a golden ingredient of chowder or tofu and broccoli salad. A pound of fish could be transformed into a fish and potato stew or a fish and noodle salad with a dill dressing.

Fig. 19   Rice and beans—"Cooking ahead." This illustrates the variations possible from one pot of rice and one pot of beans. A pot of rice and one of beans is the inspiration for many meals.

Fig. 21   Rice Salad.

Fig. 20   Rice with Bean Croquettes.

Fig. 22   Rice Ring.

Fig. 23   Raisin and Rice Pudding.

Fig. 24   Bean Dip with Chips.

Fig. 26   Rice Salad in a Pita.

Fig. 25   Norimaki.

Fig. 27   Stuffed Squash.

Supper's Ready!

Dinner is the greatest challenge for all cooks. It's easy to fall into the habit of grabbing a sandwich, a takeout meal or a beer and popcorn. Time is a crucial factor in fixing dinner. Who wants to come home and consistently have to cook a full-course dinner from scratch? Try to set up grains and beans in the morning or evening. It's comforting to come home and know dinner will be ready in an hour, with a minimum of effort.

My training as a professional chef instilled in me a sense of timing. I learned to estimate how much food could be prepared in half-hour blocks of time. Cooking a whole-grain meal from scratch takes between one and two hours. If there is enough for subsequent meals, tomorrow's dinner is a quick stir-fry or refried beans wrapped in tortillas. If I arrive home starving, to an empty refrigerator, noodles to the rescue! In ten minutes I can sit down to a steaming bowl of noodles in tamari broth.

Each week I alternate these types of meals. For example, on weekends I may make condiments, pickles, a batch or two of cookies and a pot of baked beans. This may sound like a lot of cooking, but it isn't. Fixing many dishes at once is a time-efficient and economical way to cook.

One or two nights a week, I may cook a pot of rice and one of beans. The other nights, I'll make croquettes, burgers or soup, from the food cooked ahead. The gaps are filled in with quick-cooking dishes: couscous, soy foods or fish dinners. If you cook for a large group or for someone who is on a healing diet, you may choose to cook their meals from scratch every night. Freshly-cooked food has more energy than reheated food, and therefore a greater healing or strengthening quality.

All natural foods are nutritious, alone or in combination. By keeping meals simple and not mixing too many ingredients together in each dish, you can be sure of success. The time-honored grain and bean combinations are a source of inspiration for contemporary cuisine. Somehow, nothing satisfies a hungry crowd like this southern specialty: steaming chili, corn bread, and sliced avocado salad. From the Middle East, a banquet of rice-filled grape leaves, chickpea falafels, couscous cake and lemon pudding is easily adapted to our taste.

When I feel creative, I may combine foods from different parts of the world with basic cooking skills. My favorite summertime "grain-bean-green" combination mixes Japanese-style marinated tofu, New England corn, and broccoli with an Italian basil dressing. Another savory dish is delicate black arame, a sea vegetable from Japan, seasoned with ginger and lemon and stuffed into mushroom caps, an unusual food in a familiar format. Indonesian tempeh, a high protein soy food, takes on an American flavor in my tempeh and potato cakes.

A grocery list is time-saving; make one up before heading to the natural foods store. Jot down the staples needed, but wait till you're in the store to decide on the freshest produce. When you shop, buy what is in season and adjust the menu suggestions in this book. I'm never certain how my menus will end up. Will that pound of tofu be fried and served with a teriyaki sauce, sautéed with garlic and cumin, or added to the cake batter for a moister dessert?

The Whole Grain-Whole Meal —————————————————————

The foundation of vegetarian cuisine, a whole grain meal takes approximately one to two hours to cook. Presoaking these foods or using a pressure cooker will shorten the cooking time. Wash and soak rice, barley, rye or wheat berries in the evening to cook the next day. Chickpeas, black beans, red beans and navy beans also benefit from soaking 12 to 24 hours. Hearty, slow-cooking casseroles such as "3 Sisters" Casserole, Chili or Chulent fall into this category along with special dishes such as pizza.

Whole Meal Suggestions:

Bean:	Chickpea Stew	Miso-Tofu Soup	Chili
Grain:	Rice Pilaf	Rice and Rye	Corn Polenta
Vegetable:	Mediterranean Salad	Kale with Carrots	Collard Greens

Quick Meals

Many people allow 20 to 40 minutes for meal preparation. In that time they can prepare quick-cooking whole grains: millet, buckwheat, cracked wheat or corn-on-the-cob. Red or brown lentils may cook in 30 to 40 minutes if they have been presoaked. A few beans, such as navy, pinto or adzuki beans, may be pressure-cooked (if presoaked) in this amount of time. However, I find slow-cooked beans more digestible.

Soy foods lend themselves to quick cooking. Tempeh can be braised, fried or baked. Tofu makes marvelous burgers with cooked rice and spices. Skewed on kebabs, marinated or pan-fried, tofu offers limitless possibilities for quick meals. Whole grains and beans which were cooked ahead can be stuffed into peppers or squash, formed into croquettes, wrapped in chapatis or rolled in grape leaves.

Quick Meal Suggestions:

Bean:	Red Lentil Soup	Tempeh "Turkey"	Tofu-Rice Burgers
Grain:	Kasha Croquettes	Millet "Mashed Potatoes"	Sesame Onion Rolls
Vegetable:	Cucumber-Dill Salad	Broccoli	Salad with Tahini Dressing

The Instant Meal

The answer to everyone's prayers—a hot tasty meal in the time it takes to boil water! Here are a few ideas, but they don't include a whole grain, unless it was cooked ahead. Grain products such as noodles, couscous, bulghur, breads and muffins can all be ready in less than 30 minutes. Corn-on-the-cob is my favorite quick grain, but unfortunately it's not available all year.

Fish is an instant source of protein. Pan-fried or broiled, it takes only 5 to 10 minutes. Nuts or seeds can be roasted in a short time, too. Cooked rice or other grains can be fried (a fried rice dinner for two takes only 15 minutes), steamed or made into a salad. A pot of cooked beans will disappear in stews or wrapped in a corn tortilla. Sandwiches are not the only instant meal.

Quick Meal Suggestions:

Bean:	10-Minute Tofu with Swiss Chard	Jane's 10-Minute All-in-One Meal	Pan-Fried Fish
Grain:	Corn-on-the-Cob		Noodles
Vegetable:	Steamed Squash	Cabbage Salad	Basil Sauce

Tips for instant meals:
- Make certain you have a well-stocked pantry, refrigerator and freezer.
- A pot of rice and one of beans can be transformed into ethnic meals in minutes with a few special ingredients.

- Keep on hand: corn tortillas, whole wheat chapatis, pita bread, and grape leaves.
- Season grains and bean dishes with: salsa, mustard, horseradish, falafel mix, miso, mirin or umeboshi.

Lunch Ideas

Sandwiches are usually the number one choice in my house at lunchtime. To begin creating high quality sandwiches, let's consider breads.

Stone-ground whole wheat bread, fresh from the bakery or homemade and naturally leavened, leads the list. Pita or pocket bread is another good choice for all types of fillings. Find a brand which doesn't fall apart when filled. This bread can be filled with protein-rich tempeh or tofu dishes. Vegetable salads can be neatly tucked into a pita with lettuce or sprouts.

If you don't bake your own, look for the freshest breads in your area: sour dough (wheat or rye), sprouted wheat, whole wheat or corn breads can be interchanged in lunchbox meals. The following recipes make savory sandwiches.

Soy Foods:
Tofu Cheese, Avocado Tofu Dip, Lorraine's Tofu Salad, Tofu Spread (for canapés)
10-Minute Tofu with Swiss Chard, Scrambled Tofu
Tempeh "Turkey," Tempeh "Bacon," Barbecued Tempeh
Miso-Tahini Spread with sprouts or salad

Bean and Grain Fillings:
Hummus, Baked Beans, Chili or Refried Beans
Rice Salad, Spicy Tofu and Rice Burgers, Millet Croquettes, Swedish Wheat Balls
These grain dishes along with a basil or Tahini-Onion Sauce could fill a pita.

Vegetables:
Serve the usual salad fixing of lettuce, sprouts, sliced cucumber, onion and radishes. Cooked vegetables make juicy, flavorful additions to sandwiches. Try: steamed kale, sautéed collards, Himalayan Greens, Stewed Broccoli-Rabe, Quick Cabbage Salad, Dilled Cucumber Salad or Braised Red Cabbage.

Sea vegetables are an unusual, nutritious sandwich filling. Try arame or hijiki seasoned with onions and lemon and served with a creamy tofu dressing.

Fish:
Fish salad in a pita or Fish Croquettes with Tartar Sauce and pickles is a satisfying lunch at home or the office.

Soup and Sandwich Ideas:
Everyone loves a bowl of homemade soup and a sandwich layered with crisp vegetables. I usually combine a bean sandwich, such as tofu, with a grain or vegetable soup, say, corn chowder or leek and barley. A hearty bean soup of lentils pairs nicely with a grain burger or rice salad. Here are a few of my lunch combinations.

Soup	—With—	*Sandwich*	—Or—	*Salad*
Miso Soup		Tofu "Cheese" Sandwich		Tofu Salad
Cabbage and Corn Soup		Arame Sandwich		Hijiki Noodle
Leek and Barley Soup		Hummus and Pita Bread		Chickpea Salad
Red Lentil Soup		Rice Burger		Rice Salad
French Onion Soup		Fish Filet Sandwich		Fish Salad
Chickpea Stew		Himalayan Greens		Mediterranean Salad

Breakfast

Breakfast should help you balance your day's activities. It can be either a substantial meal for a busy day, or a light breakfast for a quiet morning. Whole grains are a healthy way to start the day. Here are a few suggestions.

Instant Breakfast: Toast, with a variety of spreads, and tea is a quick meal. Choose a whole grain bread and make your own spreads. Try: Miso-Tahini, Apricot Spread, Raisin (Fruit) Purée, Gingery Stewed Fruit. For a hot breakfast try miso soup, noodles in broth, couscous or oatmeal. Fruit salads, kantens, or applesauce with crunch is a sweet, light meal in warm weather.

Quick Breakfast: In the time it takes you to shower and dress, a hearty pot of whole grain can be ready if it was washed and soaked overnight. Oatmeal, corn grits, millet, buckwheat and cracked wheat are creamy and nutritious topped with toasted seeds, raisins or a touch of barley malt. Fresh, hot muffins are popular, along with Stewed Fruit, Scrambled Tofu or Tempeh "Bacon."

Whole Grain—Whole Breakfast: Whole oats, rice, wheat or barley require long, slow simmering in lots of water to become a soft, easily digestible breakfast grain. To make "soft grain," wash, rinse and simmer 1 cup of grain in 4 or more cups of water for 2 to 3 hours. You can make a soft cereal from grains cooked ahead of time. Place 2 cups of cooked grain in a pot with 4 to 5 cups of water (or apple juice for a sweet taste), simmer on a low flame 1 hour or more until soft. Dried fruits, nuts, seeds or a spoonful of maple or rice syrup on cereal will entice your family to the breakfast table.

When preparing meals try to keep in mind these few simple guidelines:
- Use more whole grain and vegetable carbohydrates than bean, nut or fish protein.
- Try not to mix more than two protein-rich foods, such as beans, nuts or fish, in one meal.
- Eat vegetables in a variety of cooked forms, but definitely include raw, steamed and pickled forms, according to seasonal and personal needs.
- Raw fruits are best eaten alone, not in combination with or immediately following a meal.
- When it comes to seasoning, a light hand brings out the true flavor of the foods.

Planning for Family, Health and Fun————————

My years of teaching cooking classes has acquainted me with the special needs of a variety of people. Children are often advised to eliminate refined foods from their diets to lose weight or control their allergies. Athletes and entertainers seek low-fat, high-carbohydrate diets to maintain their high energy levels. Finally, many people are advised by nutritional counselors to limit their diet and restrict their use of familiar seasonings and favorite foods. Special diets are designed to meet the needs of a particular person and will change as he or she improves.

No matter what the need, it will require time, patience and cooperation among all family members. The unity of eating together as a family is as important in healing as is food. The basic recipes and cooking skills in this book will enable families to become adept at whole foods cookery and still meet the varied needs of individual family members.

Children's Needs————————————

Parents today are increasingly aware of the importance of feeding their children un-refined, unadulterated foods. Weaning children from fast foods *can* be done successfully with patience, creativity, humor, and the active involvement of the children themselves. Here are some pointers I've found useful.

Begin by eliminating processed foods from their diet and replace these with whole foods: fresh juices for soft drinks, whole grain cereal for the sugar-coated kind, fruit kantens in place of puddings and ice cream.

Try to prepare foods that are familiar in appearance and taste. Pizza, noodles with sauce, and chili with corn bread are always hits. Salads of all kinds are well received if vegetables are sliced to be picked up and eaten with the fingers. The sweet tastes of yams, squash, carrots or sweet potatoes are pleasing when made into soup, sauces or pies. Corn-on-the-cob is the most popular grain to begin serving your children.

Be cautious with salt when cooking for kids. They should not have very much until the age of two. Don't allow them to season their own foods with salt or shoyu at the table. By imitating adults, they may become hooked on salty tastes. It's best to remove their portions from soup, beans or other dishes before seasoning the foods with salt or herbs. Try to avoid spices, also. Your children will learn to appreciate the unique taste of each fruit and vegetable.

Your child will inevitably eat away from home—at school, a friend's home, with relatives or at the corner candy store. There are many ways to handle these situations. First, don't be upset or afraid. Trust your children. You can feed them a good breakfast or lunch before they go. It's good to offer either a sweet or snack before they leave or one to take along, so they will be less tempted by poor quality goodies.

If they are off to a friend's house, pack a tasty treat the children love, one that will be enjoyed by their friends as well. Bake a batch of cookies or a pie for your children to share. Wish them well, and encourage them to have a pleasant time, even if their friends eat foods different from yours. Make a pot of miso-vegetable soup to serve when they return. Miso is a good alkalizer to balance the refined foods or sugars eaten outside the home.

Make your children's lunchboxes varied, delicious and familiar looking. Pack them a fun lunchbox of easy-to-eat, light foods. Here again finger foods win out. Foods that are easy to handle and chew are the best choice: sandwiches, rice cakes, corn-on-the-cob, and fruit.

Offer them alternatives their friends will accept. Your hot air popcorn popper fills in the after-school or evening gap. Roasted seeds, fruit kebabs and sliced vegetables are snacks kids can help make. Desserts such as couscous cake or carrot pudding are nutritious choices for between meals. Making finger foods or individual portions shows that special care has been taken. Look at the party section for further suggestions.

Encourage children to assist you in washing grains and beans. Their nimble fingers can pick up tiny stones or unhulled grains while you sort them. Place a chair at the sink and allow them to scrub vegetables with a brush and place them in a colander to drain. This is fun for little ones who can't cut with a knife yet. When children are old enough to handle a knife, buy them their own—small vegetable or paring knives. Teach how to use them and keep them in a special, safe place.

At times you may be too rushed to let them help, so try to plan extra time for dinner preparation to involve them. It gives them a good feeling and before you know it, they'll put supper on for you!

High Flavor-Low Fat Meals

In my cooking classes someone always asks, "My spouse has been advised to reduce salt, sugar and meat from daily meals. How do I make whole grains taste good for a strictly meat-and-potatoes eater?" I tell them they must want to change their food habits and be willing to try new things. They will discover, as we all do, that contrary to popular belief, tastes can and do change given time and well-prepared food.

As with children, it is important to introduce whole foods slowly. Try cooking grains such as buckwheat or millet with potatoes at first. Start with long grain rice or rice pilafs. If you cook for someone who loves garlic and onions, continue to include these foods. Don't fall into the trap of covering everything with tomato sauce; try Red Velvet Soup, Estella's Red Sauce or Gingery Carrot Sauce. Many adults don't like the taste of soy sauce (usually because they have sampled poor quality, commercial products in restaurants), so use plenty of herbs or try miso. Some people become "soy sauce junkies." If so, you can add water to their bottle of soy sauce.

Once again, serve whole foods in as many familiar ways as possible. Creamy bean dips go well with chips. Simply mix cooked beans such as pinto, kidney or red beans in a blender with salsa or hot sauce to taste. Vegetable sticks are fun to dip into tofu or bean spreads.

When reducing salt and high protein foods, go for all the flavor. Ginger, mustard and horseradish add zest. Look for fresh herbs in your market, or start a window-box garden. If you pack your lunch, try a fish salad sandwich, tofu with sprouts, or rice croquettes with tahini sauce. Keep plenty of snack foods around, such as roasted seeds, muffins or cookies, as you may feel hungry while adjusting to the new, light feeling from eating whole foods.

Healing Diets

A simple diet of grains, beans and vegetables, free of spices, oils and baked flour products is part of a healing diet frequently recommended by macrobiotic and other nutritional counselors. Each diet is tailored to the individual's specific condition. The foods advised must be prepared according to instructions with a peaceful attitude and lots of love. While one person in the family is eating a healing diet, other, more varied cooking may be needed to satisfy the rest of the family. Cooking ahead lends itself to this situation. The whole grains, beans and vegetables allowed on this diet can be cooked simply, without extra seasonings. Remove one portion for the dieter, and for the rest of the family, add extra spices, ingredients or sauce. This is one way to keep the entire family happy while you prepare the same basic foods. Look for condiment ideas in Chapter 3.

When someone is eating simply and others are eating more broadly, it is supportive to make the person on a restricted diet feel satisfied. Try attractively garnishing his plate. If small portions are advised, use or buy small dishes to serve foods with appeal. Find a small bud vase and keep a flower or two in it. This adds a fragrant touch to a meal. Make mealtimes as pleasing a ritual as possible.

Party Ideas

The key to serving a stand-up gathering, open house or buffet party is having foods which can be eaten with ease. Ever try to hold a drink and a plate of goodies and manage a fork (or chopsticks) at the same time?

"Finger foods" take a little longer to prepare but the extra effort is worthwhile. With imagination, most foods can be transformed into easily held snacks that are perfect for lunchboxes too. Let's look at the possibilities from grains to desserts:

Grains: Shape mini-rice balls, Millet Croquettes, Falafels, Fish Croquettes, Norimaki or Stuffed Grape Leaves, all made from a pot of cooked grain. Crackers, rice cakes, croutons, corn chips or popcorn are light-eating grains for parties.

Beans: Tofu and tempeh can be sliced and seasoned in a myriad of ways. Create an antipasto platter with Marinated Tofu or tempeh cubes, Tofu Cheese, Tempeh "Bacon," fried tofu cubes on toothpicks with a Teriyaki Sauce, tempeh "chips," or hummus dips with crackers.

Vegetables: Arrange a platter or basket of thinly sliced, raw or steamed vegetables. Lightly marinated pickles go well with drinks. Kebabs are quick to make and serve, combining soy foods with mushrooms, cherry tomatoes and scallions. Don't overlook "Veggie Rolls," they can be prepared ahead of time and fried to golden brown when your guests arrive. Thin slices of cucumber, radish, celery or daikon can be topped with a tofu dip or a tahini-miso spread and a fresh herb garnish.

Sea Vegetables: Arame-Stuffed Mushroom Caps are a sea vegetable success at my dinner parties, served as an appetizer or as a dramatic garnish to a fish entrée. Nori-maki or strips of toasted nori are a pleasing introduction to these foods.

Fish: Large, flaked fish fillets can be cubed for fish kebabs. They can be baked and mixed in fish-and-potato cakes or as mini fish and rice croquettes. Smoked salmon or lox is delicious on pumperknickel bread with a tofu spread.

Nibbles: Shoyu-roasted nuts or seeds, mixed dried fruits, Good Crunch, or Stuffed Dates.

Desserts: Cookies can be made small and bite-sized, or cakes can be baked in a jelly roll pan and cut into small pieces. Couscous Cake or Fruit Kebabs are colorful and easy-to-serve desserts.

Drinks: Herb teas, bancha tea with lemon, hot cider with cinnamon stick, or sparkling water mixed with fresh fruit juices.

Tips for Coordinating Meals

Involve your family in shopping, storing and preparing foods. Encourage housemates and children to learn to cook and help in the kitchen. If meals are eaten away from home, it's helpful if each family member has a thermos and a special container which he is responsible for.

- Keep a notebook in your kitchen. Include a list of your family's special needs—foods that are essential and those to be avoided. Record your family's eating schedule and when individuals need food packed for school, work or outside activities. A meal schedule posted on the refrigerator enables family members to help prepare food for others.
- Sharing meals together is as important as wholesome ingredients. If the whole family can't always eat together, try to share a meal with one other family member whenever possible.
- Plan each menu before you begin. Jot down the sequence of dishes to be prepared, according to their cooking times.
- When ready to cook, clean the kitchen. Wash all the dishes and utensils, empty the dish washer, clear the drain rack.
- Tie your hair back or cover it if it's long. Put on a clean apron. Relax your mind, let all outside thoughts rest, and think about putting your best energy into the food.
- Sharpen your knife—a daily task.
- Start the grains and beans simmering.
- If making a dessert, such as kanten, start it first, as it needs time to cool.
- Wash all vegetables, including sea vegetables. Place in colanders or baskets to drain.
- Begin to slice vegetables according to the work flow chart.
- Place each group of cut vegetables on a plate or in a bowl.

- Keep them separate until ready to use them. Wipe the cutting board and knife between each vegetable.
- Begin to cook vegetables, starting with longer-cooking ones.
- When grains and beans are ready, remove portions for children or family members on special diets.
- Season the dish to your taste.
- Clean as you go. Transfer the cooked foods to serving platters and garnish.

Fig. 28   Party Platter. Norimaki, raw vegetables, pickles and olives to accompany dips.

Sensual and Satisfying Dining

Memorable meals require more than choosing one food from each group of grains, beans and vegetables. When my family sits down to a meal, they do not consume a plate of proteins, carbohydrates, minerals and vitamins. Neither do they feel awkward because the dinner is good for their health.

An enticing aroma from the kitchen will lure your family to mealtimes. An attractive table, a peaceful atmosphere, appealing food and the gracious spirit of the cook and diners combine to nourish us on all levels.

The following sections briefly describe color, taste and texture. These elements are consciously or intuitively combined in all cuisines. As you read about them, it's helpful to visualize as you plan. One practice I continue from my culinary training is to draw a sketch of a meal, indicating the color, taste and texture of each dish. I find this helpful to blend all these sensual aspects.

Taste

The secret of a satisfying meal is a subtle blend of five tastes: sweet, sour, salty, bitter and pungent (spicy). Master chefs and intuitive cooks instinctively weave these delicate tastes together when cooking.

In my observation, people often feel hungry after eating a substantial meal if it lacks tastes from these five groups. A grain-centered diet is rich in sweet tastes. Brown rice, wheat, corn, millet and oats, along with desserts, fruits and sweet root vegetables, tip the scales to the sweet side.

Salty condiments, such as shoyu, miso, sesame salt, sea vegetables and pickles act as a balance for sweet tastes. Often a sweet-salty seesaw can occur in your cooking and cravings. Too much of one taste usually results in a desire for the other. In your meals take special care to use the less familiar tastes—sour, bitter and spicy. For instance, sprinkle grains with chopped scallions, add a teaspoon of ginger juice to bean soups or casseroles, or add lemon juice or vinegar to a salad dressing. Try umeboshi's salty, slightly sour taste which blends uniquely with many foods for a new flavor.

A condiment tray offering a variety of different tasting foods, such as mustard, horseradish, sesame salt, fruit chutneys or roasted sunflower seeds, allows each person to balance his or her own plate. When planning meals, keep these tastes in mind. Try to use the five tastes, if not in every meal, then combined throughout the day.

Sample of Five Tastes:

Sweet: most whole grains, carrots, squash, grain sweeteners, most root vegetables, fruit, dried fruit

Salty: sea salt, shoyu, tamari, miso, pickles, sea vegetables

Bitter: watercress, mustard greens, chicory, grain coffee, dandelions

Sour: lemons, limes, vinegar, pickles, umeboshi, cranberries

Pungent: scallions, daikon, ginger, mustard, garlic, horseradish

Color

A meal that is visually pleasing tends to be balanced in nutrients, tastes and textures. A plate of rice, boiled cauliflower and tofu may be a balanced grain-bean-vegetable meal, but it's all white. Just as grains are the center of whole foods cuisine, their neutral tones (beige, amber, golden, light brown) provide a base around which a colorful array of beans and vegetables are assembled.

A dish of brown rice served with a green string bean salad and bright orange "Vichy" carrots looks dramatic when garnished with black olives and sliced scallions. Spicy black beans spooned over golden corn bread, served with a slice of orange squash and a crisp green salad with red onions, is a feast for the eyes.

Nature provides us with a rainbow of colorful foods. By selecting a wide variety of foods in appealing combinations, you are sure to satisfy your visual as well as nutritional needs. The following chart is purely to inspire you when planning menus.

A Rainbow Selection of Whole Foods:

White: tofu, navy and lima beans, cauliflower, daikon, mung sprouts

Red: red lentils, kidney beans, adzuki beans, beets, red cabbage, radishes, red onion, red pepper, strawberries, apples

Orange: carrots, squash, pumpkin, oranges, tangerines, peaches

Yellow: corn, summer squash, wax beans, lemons, yellow split peas, millet

Green: split peas, mung beans, string beans, all leafy green vegetables, broccoli, brussel sprouts, snow peas

Blue: blueberries

Purple: dulse, grapes, turnips, plums

Brown: nuts, seeds, lentils, whole wheat, buckwheat, mushrooms, burdock

Black: sea vegetables (nori, arame, hijiki), black beans, olives, soy sauce

Texture

The final element in composing memorable meals is texture. Since whole foods are high in fiber, they offer a surprisingly sensual texture to persons accustomed to processed foods. Bleached white flour, white rice, and white sugar products tend to melt in the mouth. Chewed properly (that is, more than the bite and swallow habit), brown rice releases its sweet delicious flavor.

Textures should balance in a meal, like colors and tastes. Chewy grains and soft, creamy beans are complemented by a crisp salad. Creative cooks can enhance or change the texture of foods to harmonize in their menus. Carrots are crunchy served raw or steamed. Boiled and puréed, carrots make a velvety smooth, orange-colored sauce. Deep-fried, tofu is crisp and golden; blend soft tofu with seasonings and you have a pourable dressing. These are two of tofu's myriad of possible textures. Grains are inherently chewy, but they become crispy when formed into croquettes and fried. Rice, barley and oats, for example, become creamy if simmered in lots of water. Soft breakfast grains are appealing with crunchy nuts or seeds as a garnish. Blend the textures in your desserts. Hot spicy apple sauce or fruit kanten is enhanced by chopped nuts or crunchy granola.

Creating an Atmosphere

Once you make the effort to cook food lovingly, take the final step to enhance the atmosphere of the meal. Professional chefs and caterers all have their own styles of presenting food. Each chef has a special signature or trademark, such as a centerpiece of whimsically-carved vegetables arranged in a squash vase, or fresh cut flowers selected to harmonize with the meal, or an enticing fruit basket full of apples, grapes and cherries. The serving ware is often a secret of successful parties. One caterer may favor baskets of many shapes and sizes, another will present food on silver trays passed by waiters, a third may favor handmade ceramic dishes in pastel colors to complement the food.

The appropriate serving platter can highlight simple food. Imagine serving brown rice in a brown wooden bowl with only a wooden spoon—a bit austere for every day. Now picture the same brown rice in a royal blue and white ceramic dish, garnished with a red radish flower and a sprig of parsley, and surrounded by crisp green snow peas.

Simple foods are appealing on plates with colorful borders and garnishes. The reverse holds true for bright, Chinese-style vegetable dishes in a shiny kuzu sauce; these need a solid-colored, simple platter.

To choose a garnish, think of the meal as a whole—the colors, tastes, textures. Consider all the elements. Is there anything missing? Is the meal too pale or softly textured? Does it rely on the sweet tastes of grains and vegetables? Try to plan the garnish as part of the meal, not as an afterthought. A few slices of raw or steamed vegetable, such as carrot flowers, radishes, cucumber or zucchini, can be alternated to border a dish. Steamed leafy greens, such as curly kale or smooth collard greens, can line a platter. Snow peas, strips of red pepper or matchstick carrots can add an exotic look to grain or noodle dishes.

Remember that garnishes are decorative touches and should not overpower your meal presentation. Asymmetrical designs can be more aesthetic than symmetrical arrangements. Parsley and scallions are the familiar finishing touches, but don't limit yourself to the traditional accents. Scallion flowers are quick, impressive garnishes. For something unusual, try toasting nori (a sea vegetable) and cutting it into attractive shapes with scissors. Use a few carrot flowers to garnish your soup, or sautéed mushrooms to top the tempeh. Pink umeboshi radishes brighten a salad or sandwich plate.

Choose an attractive and appropriate tablecloth or table mats to show off the platters of food. Don't use a busy print that clashes with the food presentation; try a solid, cool color like pale green or blue. Neutral cloths or pastel shades with a texture enhance your meal. When I plan a special ethnic theme, I choose a cotton spread from Mexico or India. For an Indonesian "rice table" I use a colorful batik cloth. Accent the island meal with a few exotic flowers and a basket of tropical fruits.

You can create seasonal table settings with a few branches of holly or evergreens in winter, tulips and daffodils in spring, or red and golden autumn leaves in the fall. You might keep on hand an assortment of bud vases, bottles or unusual jars to hold greenery or flowers.

Candles and music may seem romantic for everyday use, but candles have been a sign of light and hope throughout history. A floral centerpiece and candles add a sense of ritual to everyday or holiday meals. Soft, relaxing music soothes children and parents after a busy day, setting a pleasant atmosphere for dining.

3. Snacks, Condiments and Pickles

Where do I begin?—Now that you've read about the basic skills of vegetable cutting and concepts of menu planning, this chapter will help you to develop some cooking skills. For those with little or no experience there are recipes that require minimal preparation and cooking time. A blender and toaster oven are good tools for starting out.

Tofu, tahini, miso, beans, stewed fruit and diced vegetables can be whipped or puréed, in a blender or food processor, into spreads, sauces and dips in seconds. Not all together, of course.

Roasting seeds and nuts is a sensory experience—their delicious aroma fills the kitchen. One cup can be roasted in a toaster-oven tray in less time than in the oven. Roast seeds or nuts in small quantities and keep them refrigerated. Besides being quite salty and expensive, store-bought seeds or nuts roasted in oil often go rancid if not refrigerated. Once you roast your own seeds, store-bought ones will never have the same appeal.

An artful arrangement of vegetables with a tofu or tahini dip attracts after-school munchers or before-dinner nibblers. Remember to have plenty of these snack foods on hand while you are tapering off processed foods. Share these simple recipes with children—get them involved.

Roasting/Toasting Grains, Nuts and Seeds

Equipment: Mesh colander, bowl of water, sheet pan or baking dish, cast-iron skillet or heavy-bottomed pot.

Set-up: Wash nuts, seeds or grain in bowl of water. Drain thoroughly in mesh colander; spread evenly on pan or baking dish for oven or cast-iron pan for stove.

Procedure:
1. For roasting (oven): Preheat oven to 325° F. Stir or shake the pan often to prevent burning. Roast until they are golden brown outside. Test by splitting them in half: nuts should be light brown, not white, in the center.
2. For toasting (stove-top): Use a medium flame. Stir or shake the pan to prevent burning or sticking. Remove from pan when browned.

Tip: Roasting brings out a rich, nutty flavor in grains (rice, millet, etc.). Roast first; continue with the recipe. Nuts and seeds change flavor when roasted. This is a necessary step before grinding into nut butters.

Roasted Sunflower and Pumpkin Seeds————————————

To satisfy the need for "crunch," serve roasted seeds with grain and vegetable dishes. My parties aren't complete without them. It is a must, too, for outings and hikes.

Servings: 2 cups
Time: 30 minutes

Equipment:
strainer, baking dishes

Ingredients:
1 cup sunflower seeds
1 cup pumpkin seeds
2 tsp. shoyu (optional) or
pinch of sea salt

Procedure: Rinse seeds in strainer. In separate baking dishes, spread seeds out evenly. Bake in 325°F. oven. Stir 2 or 3 times to roast evenly. Check after 10 minutes. When seeds are golden brown, sprinkle with shoyu and stir. Return to oven for 2 minutes. Allow to cool. Store in a jar. (Seeds or nuts can be roasted 3 to 4 days ahead of party.)

Variations:
- Almonds, pecans or filberts can be shoyu-roasted also.
- Add a pinch of curry, ginger or chili powder to shoyu to make spiced "cocktail" seeds.
- Omit shoyu.

Menu Suggestions:
- Sprinkle on breakfast cereals.
- Serve with meals for crunch, variety and protein.
- Add to trail mixes.
- Serve with drinks as snack.

Shoyu-Roasted Cashews or Almonds————————————

Roasted nuts are an irresistible addition to meals. Bring a jar to get-togethers, if you can refrain from eating them before you get there.

Servings: 2 cups
Time: 15 to 20 minutes

Equipment:
baking dish, small bowl, wooden spoon

Ingredients:
2 cups cashews
2 to 3 tsp. shoyu
1/2 tsp. coriander
(optional)
1/2 tsp. powdered ginger
(optional)

Procedure: Roast cashews in 300°F. oven until golden, stirring occasionally. Mix shoyu and spices together; pour over roasted nuts and stir. Return to oven for 1 minute to allow shoyu to dry. Cool in baking dish; store in jar.

Variations:
- Add other spices: a pinch of cumin, allspice or curry powder.
- A jar of Spicy Cashews makes a quick, welcome gift from the kitchen for holidays or birthdays.

Tip: To coat nuts evenly with shoyu, pour shoyu in a clean spray bottle and "mist" nuts after they have been roasted.

Miso-Tahini for Sauce or Spread

Tahini, a paste of ground sesame seeds, is roasted and mixed with miso. Serve as a spread on bread or crackers. Thin with water to make a creamy sauce. Miso-Tahini can keep up to 1 week refrigerated, but it never lasts that long in my house.

Servings: 6 or more
Time: 15 minutes

Equipment:
  skillet, mixing bowl or
  blender, wooden spoon

Ingredients:
  1 cup tahini
  2 to 3 tbsp. miso
  1 lemon, juiced
  water, to thin

Procedure: To roast tahini, pour it into a pan, stir over a low flame with a wooden spoon. Continue to stir until tahini begins to turn a slightly darker color. A nutty, rich aroma will arise after 3 to 5 minutes. Allow to cool before blending. Place in mixing bowl or blender, add miso, lemon juice and water. Blend or purée until creamy smooth for a spread or add more water for a pourable consistency.

Variations:
- Tahini-Basil: add 1 to 2 tbsp. chopped, fresh basil.
- Tahini-Garlic: add 2 to 3 cloves minced garlic to tahini while it roasts.
- Herbal Dressing: add 1 tsp. of favorite herbs— oregano, dill, thyme, etc.
- Substitute rice vinegar for lemon juice.

Menu Suggestions:
- Serve Miso-Tahini spread with crackers or bread for parties, snacks or meals.
- Sandwiches: spread Miso-Tahini on breads, garnish with sprouts, radish, lettuce and cucumber.
- Miso-Tahini Dressing: serve over grain or noodles; steamed vegetables and tofu; salads.

Avocado-Tofu Spread with Salsa

Salsa adds a kick to this memorable mix. Tofu blends with the luscious texture of avocado for a lighter dip or sandwich spread.

Servings: 2 cups, approxi-
  mately
Time: 5 minutes

Equipment:
  blender, small bowl

Ingredients:
  1 ripe avocado, peeled
    and seeded
  1/2 lb. tofu, drained

Procedure: Mash avocado with tofu in a bowl. Add lemon juice, sea salt and salsa; mix. Purée in blender or food processor until smooth, adding water if needed. Adjust seasonings.

Variations:
- Instead of salsa, add extra lemon and a pinch of sea salt.
- Omit salsa, sauté onion with 1/4 to 1/2 tsp. curry powder; purée briefly in blender.

1 lemon, juiced
pinch of sea salt or 1 tsp.
   shoyu (optional)
1 to 2 tbsp. salsa, or to
   taste
water, if needed for
   consistency

Menu Suggestions:
- Serve as a dip with rice crackers or corn chips.
- Use as a sandwich filling with sprouts and sliced tomatoes.
- Add extra water to make a sauce; serve with rice or steamed vegetables.

Lunch:
Cabbage-Corn Soup
Avocado-Tofu Sandwich
Fruit Kanten

Party:
Avocado-Tofu Spread
   with Vegetable Sticks
Chili
Corn Chips or Corn
   Bread
Salad with Sprouts,
   Red Onion

Poppy Seed-Tofu Dip

A delightful pairing of sliced vegetables and an unusual tofu dip, for a first course or party treat.

Servings: makes 1 1/2 cups
Time: 20 minutes

Equipment:
   blender or mixing bowl,
   skillet, platter

Ingredients:
Poppy seed-Tofu Dip:
   1/2 lb. tofu
   2 tbsp. tahini
   2 tbsp. miso, (shiro or
      kome) or pinch of sea
      salt
   2 to 3 tbsp. vinegar or
      lemon juice
   1/4 to 1/2 cup water
   2 tbsp. poppy seeds,
      roasted
   2 tbsp. chopped parsley

Vegetables:
   2 or 3 carrots, cut into
      sticks
   4 or 5 stalks celery, cut
      into sticks
   1 small zucchini, cut into
      rounds

Procedure: Mash tofu with fork. Roast tahini in skillet 2 to 3 minutes. Mix tofu, tahini, miso, vinegar and 1/4 to 1/2 cup water in blender. Roast poppy seeds in skillet; stir to prevent burning. When seeds smell nutty, add to tofu mixture in blender; purée. Chop parsley and add to dip. Adjust seasonings. Arrange sliced vegetables around a bowl of dip.

Variations:
- Broccoli, cauliflower, green beans, lightly steamed or raw, can be used.

1 bunch radishes, cut into
   flowers
2 cucumbers, cut into
   rounds
1 small bunch scallions,
   cut into 3-inch pieces
   for dipping

Tofu Canapés

Tofu canapés are the new wave of New Age entertaining.

Servings: 8 or more
Time: 15 minutes

Equipment:
   blender, skillet, toaster or
   oven, serving platter

Ingredients:
   8 slices whole wheat
      bread, toasted
   1/2 lb. tofu
   2 tbsp. miso
   1/4 cup tahini, roasted
   2 scallions, diced
   2 tbsp. vinegar
   curry and herbs (optional)

Garnish:
   1 celery stalk, sliced for
      garnish
   1 carrot, sliced for garnish
   fresh dill, radishes,
      toasted nori cut into
      shapes, fresh parsley

Procedure: Toast bread in toaster or oven. Cut each slice of bread into quarters, either square or triangular, and remove crusts if you desire. Roast tahini in skillet until "nutty." In blender combine tofu, miso, tahini, vinegar, scallion and seasonings. Wash and slice vegetables on bias into thin matchsticks, rounds or finely diced. Spread toast with tofu mixture. Garnish canapés with vegetables, paying attention to color and shape for an eye-appealing arrangement.

Variations:
• Spread tofu mixture on crackers, cucumber slices, etc.
• Garnish with lox or smoked salmon strips.

Menu Suggestions:
   For a party:
   Canapés
   Millet Croquettes with Teriyaki Sauce
   Vegetable Platter with Avocado-Tofu Dip

Japanese-Style Marinated Tofu

Tender tofu cubes marinated with ginger, shoyu and saké are a traditional Japanese summer food. In warm weather, I fill a bowl with crushed ice and arrange tofu cubes, blanched broccoli and radish flowers on top.

Servings: 6 or more
Time: 10 minute prepara-
   tion, 4 hours minimum
   marination

Procedure: Rinse tofu and press for 1/2 hour to remove water. Cut into 1-inch cubes and place in small

Equipment:
 glass or ceramic bowl or
 container

Ingredients:
 1 lb. firm tofu
 1/8 to 1/2 cup saké
 2 to 3 tbsp. shoyu
 1 tbsp. fresh ginger juice
 1/2 tsp. wasabi (dry
  horseradish)
 1/2 tsp. dry mustard
 2 cloves garlic (optional)
 water to cover

container (glass or ceramic is best). Mix marinade ingredients and pour over tofu cubes to cover completely; add extra water if needed and stir briefly. Allow to marinate 4 to 10 hours. Taste for saltiness and adjust seasonings. You may prefer more shoyu and/or ginger. Tofu in marinade will keep 3 to 4 days in the refrigerator and its flavor will become saltier.

Variations:
• Mirin can be substituted for saké.
• Vary amounts of mustard and wasabi.

Menu Suggestions:

Hijiki Noodle Salad	Marinated Tofu
Marinated Tofu	Autumn Stew or Curried
Corn-on-the-Cob	Vegetables in Sauce
Blueberry Pie	Rice Pilaf
	Greens or Salad

Herbed Croutons

Croutons add crunch to soups, salads and vegetable dishes. They will stay crisp for days if kept in a plastic bag or sealed container.

Servings: 6 to 8
Time: 30 minutes

Equipment:
 baking dish

Ingredients:
 6 slices whole wheat bread
 3 tbsp. oil
 1 tsp. shoyu or pinch of
  sea salt
 1/4 tsp. each: oregano,
  sage, thyme, basil
 2 to 4 cloves garlic,
  minced

Procedure: Cut bread into 1/2-inch cubes. Combine oil, shoyu or sea salt, herbs and garlic in baking dish. Toss bread cubes in mixture and coat well. Spread out on baking dish. Bake in 325°F. oven until golden brown (about 20 minutes), stirring occasionally. Cubes will get crisp after they cool.

Variations:
• Cut bread into strips and serve with dips.
• Use your favorite herbs in any combination.
• To make garlic toast, mix extra oil and garlic. Place bread on cookie sheet and brush with garlic oil.

Condiments

Condiments, those little jars or bowls of savory tastes, keep families and cooks from going crazy. It is impossible to please all with the same dish: it will be either too bland or too spicy. Some are on low-salt diets; others may favor the spice of Mexican cuisine. Herbs don't please some, while many can't live without them, and junk-food taste buds often complain, "This has no flavor."

Fortunately, condiments allow all to season their own plates. Looking at history, we see that this was common practice. From Indian rice tables to Middle Eastern banquets, a simple bowl of grain was the heart of the meal. Several small bowls of various other foods and condiments were offered, allowing people to balance their eating, according to need and taste.

There are condiments for every taste:

- **salty:** gomasio, shoyu-roasted nuts, toasted nori
- **spicy:** (pungent) spicy walnut condiment, scallions, mustard, grated ginger, coconut condiment
- **sweet:** chutney, sweet soy sauce
- **sour:** pickles, vinegar, lemon wedge
- **bitter:** watercress, sautéed dandelion greens, chicory
- **hot:** cayenne pepper, jalapeno peppers (approach with caution)

Tip: Make your own relish tray, with space to hold jars. Place jars in a condiment holder, something you can take from refrigerator to table. A lazy Susan is convenient for table service.

Gomasio (Sesame Salt)

Gomasio is a condiment made of roasted sesame seeds and sea salt, which are ground together. Popular in Japan and becoming better known here, this sesame salt is sprinkled on grain and vegetable dishes. The process of making sesame salt is somewhat long, and slow. Patience and practice are needed but it's worth the effort. First sesame seeds are washed and roasted, preferably in a black cast-iron skillet, then ground in a suribachi, a Japanese mortar with grooves, with a pestle. The ratio of sea salt to sesame seeds can vary from 1 to 7 to 1 to 14. Store in a jar after grinding to keep fresh. Keep in a cool place.

Servings: 1 cup
Time: 30–45 minutes

Equipment:
black cast iron or stainless skillet, strainer, wooden spoon, suribachi or mortar and pestle.

Ingredients:
1 cup sesame seeds
2 or 3 tsp. sea salt

Procedure: Wash sesame seeds carefully in a large bowl of water. Pour off water; rinse in strainer and drain. Place in skillet; dry-roast over low flame, stirring continuously. Shake pan to loosen seeds and evenly toast. Seeds will change color, becoming darker and fuller. When they give off a nutty aroma and begin popping, they are nearly done. If seeds crush easily between thumb and index fingers, they're ready to grind. Place seeds and sea salt into suribachi or grinder. Using a slow, circular motion, grind the seeds carefully. After about 5 minutes or longer, they should be coarsely ground, but not powdery. Store in jar.

Indonesian Coconut Condiment——————————

Indonesian families serve spicy condiments, enriching their rice-based diet. One recipe will keep 1 to 2 weeks in the refrigerator. A fresh bowl of rice will quickly disappear with this condiment.

Servings: 8 or more
Time: 15 minutes
           preparation, 1 hour
           roasting

Equipment:
   sauté pan, small bowl,
   large baking dish, jar

Ingredients:
   1 tbsp. sesame oil
   1 small onion (1/4 cup,
      minced)
   3 cloves garlic, minced
   1 tsp. turmeric
   1/2 tsp. powdered ginger
   1/4 tsp. powdered
      cardamon
   1/4 tsp. cumin
   1/2 tsp. sea salt
   1/8 cup sesame seeds,
      washed and rinsed
   1/2 cup peanuts, raw
   1 cup coconut (flaked or
      freshly grated)
   1/3 cup lemon juice
   1 tbsp. barley malt

Procedure: Heat oil in large sauté or fry pan. Sauté onion, garlic and spices for 3 to 5 minutes. Add sesame seeds and peanuts. Toast 2 to 3 minutes. Add coconut and stir well. Dissolve barley malt in lemon juice. Add to mixture. Turn oven on low (250° to 300°F.). Spread mixture in large baking dish. Roast slowly in oven 1 hour or more until golden and crispy. Stir occasionally. When cool, store in jar. Keep in refrigerator.

Variations:
• Experiment with quantities of spice, depending on your taste.

Menu Suggestions:

Tofu or Fish Kebabs	Black Bean Soup
Rice	Rice or Millet
Coconut Condiment	Coconut Condiment
Steamed Vegetables	Julienne Salad
Sweet-Sour Pickles	Pickles
Fruit Smoothie	

Spicy Walnut Condiment——————————

Ground, roasted walnuts with a hint of spice add crunch to mealtimes. Sprinkle on breakfast cereal, salads and desserts.

Servings: 1 cup
Time: 15 minutes

Equipment:
   roasting or cookie sheet,
   blender or suribachi

Ingredients:
   1 cup walnuts
   1 to 2 tsp. shoyu

Procedure: Roast walnuts at 300°F. for 10 minutes until golden brown. Mix shoyu and spices in bowl; toss in roasted walnuts hot from the oven and stir to coat evenly. Return to oven for 1 minute to allow shoyu to dry. Spicy walnuts can be ground in a blender or suribachi to a coarse meal, chopped by hand or left whole.

1/2 tsp. powdered ginger
1/2 tsp. powdered
    coriander
1/2 tsp. powdered cloves

Variations:
- Substitute almond or cashews for walnuts.
- Grind to a fine meal and roll grain croquettes in them.
- Add to trail mix.

Menu Suggestions:
- Serve with breakfast oatmeal or stewed fruit.
- Garnish desserts with Spicy Walnut Condiment.

Cranberry-Apple Relish

A New England holiday tradition, this tangy cranberry relish serves as a bright condiment or dessert.

Servings: 6 or more
Time: 30 minutes

Equipment:
  saucepan with cover, jar
  or serving bowl

Ingredients:
  2 cups cranberries,
      washed
  4 cups apples, McIntosh
      or Cortland, chopped
      into 1-inch pieces
  1 cup raisins
  grated peel of 1 orange
  2 cups apple juice or
      water
  pinch of sea salt
  1/2 cup walnuts, roasted
      and chopped
  1/2 tsp. cinnamon
      (optional)
  1 tbsp. kuzu, dissolved in
      1/4 cup water for
      thickening (optional)

Procedure: Put all ingredients except walnuts, cinnamon and kuzu in a heavy-bottomed saucepan. Cover and bring to a boil. Reduce flame; remove cover and simmer 15 to 20 minutes until excess liquid has evaporated—or thicken with kuzu. Add walnuts to mixture; sprinkle with cinnamon and serve at room temperature. Relish will keep in the refrigerator for 3 to 4 days.

Variations:
- Substitute orange juice for apple juice.
- Golden raisins can replace dark raisins.
- Add extra sweetener, serve as a dessert.

Menu Suggestions:

Tempeh "Turkey"	Fish with Mushroom Gravy
Brown and Wild Rice	
Steamed Kale	Millet with Potatoes
Cranberry-Apple Relish	Brussels Sprouts
	Cranberry-Apple Relish

Peach Chutney————————————————

Chutneys are sweet and spicy condiments ubiquitous in Indian cuisine. I serve them to add exotic flavor to simple dahl and rice meals.

Servings: 4 to 6
Time: 30 minutes

Equipment:
  saucepan with lid

Ingredients:
  1/2 cup raisins
  1/2 cup dried apricots
  1 orange peel
  1 cinnamon stick
  1 cup water or apple juice
  3 to 4 fresh peaches,
    peeled and diced
  pinch of sea salt
  1 tsp. kuzu dissolved in
    1/4 cup water

Procedure: Rinse dried fruit; place in saucepan with peel, cinnamon stick and water. Bring to a boil; simmer for 15 minutes. Peel and dice peaches; add to simmering fruit with a pinch of sea salt. Cook 10 minutes and thicken with kuzu if you want a thicker or smoother texture. When ready to serve, remove cinnamon stick and orange peel. Garnish bowl of chutney with slices of orange.

Variations:
• Purée and use as toast spread.
• Add roasted, chopped almonds or walnuts.

Menu Suggestions:

Breakfast:
Oatmeal Muffins
Soft Rice
Peach Chutney

Snack:
Peach Chutney
Corn Bread
Peanut Butter Cookies

Dinner:
Mung Dahl
Rice
"Himalayan Greens"
Peach Chutney

Pickles————————————————

Pickles are an important food that have almost been forgotten. They have enzymes from fermentation that aid in the digestion of all foods, especially grains. In early times, pickling or salting was a major method of preservation. All cultures had their own special style of fermenting foods. In Japan, soybeans are made into miso and shoyu. Pickles, yoghurt, sauerkraut and beer are central to European cuisine. Koreans savor kimchee—pickled Chinese cabbage with hot pepper.

Not only are pickles necessary to digestion, but they also have the sour flavor needed to satisfy one of our five tastes at mealtime.

Try to have pickles of one type or another in the house at all times. They can be added to flavor many dishes: try sauerkraut juice or pickle juice in grains, salad dressings and vegetable sauce—so don't throw that pickle juice away. Make your own pickles by adding sliced radish, daikon, carrots or onions to this juice. Marinate two days.

Sweet-Sour Pickles (Atjar)

Sweet-sour pickles are popular in the Indonesian islands. This recipe is ready in 1 day, and will keep 4 to 5 days refrigerated.

Servings: 1 qt.
Time: 15 minutes, 1 day marination

Equipment:
1 qt. jar, pot

Ingredients:
1 carrot, cut into matchsticks
1 onion, cut into 1/2-inch slices
1 small zucchini, cut into matchsticks

Marinade:
5 oz. rice vinegar
1 cup water
1 tsp. sea salt
3 tbsp. barley malt or rice syrup

Procedure: Place sliced vegetables into jar. Bring marinade to a boil and while hot pour over the vegetables; cool and refrigerate.

Variations:
• Cauliflower, celery, green beans, peppers and broccoli can be pickled, too.

Menu Suggestions:
• Serve with simple grain and bean dishes, especially tempeh.

Umeboshi Radish Pickles

Red radishes are transformed into delectable pink pickles by simmering them in water with a few umeboshi plums. Ready in minutes, these slightly salty-sour pickles aid in digestion and are a rosy garnish to meals.

Servings: 8 or more
Time: 15 minutes

Equipment:
saucepan, jar

Ingredients:
1 to 2 bunches radishes, washed and trimmed
2 to 4 tbsp. umeboshi paste or 4 to 6 plums
1 to 2 cups water

Procedure: In saucepan dissolve umeboshi paste or plum flesh in water. Add washed and trimmed radishes; if large, cut in quarters. Bring to boil and simmer 10 to 20 minutes until radishes turn pink. Cool; drain off liquid and reserve for dressings or cooking. Radish pickles keep 2 to 3 days in the refrigerator.

Variations:
• Thin slices of daikon (Japanese white radish) can be substituted for radish.

Menu Suggestions:
• These pickles lend eye appeal to grain dishes and vegetable salads.

Italian-Style Pickles with Fennel———————————

Fresh fennel and dried fennel seeds give a unique flavor to these quick pickles, inspired by Italian cuisine.

Servings: 6 or more
Time: 10 minute preparation, marinate overnight

Equipment:
1 qt. jar, pot

Ingredients:
1 celery stalk, cut into 1/2-inch diagonal slices
1 onion, cut into 1/2-inch slices
1 carrot, sliced into large matchsticks
1 cup string beans, cut into bite-sized pieces
1 cup fresh fennel, cut into bite-sized pieces

Marinade:
2 cups water
1 tbsp. fennel seeds, crushed (optional)
2 large cloves garlic, sliced
1 tsp. sea salt
sprig of basil, mint or oregano, fresh if available
juice of 1 lemon

Procedure: Cut vegetables and fill jar. Bring all ingredients in marinade except lemon juice to a boil. Add lemon juice to boiling marinade and then pour over vegetables in jar. Allow to cool overnight. It will keep in the refrigerator up to 1 week.

Variations:
• Broccoli, cauliflower and pearl onions can be used, too.

Menu Suggestions:
• Perfect for picnics and parties, they go especially well with pizza and spaghetti dinners.
• Serve with soup and sandwiches.

Mustard Green Pickles————————————————

Flavors from the "5 tastes" blend together in this 2-day pickle.

Servings: 10 or more
Time: 15 minutes, 2 days marination

Equipment:
large jar, cheesecloth, pot

Procedure: Wash and cut greens into 1-inch pieces. Pack in jar. Heat water, shoyu and rice syrup; add roasted sesame seeds and ginger juice. Pour over greens. Liquid should cover greens; add more marinade if necessary. Press greens down, so they are covered with liquid. Cover jar with cheesecloth. Keep for 2 days in cool, dark place. Refrigerate.

Ingredients:
  1 bunch mustard greens, washed and cut into 1-inch pieces
  2 cups water
  1/2 cup shoyu
  1/4 cup rice syrup
  3 tbsp. roasted sesame seeds
  1 tbsp. ginger juice

Variations:
- Daikon or turnip greens, kale or Chinese cabbage can also be pickled.

Red or White Sauerkraut

Homemade sauerkraut has a fresh, sharp taste, unlike its store-bought relatives. Red cabbage makes a tangier version with an appealing color. For successful sauerkrauting, slice cabbage thinly with a sharp knife. If the weather is too hot or humid (over 75° to 80°F.), the cabbage may sour before it ferments. Cool, dry days are ideal for kraut making. It makes a good gift for friends.

Servings: 2 to 3 qts.
Time: 2 weeks

Equipment:
  ceramic or wooden crock, wooden lid, weight, cheesecloth

Ingredients:
  4 to 6 lbs. red or white cabbage
  1/3 to 1/4 cup of sea salt

Procedure: Rinse cabbage. Slice the cabbage thinly with a sharp knife and also slice core very fine (or save it for stock). Place cabbage in crock; sprinkle with sea salt and mix well. Place a plate or wooden lid on top of cabbage with a weight resting on the lid. The plate must fit inside the crock. Use a brick or heavy stone for the weight. (I use a gallon jug filled with water.) Cover the crock with cheesecloth or gauze. Check the water level after 1 day; it should cover the cabbage. If it doesn't, add more weight. Place crock in pantry, dry cellar or dark, cool corner of kitchen. Check daily and skim any mold that forms on water. After 2 weeks, taste sauerkraut to see if it has fermented enough. Leave another few days if desired. When ready, place sauerkraut in very clean jars. Store in refrigerator. Rinse if too salty and serve. Sauerkraut can be heated and served. Add a few caraway seeds for a tasty crunch.

4. Breakfast

Whole grains, in one form or another, and vegetables or fruits, begin the day all over the world: Indians make chapatis; the British, porridge, toast and beans; rice and miso soup are favored in Japan; croissants and baguettes in France; South Americans breakfast on corn and tortillas; and Sri Lankans make special rice pancakes called hoppers. New England winters are made for steaming bowls of cereal or light vegetable soup.

Breakfast should reflect the morning's activities. For many, it is the only quiet meal of the day. A substantial breakfast of soft grain, a simple vegetable soup or steamed vegetables is my favorite; noodles in broth, along with toast and tea, fortify me through a busy day.

Hearty breakfasts which include scrambled tofu or tempeh bacon, muffins and fruit spreads sustain those in cooler climates or in labor-intensive work. Those living in warmer climates may find a light meal of fruits, or noodles and vegetables is the best way to begin the day.

Muffins, scones or couscous cake, made that morning (or the evening before), can be lingered over at the house or brought along to work with a thermos of tea or hot cereal.

Children benefit from these high-carbohydrate breakfasts; they usually prefer sweet tastes in the morning—barley malt or rice syrup on cereal, or dried fruits cooked together with grain. Apple juice or soy milk are popular on dry cereal.

Weekend brunches may feature corn bread, baked beans and salad, a rice salad with "tofu cheese," or a noodle kugel with vegetable soup.

Sweet "Breakfast" Barley

Sautéed spices and sweet dried fruit bring a Middle Eastern essence to plain barley. This fragrant barley could be served in the morning or at dinner with a vegetable or bean dish.

Servings: 4 or more
Time: 15 minutes

Equipment:
   heavy saucepan

Ingredients:
   2 cups cooked barley
      (approximately 3/4 cup
      dried)
   1 tsp. sesame oil
   1/4 to 1/2 tsp. cumin
   1/4 to 1/2 tsp. coriander
   1/4 cup golden raisins

Procedure: Cook barley according to directions or use leftovers. Heat oil in pot. Quickly sauté spices to bring out their flavors. Add dried fruit and 1 cup water. Cover and simmer 5 minutes. Add cooked barley; heat thoroughly. More water may be needed to reach desired consistency. Serve with chopped parsley or roasted nuts.

Variations:
• Dates or currants could be used in place of apricots.
• Cardamon or cinnamon may also be added.
• Garnish with roasted cashews.

**1/4 cup dried apricots,
chopped**
**1/2 cup roasted, chopped
almonds or walnuts
(optional)**

Menu Suggestions:
Dinner:
Lentil Soup
Sweet Barley
Steamed Vegetables or
  Salad
Mustard Green Pickles

Brunch:
Tempeh "Bacon"
Sweet Barley
Toast or Muffins

Corn Morning Cereal

Corn "grits" are whole corn kernels which have been crushed into small pieces, but not as finely ground as cornmeal. Soak grits overnight to speed cooking time. Look for corn grits in natural food stores or Latin markets. Brazilian friends serve a corn "pudding" with orange, coconut and nuts for breakfast or dessert.

Servings: 4 or more
**Time: soak overnight;
          simmer 20 to 30
          minutes**

**Equipment:
  small heavy pot**

**Ingredients:
  3/4 cup corn grits
  3 cups water or apple
    juice
  pinch of sea salt**

Procedure: Soak corn grits in water or juice overnight. Place on low flame; heat slowly, stirring occasionally. Add pinch of sea salt and optional ingredients. Cook 10 to 15 minutes. Serve hot as cereal or a cold "pudding."

Variations:
- Brazilian Corn Morning: add 1/4 cup toasted coconut, 1/4 cup toasted almonds or cashews, 1 tsp. grated orange peel or 1/2 cup juice.
- Indian Pudding: add 2 or 3 tbsp. barley malt or maple syrup, 1/2 cup raisins and a pinch of cinnamon.

Quick 'n' Creamy Buckwheat and Millet Breakfast

In the time it takes to shower and dress, your breakfast grain is ready. Simply soak overnight in cooking pot and simmer while you get ready or read the newspaper. A "whole grain" alternative to oatmeal.

Servings: 4 or more
**Time: soak overnight;
          simmer 15 to 30
          minutes**

**Equipment:
  small pot with lid**

**Ingredients:
  1/2 cup millet
  1/2 cup buckwheat
  3 to 4 cups water
  pinch sea salt**

Procedure: Wash grains. (Pan-roast for extra flavor.) Place in pan; cover with water and soak overnight. Next morning, place on low flame. Simmer 15 to 30 minutes. Add more water for a "creamier" consistency.

Variations:
- Cook with 1/2 cup raisins.
- Top with roasted nuts or seeds.
- Substitute cracked wheat for either grain.
- Add 1 to 2 tbsp. rice syrup for sweetness.

Oatmeal

Whole oats are steamed and rolled to make oatmeal. Toasting oatmeal and simmering for 30 minutes makes a creamy porridge. Mornings are a rush? Try 5-minute oatmeal: soak rolled oats overnight; next morning they need only to be heated.

Servings: 4 or more
Time: 30 to 45 minutes
or overnight soak
and 5 minutes
cooking

Equipment:
heavy pot with lid

Ingredients:
1 cup rolled oats
3 to 4 cups water
pinch of sea salt

Procedure: (*Optional step:* toast rolled oats in pan, stirring constantly 2 or 3 minutes until a nutty aroma arises.) Place oats and water in pot, add sea salt. Simmer 15 to 30 minutes. Adjust amount of water for desired consistency.

Variations:
- Apple-Oatmeal: use apple juice for liquid; add chopped, dried or fresh apples.
- Maple-Nut: serve with 1 tbsp. maple syrup and roasted, chopped nuts.
- Cinnamon: add a pinch of cinnamon or favorite dessert spice.
- Leftover oatmeal can be added to bread or muffin recipes.

Gingery Couscous Cake

A couscous cake that uses gingery stewed fruit serves as a quick breakfast to eat at home, while commuting to work, or at breaktime.

Servings: 6 or more
Time: 10 minutes

Equipment:
pot, serving dish

Ingredients:
5 cups apple juice
1 cup stewed fruit with
ginger (recipe on page
78)
2 cups couscous
pinch of sea salt
1/2 cup chopped nuts
(optional)
apple cider jelly or apple
butter for topping
(optional)

Procedure: Bring apple juice to a boil, add stewed fruit and a pinch of sea salt. When boiling, add couscous and stir until thickened. Pour into a glass or ceramic shallow dish that has been rinsed with water. Allow to cool. Spread with jelly (thinned with a little water) or apple butter. Garnish with chopped, roasted nuts.

Variations:
- Apple cider, pear juice or water with 1/4 cup sweetener can be substituted for apple juice.
- Add extra spice: cinnamon, allspice or grated lemon peel taste good in this cake.

Menu Suggestions:
- Enjoy for breakfast while still warm, or cool and cut into squares for a snack.
- If you prefer a softer grain (like cream of wheat), add more juice or water.

Maple-Nut Granola (Not too Sweet)————————

Everyone has a favorite granola recipe. Try this simple one and vary it to your taste. Granola is not as sweet as "crunch" recipe.

Servings: 8 or more, makes about 5 cups
Time: 1 hour or longer to bake

Equipment:
mixing bowl, baking tray

Dry Ingredients:
3 cups oatmeal
1 cup chopped walnuts
1/2 cup almonds
1/4 cup whole wheat pastry flour
pinch of sea salt
1/2 tsp. cinnamon

Liquid Ingredients:
1/2 cup maple syrup
1/3 cup corn or safflower oil
1 tsp. vanilla (optional)

Procedure: Combine dry ingredients in mixing bowl. Add liquid ingredients and mix until well coated. Spread on oiled baking tray. Bake for 1 hour at 300° to 325°F. oven. Stir occasionally to break up lumps and turn granola over. Allow to cool on tray before storing in a jar.

Variations:
- Add sunflower seeds, sesame seeds, coconut or cashews to recipe.
- Raisins or chopped dates can be added to cooked, cooled granola.

Scones————————————————————

Scones, the classic, currant-studded British biscuit, deliciously adapt to natural food ingredients. They are superb served warm with jam or spread for tea time or at breakfast with oatmeal, stewed fruit or scrambled tofu.

Servings: 16 to 20 scones
Time: 30 minutes

Equipment:
pot, blender or mixing bowl, sifter, spatula, cookie sheet, rolling pin, glass

Ingredients:
1/3 cup apple juice or cider
1/3 cup currants
2 1/2 cups whole wheat pastry flour
pinch of sea salt
1 tsp. baking soda
1 1/2 tsp. baking powder
1/4 cup corn oil

Procedure: Soak currants in 1/3 cup apple juice. Sift flour, sea salt, baking soda and baking powder together in mixing bowl. Pureé tofu, corn oil, lemon and syrup in blender until smooth. Pour liquid ingredients into dry. Add currants and juice. Mix gently until dough holds together; it may need more water. Place dough on floured pastry cloth or between sheets of waxed paper (dusted with flour). Roll dough out 1/2- to 3/4-inch thick. Using a glass, cut 2-inch circles and place with spatula on lightly oiled cookie sheet in even rows. Bake in hot oven at 350°F. for 10 to 15 minutes, or until golden on top. Glaze with maple syrup the last 5 minutes of baking. Serve warm with jam or spread.

1/4 block tofu (4 oz.)
juice and rind of 1 lemon
2 to 3 tbsp. maple or
    rice syrup

Variations:
- Chopped raisins can be substituted for currants.
- Roasted nuts give extra flavor.

My Basic Muffin Recipe

A good "muffin mix" for breakfast or snacks that bakes up quickly.

Servings: 12 muffins
Time: 30 minutes

Equipment:
  2 bowls, blender, muffin
  tins

Dry Ingredients:
  2 cups whole wheat
    pastry flour
  1 cup cornmeal
  1 tbsp. baking powder
  1 tsp. cinnamon (optional)
  1/8 tsp. sea salt

Liquid Ingredients:
  1/2 cup maple syrup
  1/2 cup corn oil
  3/4 cup water
  2 eggs or 4 oz. tofu

Procedure: Sift dry ingredients in large bowl. Mix liquid ingredients together. (If using tofu, purée in blender with wet ingredients until creamy smooth.) Add wet to dry, mix gently—don't over-mix. Preheat oven to 375°F. Oil muffin tin. Bake for 20 minutes. If batter is dry add 1/4 cup extra water. Some flours absorb more liquid than others.

Variations:
- Blueberry: add 1 cup washed berries.
- Cranberry-Nut: add 1 1/2 cups berries, 1/2 cup toasted, chopped walnuts.
- Raisin-Bran: 1/4 cup bran, 1 cup raisins soaked in 3/4 cups orange juice. Omit water.
- Substitute white unbleached flour for cornmeal, or whole wheat flour for a lighter muffin.
- Substitute honey or barley malt for maple syrup.

Maria's Corn Muffins

Corn muffins are light and not too sweet. Maria always lines her muffin tin with cupcake papers. This recipe can also be baked in a cake or bread pan for "corn cake."

Servings: 10 to 12 small
               muffins
Time: 30 minutes

Equipment:
  mixing bowl, muffin tins,
  blender

Dry Ingredients:
  1 cup whole wheat pastry
    flour
  1 cup cornmeal
  1 tbsp. baking powder
  1/2 tsp. sea salt

Procedure: Sift flours together (add sifted bran back to flour or save) with sea salt and baking powder. Blend liquid ingredients together. Add liquid to dry ingredients and mix gently. Oil muffin tins; fill 2/3 full. Bake in 375°F. oven for 15 to 20 minutes until golden brown.

Variations:
- For Blueberry Muffins, add 1 cup washed blueberries.
- For Cranberry-Orange, add 1/2 cup cranberries; substitute 1 cup orange juice for water.
- To make Corn-Sunflower, add 1/2 cup toasted sunflower seeds.

Liquid Ingredients:
  1 cup water
  1 egg
  1/4 cup corn oil
  1/4 cup maple syrup

Menu Suggestions: Corn muffins go with everything; they aren't just for breakfast. I like them with bean dishes: chili, baked beans, black bean or other thick soups.

Angie's Oatmeal Muffins

Chewy oatmeal is the mainstay of these muffins. They are lighter and nuttier than muffins made with 100% whole wheat flour.

Servings: 12 small muffins
Time: 30 minutes

Equipment:
  mixing bowl, muffin tins

Dry Ingredients:
  2 cups oatmeal
  1 cup whole wheat pastry
    flour
  1/2 cup raisins or currants
  1/2 cup roasted, chopped
    walnuts
  1 tbsp. baking powder
  1/4 tsp. sea salt
  1/2 tsp. cinnamon

Liquid Ingredients:
  2/3 cups water
  1/2 cup corn oil
  1 egg, beaten (or 4 oz.
    tofu puréed with all
    liquid ingredients)
  1/2 cup maple syrup

Procedure: Combine dry ingredients; sift flour and baking powder into bowl. Blend liquid ingredients in separate bowl. Add liquid to dry ingredients. Stir. Oil muffin tin and fill 2/3 full. Bake at 375°F. for 15 to 20 minutes, until golden. Try using cupcake papers in muffin pans.

Variations:
• Almonds or sunflower seeds can be substituted for walnuts.
• Golden raisins or chopped, pitted dates can be used instead of raisins.

Sesame-Onion Rolls

Homemade rolls for brunch or dinner fill the house with that glorious bread-baking aroma. Serve a basket of warm Sesame-Onion Rolls with meals or split them and fill with your favorite tofu or tempeh dish.

Servings: 10 to 12 rolls
Time: 2 hours

Equipment:
  small bowl, pan, 2 large
  mixing bowls, cookie
  sheet

Procedure: In a small bowl, dissolve barley malt in 1 cup of warm water. Sprinkle yeast over barley malt water and stir gently. Place near stove to "proof" (make a sponge). While yeast is "proofing," sauté onion in 3 tbsp. oil. Add a pinch of sea salt. Cook over medium heat until onions are clear and soft. Lightly

Ingredients:
1 tbsp. granular yeast
1 cup warm water
2 tbsp. barley malt
1 cup cold water
2 large onions, minced
3 tbsp. oil
3 tbsp. sesame seeds
pinch of sea salt
5 to 6 cups whole wheat
   flour: bread, pastry or
   combination of flours

toast sesame seeds and add to onions. In a large mixing bowl, place sautéed onions, seeds, 1 cup cold water and the yeast "sponge." Sift flour in separate bowl and add slowly to liquid. Mix thoroughly to form a ball; begin to knead dough in bowl. Remove and continue to knead 5 minutes on a floured board or until soft and elastic to the touch. Lightly oil a large bowl, and place dough inside; then flip dough over so the top will have a little coating of oil to prevent drying out. Cover with clean towel; place near stove or another warm place and allow to double in size, about 1 hour.

Punch dough down and remove from bowl. Place on a cutting board and flatten down. Cut into approximately 10 pieces. Form pieces into round shapes between hands. Roll them smoothly so there are no holes or creases. Lightly oil a cookie sheet. Preheat oven to 375°F. Place rolls on sheet at least 3-inches apart. Shape nicely and sprinkle sesame seeds over the tops. Allow to rise another 15 minutes. Bake 15 to 20 minutes until rolls are firm and lightly golden.

Variations:
- Onion-Poppy Seed: substitute 3 tbsp. roasted poppy seeds for sesame seeds.
- Sweet rolls: omit onion; add 1 cup raisins or currants and 1 tsp. grated orange or lemon rind.

Menu Suggestions:
- Split toasted or plain rolls and fill with tofu salad, barbecued tempeh, avocado-tofu spread or scrambled tofu.

Brunch:
Italian-Style Greens
Sesame-Onion Rolls
Tofu Cheese or
   Scrambled Tofu

Picnic:
Barbecue Tempeh with
   Orange-Barbecue Sauce
Onion-Sesame rolls
Salad, Pickles
Blueberry Pie or
   Couscous Cake

Apricot Spread

Homemade spreads are easy to prepare, as well as tastier and cheaper than store-bought varieties. Spread them on toast, muffins or cakes.

Servings: 1 to 2 cups
Time: 15 minutes

Procedure: Simmer apricots in juice until soft. Purée in blender or food mill or finely chop. Dissolve

Equipment:
    blender or food mill, pan,
    wooden spoon

Ingredients:
    1/2 lb. dried apricots
    apple juice to cover
    1 tbsp. arrowroot
    1 cup apple juice
    pinch of sea salt

arrowroot in cup of apple juice in saucepan. Stir; then bring to boil. Add a pinch of sea salt; add puréed apricots. Stir until mixture thickens. Keep refrigerated.

Variations:
- Mix dried fruits together: dried apples, raisins, etc.
- Add lemon or orange juice for flavor.
- Add pinch of spice or ginger juice.

Stewed Fruit

The sweetest dessert is also the easiest. Simply cover dried fruit with water and simmer until plump and juicy. Keep a variety of dried fruits on hand for a breakfast treat or dessert that satisfies your sweet cravings.

Servings: 6 or more
Time: 1/2 hour

Equipment:
    pot with cover

Ingredients:
    2 cups dried fruit, any
        assortment of apples,
        apricots, dates,
        peaches, raisins, etc.
    water to cover
    pinch of sea salt

Procedure: Rinse fruit in strainer; then place in pot and cover with 1 inch water and pinch of sea salt. Cover pot and simmer slowly for 1/2 hour or until fruit is soft. It can be cooked longer, to make purée.

Variations:
- Season with lemon juice and/or cinnamon or vanilla.
- Purée mixture and spread on toast or muffins. Make extra purée to have on hand as this keeps for a week.
- "Ice" cake with purée; garnish with toasted coconut, roasted nuts or orange slices.

Menu Suggestions:
- Serve with scones or muffins. Top with crunch or toasted nuts.

Gingery Fruit Chutney

Fill the house with the sweet-spicy aroma of chutney, an exotic complement for toast and muffins. Serve it in the morning, or serve with dinner for a taste of India.

Servings: 4 or more
Time: 45 minutes

Equipment:
    saucepan, grater, bowl

Procedure: Rinse fruit in a strainer. Place all ingredients in a saucepan and bring to a boil slowly. Simmer 30 to 40 minutes. Remove cinnamon stick. Ginger can be sliced into thin slivers and returned to fruit. Cool; place in jar and keep refrigerated until used.

Ingredients:
1 cup raisins
1/2 cup dates
1/2 cup golden raisins or
apricots
1 cinnamon stick
1/4-inch piece of fresh
ginger root, peeled
1 lemon or orange peel,
grated
2 1/2 to 3 cups water
pinch of sea salt

Variations:
- Roasted nuts can be added.
- Vary combinations of dried fruits.

Peaches 'n' Pears

Sliced fruit served in juice or sauce disappears faster than whole fruit in a basket.

Servings: 4 or more
Time: 10 minutes

Equipment:
serving bowl, spoon

Ingredients:
3 ripe peaches, sliced
3 ripe pears, sliced
2 cups apple or pear juice
1 tbsp. lemon juice
pinch of sea salt
2 tbsp. kuzu (optional)

Procedure: Rinse and slice fruit. Place in bowl; cover with juices and sea salt; toss and chill. Juice can be thickened for a rich sauce. Dissolve kuzu in juice; heat slowly in saucepan. Stir until thick; pour over fruit. Cool.

Variations:
- Add 1/2 cup raisins or chopped nuts.
- Serve fruit and sauce over hot cereal.

Menu Suggestions:
- Serve as light breakfast, snack or dessert.

A-B-C Fruit Salad

A is for apples, B is for blueberries, C is for the vitamins in lemon juice. The grapes are an extra breakfast bonus.

Servings: 4 or more
Time: 10 minutes

Equipment:
mixing bowl

Ingredients:
3 to 5 apples (McIntosh,
Cortland, Delicious)
1/2 pt. blueberries
1/2 lb. seedless grapes
2 to 3 cups apple juice or
cider
1 lemon, juiced
pinch of sea salt

Procedure: Wash all fruit. Chop apples into small pieces; place in mixing bowl. Combine all ingredients. Refrigerate until served.

Variations:
- Add diced pears, pitted cherries or peaches.
- Garnish with coconut or toasted nuts.

Menu Suggestions:
- Serve for breakfast, snack or dessert.
- Remember it's best to eat raw fruits alone, not combined with cooked foods.

Blackberry Juice

Fresh from our blackberry bushes, my dad and I savor this drink in the last days of August.

Servings: 6 or more
Time: 15 minutes

Equipment:
  pot, blender or food processor, strainer

Ingredients:
  1 qt. blackberries
  1 pt. water
  pinch of sea salt
  2 to 3 tbsp. rice syrup (or maple syrup) to sweeten

Procedure: Wash blackberries; drain; place in pot with 1 pint of water and bring to a boil. Remove from the flame and purée in blender or food processor. Strain seeds out of the juice by pouring purée into wire strainer and pushing through with a spatula. Juice can be sweetened with syrup or used as is. The taste is slightly tart.

Variations:
- Blackberry kanten can be made from juice, thickened with agar.
- Couscous cake will take on a lovely pink color from the juice.
- Add kuzu to make a smooth sauce to serve over cake or puddings.

Scrambled Corn-Tofu-Red Pepper

Golden crisp kernels, soft white tofu and bright red pepper sautéed together are garnished with scallions for a fast, appetizing breakfast or light meal.

Servings: 4
Time: 15 minutes

Equipment:
  saucepan or skillet

Ingredients:
  1 tsp. sesame oil
  3 or 4 scallions, finely sliced
  1 red pepper, cut into 1/4-inch diced
  2 ears corn, cooked and cut off cob
  1/2 lb. tofu
  pinch sea salt

Seasoning:
  1 tbsp. chopped fresh dill or basil

Procedure: Heat oil in pan; sauté vegetables, beginning with scallions. Pepper and corn are next: sauté until pepper begins to get soft (a pinch of sea salt will help.) Crumble tofu over vegetables. Continue to cook for 5 minutes over low heat. Fresh herbs can be added at the end. Adjust seasonings. Shoyu can be used, but it will darken the bright colors.

Variations:
- Onion, garlic or carrot can be substituted for red pepper or scallion.
- Sliced black olives further color and flavor this dish.

Menu Suggestions:

Breakfast/Brunch:
Scrambled Corn-Tofu-
  Red Pepper
Toast or Muffins
Chutney or Fruit Spread

Lunch:
Squash Soup or
  Escarole Italian-Style
Scrambled Corn-Tofu-
  Red Pepper
Pita Bread
Sprouts, Pickles

Scrambled Tofu

Grated carrots give tofu a golden color and crunch. Turmeric or curry add spice. A quick dish for breakfast, light meals or sandwich fillings.

Servings: 4
Time: 15 minutes

Equipment:
  grater, sauté pan

Ingredients:
  1 onion, minced
  1 carrot, grated
  1 celery stalk, finely diced
  1 tsp. sesame oil
  1/4 tsp. turmeric or curry
    for color and flavor
    (optional)
  1/2 lb. tofu
  pinch of sea salt or shoyu
    to taste

Garnish:
  chopped parsley

Procedure: Prepare vegetables. Heat oil in sauté pan; sauté spices for 1 minute. Add vegetables, beginning with onion, carrot, then celery. Sauté for 3 to 5 minutes. Crumble tofu into bowl, add to vegetables and stir. Cover to steam for 5 minutes, stirring occasionally. Season with sea salt or shoyu. Garnish with parsley.

Variations:
• Add 2 to 3 tbsp. soy mayonnaise for extra creaminess; makes a great sandwich filling.
• Garlic or fresh herbs could be added.
• Vary or omit spices.

Menu Suggestions:

Breakfast/Brunch:	*Light Meals:*
Scrambled Tofu	Gingery Miso Broth
Toast	Scrambled Tofu
Miso-Tahini Spread	Norimaki or Millet
Sprouts or Cucumber	Croquettes
Slices	Steamed Vegetables or
	Salad

Tempeh "Bacon"

Braised and broiled tempeh is quick, scrumptious and digestible! Tempeh prepared in this method can be used to make new dishes: "T. L. T.'s" (tempeh, lettuce, tomato sandwiches), or tempeh cacciatore.

Servings: 4
Time: 30 minutes

Equipment:
  sauce pot, baking dish

Ingredients:
  1/2 lb. tempeh, cut into
    1/4 × 2-inch strips

Broth:
  2 cups water
  2 tbsp. miso (kome or
    shiro), or pinch of sea
    salt

Procedure: Cut tempeh into strips. In a sauce pot, dissolve miso in water, add seasonings and tempeh. Cover and simmer slowly for 10 to 15 minutes. Oil baking dish and line drained tempeh pieces on dish. Place under broiler for 5 minutes on one side, then turn over and bake 3 to 5 minutes more.

Variations:
• Shoyu can be substituted for miso. Spices such as cumin, coriander or turmeric can be sautéed first and then added to broth.

1 tsp. mustard
2 bay leaves
3 cloves garlic, sliced
1/4 tsp. white pepper
1 tbsp. sesame oil

Menu Suggestions:

Breakfast:
Oatmeal
Tempeh "Bacon"
Toast

Dinner:
Barley-Leek or Vegetable Soup
T.L.T. (tempeh, lettuce,
        tomato)
Gingery Couscous Cake

5. Stocks, Sauces and Soups ────

Stocks are the foundation of soup making. There are three types of stock I make on a regular basis: kombu-shiitake mushroom, fish (see Chapter 8) and vegetable stock.

It's a good feeling to use all parts of vegetables; a special container is helpful to collect peels and scraps for stock. The scraps will keep for several days in the refrigerator. Once stock has been made, the cooked scraps can be added to your compost heap.

Tips:
- The color of soup or stock is influenced by seasonings. A pinch of sea salt will keep colors bright. Shoyu will darken soup (not always desirable). Miso blends into soup but needs to be stirred before serving.
- A golden onion stock can be made by washing onions before peeling and simmering the peels with other trimmings.
- Water from soaking or cooking sea vegetables such as kombu or wakame can be used as stock.
- Allow stock to cool before refrigerating.
- Never pour hot stock (or any hot food) in plastic containers.

Basic Vegetable Stock ────

Equipment: 2 large pots, colander
Set-up: Place 1 pot on stove. Place colander over second pot.

Procedure: Place all vegetable peels, skins, ends and sea vegetables into a stock pot. (Do not use bitter or sour foods like mustard greens, beet greens, lemon peel or waxed, moldy or spoiled pieces.) Cover with twice as much water. Cover pot; bring to a full boil over high heat. Reduce heat and simmer 1/2 to 1 hour. Strain through colander into the second pot.

Tips:
- Organic vegetables are best (wash well with vegetable brush). You may not want to use trimmings of commercial vegetables.
- Suggested vegetables: onions, onion peels, greens, celery, squash ends, tomatoes, cabbage cores, wilted lettuce or watercress, parsley stems.
- Aromatics (add these in the beginning): bay leaf, rosemary, thyme, peppercorns, cumin seed, celery seed, coriander seed, sage.
- Use stock in place of water in any recipe, especially for grains, soups, sauces and gravies. Make extra stock for future use.
- Cook stock ahead and keep refrigerated until use. Always taste stock before using it.

Kombu-Shiitake Stock————————————————

Japanese cuisine relies on this stock for miso soups, sauces and noodle dishes. Quickest to make of all stocks, simply simmer these two ingredients in water.

Servings: 2 qts.
Time: 30 minutes

Equipment:
  soup pot, colander

Ingredients:
  3 to 4 strips of kombu
    (6- to 8-inch pieces)
  4 to 5 shiitake mushrooms
  6 to 8 cups of water

Procedure: Rinse kombu and shiitake mushrooms; place in soup pot; cover with water. Bring to boil; simmer 1/2 to 1 hour until vegetables are very soft. Strain stock. Kombu and shiitake can be sliced and added to soup or other dishes.

Sauces————————————————————————

Sauces have traditionally been used in a supporting role with the main course. Now they are coming into their own as an integral part of good cusine. They add nutritional value as well as enhance flavor and visual appeal. For example, a tahini, bean or peanut sauce over grain provides a balanced protein dish.

A meal of pale yellow millet, golden fried tempeh and steamed greens is enlivened by the sunny glow of carrot or squash sauce. Bright Green Basil or Estella's Red Sauce dresses up noodles, rice, millet or tofu dishes.

By mastering four basic types of sauces, the home cook can create exciting and wholesome meals. Sauces are helpful, for they allow the core foods to be served differently each day without ever having to repeat a menu. Each meal becomes an adventure.

Vegetable-based Sauces: Green, red, orange, yellow or white vegetables make the easiest sauces, sautéed and simmered or pressure-cooked with a small amount of water until they are soft. Purée them in a blender, food processor or food mill; season with herbs, miso, sea salt or shoyu. Don't overcook them or keep them on the stove warming for longer than 20 to 30 minutes, as the bright colors will fade. For extra body, kuzu or arrowroot can be added, but it's not needed. Just use a small amount of liquid when blending the sauce and it won't be too runny. Examples are Gingery Carrot Sauce and Primavera Sauce.

Reduction Sauces: Flavorful liquids such as shoyu, vinegar and rice syrup or barley malt are boiled down to syrupy sauces which require no thickener. This technique is traditionally used in Japanese cooking to create teriyaki sauces.

Clear Sauces: Kuzu is the single most exciting ingredient I have come across in natural foods cooking. A chalk-like powder made from the root of a hearty vine, kuzu is dissolved in cold water, then added to vegetables that are sautéing or simmering in liquid to make a gravy. Kuzu provides a lovely glaze for vegetables dishes, and has a unique, satiny-smooth texture. Two kuzu sauces—Onion and Mushroom—can be varied by adding spices or herbs, or peppers, garlic, shallots, scallions, wild onions and fresh shiitake mushrooms.

Mixed or Blended Sauces: These sauces need no thickener or reduction. Two or more ingredients are combined. They are usually not cooked, just blended as in basil or tofu sauces, or mixed in a bowl. Others, such as tahini and peanut sauces, are heated and blended. Beans can be puréed in the blender with herbs, spices or salsa for a thick sauce. Avocado or jalapeno pepper are good in mixed sauces, with tofu or beans, respectively, served over grains and vegetables for Latin flair.

Green Sauce Primavera

The "Green Temptation" is for those who love sauces, but shy away from greens; Primavera elevates them from ho-hum-dom to stardom. When you don't know what to do with those greens wilting away in the refrigerator, try it.

Servings: 6
Time: 20 to 30 minutes

Equipment:
   bowl, pot with cover, pan, blender or food mill

Ingredients:
   1 small bunch broccoli
   1/2 cup chopped parsley
   1/2 bunch watercress (or
      other greens)
   1 onion, chopped
   4 oz. tofu
   2 tbsp. tahini
   pinch of oregano, basil
      or tarragon
   1 to 2 tbsp. miso
   1 tsp. olive oil
   1 tbsp. arrowroot,
      dissolved in 2 tbsp.
      water (optional)

Garnish:
   1 red pepper, sliced into
      strips
   1 yellow squash, cut into
      half moons (optional
      for color)

Procedure: Cut flowerettes off broccoli, reserve for garnish. Chop stalks and leaves of broccoli. Chop onion, watercress and parsley. Combine tofu, miso, tahini and herbs in a bowl. Heat oil in large soup or sauce pot. Sauté onion and broccoli stems for 2 to 3 minutes. Add 1 cup water and simmer 2 minutes. Add parsley and watercress. Cover and cook until greens are soft, but still bright. Add tofu mixture. Purée sauce in a blender or food mill. This basic recipe should be thick, but you can thin it down if you desire. Slice red pepper into thin strips. Slice squash into half or quarter moons. Bring 4 cups of water to a boil to blanch these vegetables. Separately blanch broccoli flowerettes, red pepper and squash. Rinse under cold water to stop cooking. Use to garnish sauce.

Variations:
• Rice and pasta also blend beautifully with sauce. Add garnish.
• Fresh basil can be added for a rich flavor.
• Sprinkle dish with roasted pine nuts.
• Sauce can be served in pita bread or chapatis, with fried tofu or tempeh.

Menu Suggestions:

Navy Bean and
   Leek Soup
Rice

Miso Soup
Millet and Lentil
   Croquettes

Green Sauce Primavera
with Vegetables

Green Sauce Primavera
with Vegetables
Olives

Estella's Red Sauce

A tomato-free version of the classic Italian sauce. With this sweet, rich combination of vegetables the tomatoes won't be missed. Beets lend color, herbs and garlic add authentic flavor. Similar to Red Velvet Soup, Red Sauce can be served in place of tomato sauce.

Servings: 6 or more
Time: 1 to 1 1/2 hours

Equipment:
heavy pot with lid or
pressure cooker, blender,
sauté pan

Ingredients:
1 to 1 1/2 lbs. carrots, cut
in large chunks
2 or 3 beets, large dice
2 or 3 onions, large dice
2 or 3 celery stalks, cut in
large chunks
2 bay leaves
2 tbsp. red or kome miso
2 to 3 cups water to pressure-cook (more if
boiling)

Seasonings:
2 to 4 cloves garlic,
minced
1 to 2 tbsp. olive oil
1 tsp. oregano
1/2 tsp. basil, marjoram or
thyme
2 tbsp. arrowroot or kuzu,
dissolved in 1/4 cup
water

Procedure: Scrub vegetables; cut into large chunks. Peel rough end of beets. Place vegetables, bay leaves, miso and water in pressure cooker. (If boiling, add water to cover; boil until very soft.) Bring to pressure, cook 15 to 20 minutes. Remove bay leaves. Purée vegetables, using red broth as needed. Return to pot. Sauté garlic and add to sauce along with seasonings. Arrowroot or kuzu can be added at this point for a glossy sheen and extra body. Simmer 15 to 30 minutes, allowing flavor to improve. Adjust seasonings.

Variations:
- Vary vegetables in sauce: try parsnips, zucchini, mushrooms or peppers.
- 1 tsp. umeboshi lends "zip" that tomatoes would otherwise give.

Menu Suggestions:

Polenta or Millet with
Estella's Red Sauce
String Bean Sauté or
Salad
Olives, Pickles

Pizza with
Estella's Red Sauce
Mediterranean Salad
Pear Parfait

Gingery Carrot Sauce

A rich relative of carrot soup, Gingery Carrot Sauce imparts an orange glow to amber grains.

Servings: 4 or more
Time: 30 to 60 minutes

Procedure: Heat oil. Sauté carrots and onions 3 to 5 minutes, until they smell sweet. Add water and sea

Equipment:
soup pot with lid or
pressure cooker, blender

Ingredients:
1 tsp. oil
1 to 1 1/2 lbs. carrots,
chopped
1 to 2 onions, diced
water or stock to cover
pinch of sea salt

Seasonings:
1 to 2 tbsp. white or light
miso or pinch sea salt
1 tsp. ginger juice
(optional)
1 tbsp. kuzu, dissolved in
1/4 cup water

salt and pressure-cook 15 minutes or boil until very soft. Purée carrots, using carrot broth as needed. Return to pot; add seasonings and thicken with kuzu. Stir and simmer 10 to 15 minutes. Adjust seasonings.

Variations:
● Orange-skinned squash or yams can be combined with carrots.
● Natto-miso or umeboshi can be used for seasoning.
● Spicy Sauce: add pinch of cumin, coriander or cardamon to carrots as they sauté.

Menu Suggestions:

Millet 'n' Cauliflower	Swedish Wheatballs
Carrot Sauce	Carrot Sauce
Arame with Tofu	Braised Greens
Greens, Salad	Cranberry Kanten

20-Minute Fresh Tomato Sauce

Overripe tomatoes from our garden are transformed into a velvety sauce. Miso and kuzu are used to mellow the acidity of the tomatoes and thicken the sauce.

Servings: 4 to 6
Time: 20 minutes

Equipment:
stainless steel pot
or saucepan

Ingredients:
3 lbs. overripe tomatoes,
chopped
1 tsp. olive oil
1 green pepper, diced
1 onion, diced
3 cloves garlic, minced
1/4 cup fresh basil,
chopped, or 1 tsp. dried
basil (optional)
2 tbsp. kuzu, dissolved in
1/4 cup water
2 tbsp. miso, (kome or
red variety) or pinch of
sea salt

Procedure: Peel and chop tomatoes. If they are very ripe, the skin should come off easily; if not, cut an "x" on the bottom of the tomatoes and drop into boiling water for 30 seconds and peel. Remove seeds. Then chop tomatoes. Sauté diced pepper, onion and garlic in oil for 2 minutes. Add chopped tomatoes and cover; simmer for 10 minutes. Dissolve miso and kuzu together and add to sauce. Stir until thick. Finish with chopped basil; adjust seasonings and remove from heat.

Variations:
● Add mushrooms, diced zucchini or yellow squash.

Menu Suggestions:

Corn Polenta	Pan-Fried Fish
Fresh Tomato Sauce	Pasta
Green Salad or	Fresh Tomato Sauce
Brussel Sprouts	Broccoli or Salad
Pickles	Blueberries in
	Lemon Pudding

Sweet Soy Sauce

Barley malt's sweetness mellows the strong flavor of shoyu. Mix them and simmer for a quick sauce. Brush sauce on tofu or tempeh; then bake or broil. Steamed or sautéed vegetables are enhanced by adding 1 to 2 tbsp. of Sweet Soy Sauce for a glaze.

Servings: 1/2 cup
Time: 15 minutes

Equipment:
small saucepan, wire
whisk or wooden spoon

Ingredients:
1/3 cup shoyu
1/4 cup barley malt

Procedure: Mix shoyu and barley malt in saucepan with whisk or wooden spoon. Slowly simmer 15 minutes. Stir occasionally. Sauce will thicken and reduce slightly.

Variations:
• Add 1/2 tsp. ginger juice.
• Add 1/2 tsp. rice vinegar.

Menu Suggestions:
• Brush sauce on fish, seitan, tofu or tempeh; bake or broil.
• Brush on squash, onion, or other root vegetables; bake until soft.

Quick Teriyaki Glaze

An instant glaze to pour over fish, tofu or vegetables, adding Japanese flavor to your meals.

Servings: 1/3 cup
Time: 10 minutes

Equipment:
small saucepan

Ingredients:
2 tbsp. rice syrup
2 tbsp. shoyu
1 tbsp. rice vinegar
2 1/4-inch slices of ginger
root

Procedure: Combine rice syrup, shoyu and rice vinegar in saucepan; place on medium flame. Slice 2 thin pieces of ginger root, approximately 2-inch $\times$ 1/8-inch. Add ginger root to the saucepan; simmer for 5 to 10 minutes. Reduce the sauce slightly, but don't burn. Remove ginger pieces and spoon glaze over fish, tofu, tempeh or vegetables. Bake or heat and serve.

Variations:
• Use 1/8 tsp. of fresh ginger juice in place of ginger slices.
• Add a pinch of wasabi or dry mustard powder for a piquant taste.
• Serve with fresh rice, greens and toasted nori on the side.
• Use to flavor fried rice or noodles.

Menu Suggestions:
Baked or Pan-Fried Fish   Pan-Fried or Baked Tofu
with Teriyaki Glaze   with Teriyaki Glaze

Rice or "Sweet" Barley   Rice or Noodle Salad
Broccoli or Greens   Greens or Salad

Orange-Miso Barbecue Sauce

What's a barbecue without sauce? Simply combine ingredients, thicken with kuzu and baste kebabs on the grill or pour over tofu burgers or croquettes.

Yield: 1 cup
Time: 15 minutes

Equipment:
   measuring cup, saucepan,
   wire whisk or wooden
   spoon

Ingredients:
   2 tbsp. apple cider jelly
   1 tbsp. umeboshi paste
   1 tsp. mustard
   1 tsp. miso
   1 tsp. rice vinegar
   juice and rind of 1 orange
   1 heaping tsp. kuzu (or
     1 tbsp. arrowroot)
     dissolved in 1/4 cup
     water
   water to measure 1 cup

● **Procedure:** Combine first 6 ingredients in a measuring cup. Add kuzu dissolved in water; then fill with water to make 1 cup. Pour mixture into saucepan and heat slowly, stirring with wire whisk or wooden spoon to prevent lumping. Simmer 5 minutes and adjust seasonings.

Variations:
● Rice syrup can be substituted for cider jelly.
● Vary quantities of ingredients. Double recipe for family gatherings.

Menu Suggestions:
● Serve with Tempeh Kebabs or deep-fried tofu. It's wonderful on grains and vegetables, too.

Cookout:
Tempeh or Tofu Kebabs
Orange-Miso Barbecue Sauce
Baked Corn or Rice Salad
Tossed Salad
Melon Kebabs or Kanten

Mushroom Sauce

One-half pound of fresh, sliced mushrooms quickly sautéed, a little kuzu and presto . . . a fancy sauce to dress up simple meals.

Servings: 4 or more
Time: 15 minutes

Equipment: saucepan

Ingredients:
   8 to 12 oz. fresh
     mushrooms, sliced
   1 tsp. oil
   1 to 2 tbsp. kuzu,
     dissolved in water

Procedure: Slice mushrooms. Heat oil in fry pan; add mushrooms and stir. The heat should be hot enough to sear or brown the mushrooms to keep them from losing water and to enhance their flavor. Continue to sauté on high heat for 2 to 3 minutes, stirring often so they do not burn. Lower flame when mushrooms are tender. Dissolve kuzu in water; add to mushrooms; stir until thick and clear. Season with shoyu or sea salt.

2 cups water or stock
pinch of sea salt to taste
   or 2 tsp. shoyu

Variations:
- Add 3 to 4 cloves of minced garlic.
- Add 1 tbsp. chopped fresh basil, dill, parsley or scallions.
- Season sauce with 1 tsp. miso.
- Pour over fried tempeh, tofu, or fish; then bake.

Menu Suggestions:

Buckwheat Croquettes	Fried Tempeh or
Mushroom Sauce	Tempeh "Bacon"
Steamed Vegetables	Mushroom Sauce
Sauerkraut or Pickles	Rice Pilaf
	Steamed Greens or Salad

Shiitake Mushroom Sauce

Shiitake are dried mushrooms imported from Japan. Like ginger root, they are used for both culinary and medicinal purposes. A few of these costly mushrooms are sufficient to flavor a pint of sauce. I serve Shiitake Sauce with fish or fried foods.

Servings: 4 or more
Time: 30 to 45 minutes

Equipment:
  saucepan, bowl

Ingredients:
  6 or 7 shiitake mushrooms, soaked and sliced
  2 to 3 cups water
  1 to 2 tbsp. kuzu, dissolved in 1/2 cup water
  pinch of sea salt or 1 tsp. shoyu

Garnish:
  sliced scallions or parsley

Procedure: Soak shiitake mushrooms in bowl of water until they are soft enough to slice, 10 to 20 minutes. Cut off stems (save for stock) and thinly slice mushroom caps. Place in saucepan with water. Bring to a boil and simmer 15 to 20 minutes until very soft. Dissolve kuzu in water; add to saucepan and stir until clear. Season with sea salt or shoyu. Keep warm until served.

Variations:
- Ginger-Mushroom Sauce: add 1/2 to 1 tsp. ginger juice.
- Kombu Stock: use kombu stock for water.
- Matchstick-cut red pepper may be used for color and flavor.

Menu Suggestions:

Fish or Fried Tempeh	Millet Croquettes or
Shiitake Mushroom	Kasha Knishes
Sauce	Shiitake Mushroom
Rice Salad	Sauce
Pickles	Steamed Vegetables or
	Julienne Salad

French Onion Sauce

The technique of making a good onion sauce is similar to French-Style Onion Soup: lots of onions and long, slow sautéing. When looking for a different sauce for grain, bean or vegetable meals, try variations of this recipe.

Servings: 4 to 6
Time: 30 to 60 minutes

Equipment:
  skillet or saucepan,
  wooden spoon

Ingredients:
  1 tsp. sesame oil
  1 to 1 1/2 lbs. onions,
    thinly sliced
  pinch of sea salt
  2 to 3 cups water or stock
  1 tbsp. kuzu, dissolved in
    1/4 cup water
  2 tbsp. miso (light is best)
    or pinch of sea salt
  2 tsp. rice vinegar
    (optional)

Procedure: Heat oil in saucepan; sauté onions over a low flame. Add pinch of sea salt; stir. Continue to sauté until they turn a golden color, 15 to 20 minutes. Add water; simmer 5 minutes. Dissolve kuzu, add to onions and stir until thick. (Add more kuzu for a thicker sauce). Season with miso or sea salt and vinegar, if you desire. Taste and adjust seasonings if necessary.

Variations:
● Garlic-Onion Sauce: add 2 or 3 cloves of minced garlic.
● Dill-Onion Sauce: add 1 or 2 tbsp. freshly chopped dill (basil or tarragon).
● Spicy Onion Sauce: add 1/2 tsp. of either curry, turmeric, cumin or coriander, 1/4 tsp. nutmeg.

Menu Suggestions:
● Try Onion Sauce over grain dishes. Pour over fried tofu or tempeh and heat slowly.

Grain Croquettes or Burgers	Fried Tofu or Tempeh
Onion Sauce	Onion Sauce
Beets and Greens	Greens, Salad
Salad, Pickle	Cranberry Sauce or Chutney

Teriyaki Kuzu Sauce

Kuzu thickens this satiny smooth sauce which is ready in minutes. Use as a dip sauce for croquettes, or pour over stuffed peppers or cabbage rolls and bake.

Servings: 1 cup
Time: 20 minutes

Equipment:
  saucepan, wooden spoon

Ingredients:
  1 cup apple juice or apple
    cider
  2 tbsp. shoyu
  1 tbsp. lemon juice

Procedure: Place apple juice, shoyu and rice syrup in a small saucepan. Simmer gently on a low flame to reduce volume slightly. Thicken with kuzu. Add the ginger juice. Adjust flavor.

Variations:
● Use mirin instead of rice syrup.
● Add sautéed garlic.

1 tbsp. rice syrup
  (optional)
1 small piece ginger root,
  grated (yields about 1/2
  tsp. juice)
1 tsp. kuzu or arrowroot
  (optional), dissolved in
  a little water

Menu Suggestions:
• This sauce can be used to marinate fish or tofu.
Simply place fish or tofu in a shallow pan or baking
dish, cover with sauce and allow to absorb flavor
for 1/2 hour. Once the flavor has been absorbed, bake
at 350°F. for 15 minutes or serve with croquettes, fried
tempeh or noodles.

Tahini-Onion Sauce

Tahini sauces and dressings have that unctuous quality that was thought attainable only
with dairy foods such as cream and butter.

Servings: 1 1/2 cups
Time: 15 minutes

Equipment: skillet

Ingredients:
  1 tsp. sesame oil
  1 onion, finely minced
  4 scallions, minced
  2 cloves garlic, minced
    (optional)
  1/2 cup tahini
  3/4 cup water
  1 tbsp. miso or sea salt to
    taste
  pinch white pepper
    (optional)
  pinch herbs

Procedure: Heat oil in skillet; sauté onion and
scallions until soft. Add tahini and stir until lightly
roasted. Dissolve miso and seasoning in 3/4 cup water.
Stir into tahini. Simmer 5 minutes and serve. Do not
boil.

Variations:
• Add 1 tsp. rice vinegar.
• Add fresh or dried chopped basil, dill or oregano.

Menu Suggestions:

Spicy Tofu and	Stuffed Cabbage or
Rice Burgers	Squash
Tahini-Onion Sauce	Tahini-Onion Sauce
Salad "Fixings"	Dulse-Red Onion Salad
Pita Bread for	Greens
Sandwiches	Fruit Pie or Kanten

Spicy Peanut Sauce

Decadently thick and spicy, peanut sauce is found in cuisines from Indonesia to Africa.
It will keep up to a week if refrigerated, and can be reheated. Try as a party spread for
rice cakes or corn bread.

Servings: 2 1/2 cups
Time: 10 minutes

Equipment:
  blender or whisk,
  saucepan

Ingredients:
  1/2 cup peanut butter
  1 tbsp. mustard

Procedure: Combine all ingredients in blender.
Purée until smooth. Pour in saucepan and slowly heat
over low flame, stirring constantly. Be careful not to
let it boil or burn. Add water to obtain desired
consistency.

Variations:
• Hot and Garlicky Peanut Sauce: omit mustard;
  sauté 2 or 3 cloves of minced garlic in 1 tsp. oil.

1 tbsp. miso
1 tsp. ginger juice
1 tsp. rice or umeboshi
   vinegar
1 1/2 to 2 cups water

Add 1/2 tsp. red pepper; add remaining ingredients.

Menu Suggestions:

Tofu or Tempeh Kebabs	Millet
Spicy Peanut Sauce	Spicy Peanut Sauce
Yellow or Basmati Rice	Baked Yams or Squash
Julienne Salad	Collards or Kale
Tropical Island	Pickles
Fruit Fantasy	

Basic Basil Sauce

Emerald green, rich and tasting of summer, Basic Basil Sauce is a simpler sister of pesto. A little of this flavorful sauce goes a long way. Add a dollop to soups at serving time and use as traditional pesto. "Summerize" steamed vegetables or grain salads.

Servings: 6 or more
Time: 10 minutes

Equipment:
   blender or food processor

Ingredients:
   1 cup fresh basil (roughly
      1 large bunch)
   1/2 cup olive oil or oil of
      your choice
   1/2 cup water
   2 to 3 tsp. umeboshi
      paste or 2 to 3 plums

Procedure: Wash and chop basil. Place in blender with oil, water and umeboshi. (If using food processor, basil need not be chopped.) Blend on a high speed until the sauce is a smooth satiny consistency. Store refrigerated in jar up to 2 or 3 days.

Variations:
• Sea salt and vinegar or lemon juice can be substituted for umeboshi.
• Dress up tofu and noodle dishes.
• Add fresh, chopped parsley or scallions to basil.
• Add garlic or roasted pine nuts; reduce water.

Menu Suggestions:

Pasta	Salmon or Fish Filets
Basil Sauce	Boiled Potatoes
Mediterranean Salad	Basil Sauce
Lemon-Walnut Cake	Corn
	Salad
	Fruit Kanten

Tartar Sauce

Tartar sauce traditionally perks up fish fillets. It improves tofu and tempeh sandwiches, too.

Servings: 2 1/3 cups
Time: 10 minutes

Procedure: Squeeze lemon and mix all the ingredients together in a blender or with a whisk in a mixing bowl. Refrigerate until served. It will keep for 1 week.

Equipment:
  blender or mixing bowl
  and wire whisk

Ingredients:
  2 cups mayonnaise
  1 lemon, juiced
  2 tbsp. mustard
  1/4 cup pickles, finely
    chopped, or relish
  1/4 cup onion, minced
  1/8 cup parsley, minced
  pinch of sea salt

Menu Suggestions:
Haddock Fillet or
  Fish Croquettes
Tartar Sauce
Rice or Couscous
Broccoli or Salad

Tofu with Red Chard
Tartar Sauce
Sesame-Onion Rolls
Blueberry Pie

Tempeh Sandwich with
  Tartar Sauce, Lettuce,
  Tomato
Date-Nut Squares

Soups

Vegetarian cuisine relies on intuition to create soups that are sensual and sensible.
A soup of diced vegetables simmered in a pot, thickened with grain or creamy beans,
seasoned with miso or sea salt, and stirred with love, is healthful and heart warming.

Soup soothes the spirit after a long day, gently awakens digestion in the morning,
and comforts with reminiscences of childhood days when chicken noodle or tomato soup
was a panacea for whatever ailed you. Smooth or chunky, its myriad textures woo the
palate.

Let's look at five styles of soup.

Miso Soup: Miso, a salty paste of fermented soybeans is used to season soups—
it's the natural "bouillon cube." The enzymes in miso are helpful to digestion if it
is added to soup just before serving and simmered a few minutes below a boil. Start
a pot of 1 1/2 to 2 quarts of water or stock boiling; add a combination of sliced or
diced vegetables, cut small for quick-cooking, and a strip or two of kombu, wakame
or dulse. When the vegetables are soft, season the pot with miso, about 1/2 to 1 tsp.
per serving, depending on the saltiness of the miso and personal taste. Garnish with
chopped scallions, parsley or watercress. Try adding tofu cubes or cooked noodles
near the end of cooking for a change.

Vegetable Soup: Layer vegetables in the soup pot and simmer without stirring for
a gentle, easy method of cooking. A piece of sea vegetable (kombu, wakame) can be
placed on the bottom, firmer vegetables such as carrots or other roots on top. If
grains such as millet, buckwheat or barley are added, they go on top of vegetables.
Water or stock is added to cover. Bring to a low boil. This soup cooks itself and is a
good choice for "batch cooking" when other dishes require more attention. Quick-
cooking vegetables or greens are added at the end along with sea salt or miso. Soup is
stirred only at the end of cooking. This peaceful, harmonious method of cooking
brings only happiness to cook and eaters.

Bean Soup: Highest in protein of all soups, they are easily digestible and an agreeable
way to serve beans. Those who politely refuse bean casseroles can't resist the colorful

temptation of bean soups such as black bean, green or yellow split pea, white navy bean or red lentil. Bean soups, like grain soup, can be made many ways. For instance, cook beans in lots of water until soft; purée part or all for a creamy base—add sautéed spices and vegetables—or—start with sautéing vegetables; add stock; then add precooked beans. Thick or thin, bean soups are a bonus of protein to complement grain and vegetable dishes.

Sautéed Vegetable Soup: The sweetest onion soup comes from sautéing onions slowly for a long time in a small amount of oil. Fill a soup pot halfway with sliced onion, carrots, celery, cabbage or a combination of these. Stir and add a pinch of sea salt to draw out juices and help caramelize the vegetables (turn starch to "sugar"). Add stock or water, herbs, grains or cooked beans. Cook until tender and season with sea salt or miso.

Grain Soup: This filling soup can be made two different ways: either from cooking grain in lots of water so it becomes creamy, then adding vegetables and seasonings; or sautéing vegetables first in a soup pot, then adding leftover grain and stock, and simmering until the flavors have mingled. Either way makes a delicious soup.

   Oats, barley and rice cook for 2 to 3 hours in a ratio of 1 cup to 5 or 6 cups of water. Millet, buckwheat, cracked wheat, corn grits or corn flour require 1 cup to 4 cups of water and 1 hour's simmering (or more) before using in soups. Couscous or oatmeal will thicken in a hurry; add 1/2 to 1 cup (dry) of either to a large pot of vegetable soup and simmer 15 to 30 minutes. Cooked grains become instant thickeners when buzzed in a blender with a little water. Soft grain soups are particularly good for breakfast.

Consommé with Carrot Flowers

Consommé, a clear soup, can be made with a fish stock using bonito flakes or fish bones.

Servings: 4 to 6
Time: 30 minutes

Equipment:
   soup pot, strainer, bowl
   or suribachi, ladle

Ingredients:
   1 1/2 qts. water
   1 to 2 strips kombu
   3 to 5 shiitake mushrooms
      (optional)
   1/4 cup bonito flakes
   shoyu or sea salt to taste
   1 carrot for flowers
   1 tsp. ginger juice
      (optional)

Procedure: In a pot, simmer kombu and shiitake mushrooms 30 minutes to an hour. Remove kombu and shiitake and cut into strips; reserve. Drop bonito flakes into hot stock. When they sink to the bottom, strain flakes and discard (or feed to cat or dog). Return stock, kombu and shiitake strips to pot. Season with shoyu. Add carrot flowers. (page 39) Simmer 5 minutes. Add ginger juice. Serve immediately; garnish with scallion.

Variations:
• Serve "clear" without kombu or shiitake.
• Add tiny tofu cubes or fresh, thinly sliced mushrooms.
• Use broth in other soups, grain or vegetables.

Garnish:
scallion or chopped
watercress

Menu Suggestions:
• Serve with hearty meals.

Consomme with	Comsomme with
Carrot Flowers	Carrot Flowers
"5 Senses" Rice	Glazed Tempeh
Veggie Rolls	Jardiniere
Greens	Rice or Noodles
Mocha Kanten	Pecan Pie

Gingery Miso Broth

Warming miso broth is quick and one of the finest first courses of any meal. Miso and ginger aid digestion.

Servings: 4 to 6
Time: 30 minutes

Equipment:
soup pot, ginger grater

Ingredients:
1 1/2 qts. stock or water
2 small strips kombu
3 to 4 dried shiitake
  mushrooms (optional)
2 tsp. fresh ginger juice
2 to 3 tbsp. miso (shiro
  or kome)
2 carrots for "flowers"
  (optional)

Garnish:
3 scallions, thinly sliced,
  or watercress

Procedure: Rinse kombu and shiitake mushrooms. Place in stock or water. Bring to a boil; lower flame and simmer 1/2 hour. Remove kombu and shiitake. Slice kombu into long 1-inch strips; then slice thinly across those strips. Cut mushroom stems off caps; slice caps thinly. Return kombu and shiitake to stock. Simmer gently. Cut carrot flower (page 39) and add to stock 10 minutes before serving (so the carrots will cook slightly). Grate ginger; squeeze juice into small bowl or suribachi. Add miso and 1/2 cup water to dissolve it in. Slice scallions thinly on an angle. Five minutes before serving, add miso and ginger juice to broth. Adjust flavor. Garnish each bowl with scallions.

Variations:
• Fresh mushrooms can be substituted for shiitake mushrooms.
• Tofu cubes could also be added.
• Include cooked noodles and watercress for quick meal.

Menu Suggestions:
• For breakfast, lunch or dinner, miso broth is warming and delicious.

Dinner:	*Brunch:*
Miso Broth	Miso Broth
Rice	Broccoli-Corn-Tofu
Adzuki-Squash	Medley
Broccoli or Cabbage	Oatmeal Muffins
Pickles	

Lunch:
Miso Broth
"3 Sisters" Casserole
Greens or Salad

Tofu-Watercress Soup

There are many types of miso: each imparts a distinctive flavor to this simple soup. Try a lighter, less salty miso in summer and a darker, stronger one in winter. Use only a small amount of miso, so its taste will not overpower that of the watercress.

Servings: 4
Time: 20 minutes

Equipment: soup pot

Ingredients:
   1 tsp. sesame oil
   2 onions, thinly sliced
   2 strips wakame, soaked
      and chopped (optional)
   1 qt. stock or water
   1 small bunch watercress
   1/4 lb. tofu, medium or
      firm, cut into 1/2-inch
      cubes
   1 to 2 tbsp. miso

Garnish:
   scallions, thinly sliced

Procedure: Heat oil in a soup pot. Lightly sauté onion; add water and wakame. Simmer 15 minutes. Add tofu and watercress; lower flame. Dissolve miso in a little warm liquid and season to taste. Garnish with chopped scallions. Serve immediately.

Variations:
• Carrots cut in matchsticks or "flowers" can be added for color and flavor.
• Any quick-cooking vegetables can be used, such as zucchini, summer squash, snow peas, mung sprouts, celery.
• For a refreshing summer soup, add a squeeze of lemon and serve cold.

Menu Suggestions:
• Good light prelude to any meal.

Tofu-Watercress Soup	Tofu-Watercress Soup
Fried Rice with	Fish or Grain Croquettes
Almonds	Baked Root Vegetables
Pickles	Cabbage Salad

Miso Soup with Daikon

Miso soup with daikon and burdock has a strengthening effect on the system, especially in regulating digestion. Look for these ingredients in Oriental and health food stores. It's easy to prepare and an excellent soup to have when feeling tired, weak or out-of-balance. As "Sunday Soup" it sets me up for the week ahead.

Servings: 4 or more
Time: 45 minutes

Equipment: soup pot

Procedure: Slice vegetables. Place in soup pot with kombu and water. Bring to a boil; simmer 20 minutes until vegetables are soft. Remove kombu. Slice kombu into strips and return to soup. During last 5 minutes of cooking, dissolve miso (to taste) in a little broth and simmer with soup. Garnish with scallions and serve.

Ingredients:
- 1 onion, sliced
- 1 small daikon, matchstick-cut
- 1 small burdock root, thin matchstick-cut (optional)
- 1 strip kombu or wakame, soaked and chopped
- 4 to 6 cups water
- 2 to 3 tsp. miso

Garnish:
- sliced scallions or collards

Variations:
- Miso Soup with Kuzu and Ginger: for extra flavor and strength, add 1 to 2 tbsp. kuzu dissolved in 1/2 cup water, plus 1 tsp. ginger juice to soup 10 minutes before serving; stir until clear.
- Miso Soup with Greens: add a handful of chopped watercress or tender kale before serving.

Menu Suggestions:

Miso Soup with Daikon	Miso Soup with Daikon
Rice	Sweet Rice, Chickpeas
Lentils and Squash	and Millet
Greens or Salad	Greens, Salad
	Pickles
	Baked Apples

Escarole Soup, Italian Style

Learning to slow-simmer greens the Italian way is one of my memorable culinary discoveries. The greens are transformed into a slightly sweet, yet distinct, flavor. They melt in the mouth and are eaten as soup for the first course or with crusty Italian bread any time of day or night.

Servings: 4 to 6
Time: 1 hour

Equipment:
- strainer, soup pot

Ingredients:
- 1 to 2 heads of escarole, washed very carefully
- 1 large onion, thinly sliced
- 2 to 3 cloves garlic, sliced
- 1 tbsp. olive oil (optional)
- sea salt to taste or 1 tsp. shoyu
- 1 1/2 qt. water or stock

Procedure: Wash greens in large amount of water, separating each leaf. Chop into 2-inch pieces. Slice onion and garlic. Place all ingredients in large pot; add water or stock, cover. Gently bring to a boil. Allow greens to cook slowly.

The juices will be released from the greens to make a delicious broth. The greens should simmer 1/2 to 1 hour, depending on your taste. The Italians season liberally with olive oil and salt, but a squeeze of lemon can be substituted. Serve as soup or drain vegetables and place in a separate dish. Drink the savory broth: it's the best part.

Variations:
- Substitute mustard greens or broccoli-rabe for escarole.

Menu Suggestions:

Escarole Soup	Marinated Tofu with
Pizza or Noodles with	Fennel
Sauce	Escarole, Italian Style
Salad	Risi-Bisi
Pickles	Mediterranean Salad
Pear Parfait	

Cabbage 'n' Corn Soup

A few ears of fresh corn-on-the-cob add a golden touch to a humble cabbage soup. It's a hearty one-pot meal on a crisp autumn day.

Servings: 4 to 6
Time: 30 minutes

Equipment: soup pot

Ingredients:
- 1 tsp. oil
- 1 onion, sliced
- 1 small cabbage, thinly sliced (about 6 cups)
- 2 carrots, diced
- 2 to 3 ears corn, cut off cob
- 2 pieces wakame or 1/4 cup dulse (optional)
- 6 to 8 cups water
- 2/3 tbsp. miso or sea salt to taste

Garnish:
- carrot flowers
- scallions or parsley, minced

Procedure: Heat oil in soup pot. Sauté onion, cabbage and carrots until soft and sweet-smelling, about 10 minutes. Add corn cut off the cob, water, and wakame or dulse. (Soak wakame 10 minutes and cut into small pieces.) Simmer 15 to 20 minutes until the vegetables are tender, but haven't lost color. Season with miso or sea salt.

Variations:
- Sage, rosemary, thyme or oregano can be used to season soup.
- Celery, parsnips or squash could be added—or try potatoes and dill.

Menu Suggestions:

Cabbage 'n' Corn Soup	Cabbage 'n' Corn Soup
Tofu or Tempeh Sandwich	Stuffed Squash
Sprouts, Pickles	Sautéed String Beans and Mushrooms
Cookies or Cake	Apple Pie

Sweet Potato 'n' Squash Soup

Everyone adores a bright, luscious soup with or without the exotic possibilities of curry spices.

Servings: 4 or more
Time: 45 minutes

Equipment:
soup pot, food mill or blender

Ingredients:
- 2 large sweet potatoes or yams, peeled and cubed
- 1 small butternut or orange-skinned squash (peeled if it has been waxed), seeded and and cubed

Procedure: Place cubed squash and sweet potatoes in a soup pot with kombu and water. Low boil until vegetables are soft. Purée in blender or food mill. (Remove kombu and cut it into thin strips.) Dissolve miso and add to soup; adjust seasoning. Garnish with kombu.

Variations:
- For Indian flavor, sauté onions with curry spices; then proceed with recipe.
- For a glossy look, add 1 tbsp. kuzu dissolved in 1/2 cup water.
- Try toasting nori (a sea vegetable) and cutting it into shapes with scissors for an unusual tasty garnish.

1 strip kombu (optional)
1 qt. water or more
1/4 cup light miso (natto
   miso is my favorite for
   this soup) or 2 tbsp.
   darker miso or sea salt
   to taste.

Menu Suggestions:
• Serve with garlic croutons or toast.

Sweet Potato 'n' Squash Soup
Kidney Beans with Rice or Rositas and Rice
Collards

Sweet Potato 'n' Squash Soup
Tempeh "Turkey" Sandwich or Tofu Sandwich
Dill Pickle or Sauerkraut

Sweet Potato 'n' Squash Soup
Chickpea Salad or Hijiki 'n' Noodle Salad
Pickles

French-Style Onion Soup (To Stir with Love)——————

In France, restaurants and country homes make onion soup in time-honored fashion: pounds of thinly sliced onions are long and slowly sautéed to bring out their natural sweetness, then simmered with a flavorful stock. Stirring and a watchful eye on the pot are needed. I usually fill my soup pot half full of onions; it cooks down to one-quarter of the volume of onions before I add stock.

Servings: 6 or more
Time: 2 hours

Equipment:
   large heavy soup pot,
   wooden spoon

Ingredients:
   1 tbsp. sesame oil
   2 lb. onions, thinly
      sliced
   pinch of sea salt to taste
      (or your favorite miso)
   1 to 1 1/2 qt. stock
      (vegetable or kombu)
   3 bay leaves (optional)

Garnish:
   herbed croutons, chopped
      parsley or scallions

Procedure: Heat oil in pot and add onions. Sauté slowly; the onions shouldn't burn or turn brown. Add pinch of sea salt. Allow onions to become clear, then golden, as they caramelize. This should take 30 to 60 minutes. Make a stock using onion peels and vegetables (or kombu with shiitake mushrooms). Add the stock and bay leaves to onions. Simmer 30 minutes to 1 hour. Remove bay leaves. Season to taste with sea salt or miso. Garnish with herbed croutons, parsley or scallions.

Variations: French onion soup is just that— simply onions—but I often add other ingredients to this rich onion base.
• Onion-Garlic: add 3 or 4 cloves of minced garlic.
• Tofu-Onion: add 1/4 lb. fried or raw tofu cubes to onion soup.
• Tempeh-Onion: add fried tempeh cubes as a garnish.
• Julienne of Vegetables: thin strips of carrots, parsnips, burdock and daikon can be added after stock and onions have simmered 10 minutes. Cook together a minimum of 30 minutes.

- Sea Vegetable-Onion: add approximately 1/2 cup sliced kombu, wakame or dulse.
- Herbed Onion: add fresh or dried tarragon, dill or basil.

Menu Suggestions:
French-Style Onion Soup
Rice with Rye Berries
Marinated Bean Salad with Tofu Cheese or
  Marinated Tofu
Carrots Vichy
Fruit Tart

Borscht

Borscht, a soul food of northern Europe, can be served hot or cold with a dollop of basil sauce.

Servings: 4 to 6
Time: 1 hour

Equipment:
  soup pot or pressure cooker, blender or food mill

Ingredients:
  1/4 head cabbage, sliced (2 to 3 cups)
  2 to 3 beets, diced in 1/2-inch pieces, ends peeled
  4 carrots, diced 1/2-inch
  2 to 3 onions, diced 1/2-inch
  2 to 3 stalks celery, diced 1/2-inch
  2 strips kombu (optional)
  2 tbsp. kuzu, dissolved in 1 cup water (optional)
  pinch of sea salt or red miso to taste

Garnish:
  pinch of herbs (optional)

Procedure: Place the diced vegetables and kombu in soup pot with water to cover. Bring to boil; lower flame and simmer until vegetables are tender. Remove kombu and dice; return to soup. Purée part or all of soup for chunky or smooth texture. Thicken with kuzu if extra "body" is desired. Season with sea salt or miso. Keep warm. Garnish.

Variations:
- Sauté vegetables in oil for extra flavor.
- Add bay leaves or herbs.
- Parsnips, garlic and potatoes can be added.
- A tablespoon of prepared mustard adds zing.

Menu Suggestions:
Borscht	Borscht
Noodle Kugel	Buckwheat Croquettes
Kale or Collards	Greens or Salad
Pickles	Apple Sauce with Crunch

Autumn Stew

The East-West Family Kitchen, a restaurant in Los Angeles, serves this rich root stew every day. Use any root vegetables on hand or take a trip to an Oriental market for lotus root, burdock and daikon. Make a large pot: there is never enough.

Servings: 4 to 6
Time: 1 hour

Equipment: soup pot

Ingredients:
  2 strips kombu, pre-
    soaked 1/2 hour
  2 large onions, thickly
    sliced
  1 small burdock root,
    scrubbed clean, sliced
    thinly on diagonal
  1 small daikon, cut in
    quarter moons
  3 carrots, roll cut
  1 small squash (Hokkaido,
    butternut or buttercup),
    cut in cubes (2 to 3
    cups)
  water to cover
  2 tbsp. kuzu, dissolved in
    1/2 cup water
  1 to 2 tsp. shoyu or sea
    salt to taste
  1 tsp. ginger juice
    (optional)

Garnish:
  roasted sunflower seeds,
    2 to 3 scallions, thinly
    sliced

Procedure: Scrub all the roots with a vegetable brush. Cut each vegetable as instructed. Place strips of kombu on the bottom of pot and layer roots in order listed. Add just enough water to cover vegetables and put lid on pot. Set the squash aside to add later. Bring the stew to a boil slowly. Simmer for 15 minutes without stirring; then add the squash. Cover. It will steam-boil on top of vegetables. Simmer for 20 minutes until all roots and squash are tender. Remove kombu, slice into thin strips, return. Add kuzu to thicken; stir. Season with shoyu and ginger. Serve with sliced scallions for a garnish.

Variations:
• Try sweet potatoes or parsnips instead of squash.
• Lotus root can be added also (fresh or dried).
• Omit kuzu for a lighter soup.

Menu Suggestions:
• Autumn stew is a warming brunch on snowy New England mornings. Serve with corn or oatmeal muffins.

Autumn Stew	Autumn Stew
Toasted Nori or	Rice and Millet
Arame with Tofu	Broccoli or Salad with
Sautéed Collards or	Tofu Dressing
Salad	Roasted Nuts or Seeds
Corn Muffins or	Pickles
Sesame-Onion Rolls	

Warming Winter Stew

Autumn's harvest is the inspiration for warming winter meals. This is a flexible recipe I use in weekly batch cooking. A large pot lasts two days. Puréeing part of the stew gives it a creamy consistency.

Servings: 4 to 6
Time: 1 hour

Procedure: Wash and dice or cube all vegetables. Sauté all vegetables in oil in order listed. Add enough water or stock to cover; add kombu and bay leaves; simmer on medium heat until soft. Remove 2 to 3

Equipment:
heavy pot, blender or
food mill

Ingredients:

Base:
1 large onion, diced
2 medium carrots, diced
1 turnip, cubed
1 rutabaga, cubed
1 parsnip, diced
1 tbsp. sesame oil
water or stock

Seasonings:
2 bay leaves
pinch sea salt or miso
to taste
1 strip kombu or wakame

Extra Protein:
1 cup beans, tofu or
tempeh

Thickener:
3 tbsp. arrowroot or kuzu
(optional)—dissolved
in 1/2 cup water

Garnish:
toasted nori,
scallions, parsley

cups cooked vegetables; purée in blender or food processor until smooth. Return to pot. This purée gives stew its "creamy" consistency. Dissolve arrowroot in 1/2 cup water; add to stew for extra thickness. Remove bay leaves. Add beans or fried tofu. Season with herbs, miso or sea salt, Keep warm on low flame.

Variations: *Endless*!
- Vary vegetables; try cabbage, potatoes and squash.
- Add spices: sauté 1/2 to 1 tsp. of your favorite spice with vegetables.
- Add 3 to 4 shiitake mushrooms, soaked and thinly sliced.
- Add 1 to 2 cups leftover grain instead of beans.

Menu Suggestions:

Winter Stew	Winter Stew
Barley or Millet	Marinated Bean Salad
Red and Green	Oatmeal Muffins or
Cabbage Salad	Rice Bread
Baked Apples or Crisp	Pickles

Red Velvet Soup

Beets turn a humble pot of pale-colored lentils into—red velvet, beckoning everyone to the start of a bright meal!

Servings: 4 to 6
Time: 1 hour

Equipment:
pot, flame tamer, food
mill or blender, wooden
spoon

Ingredients:
1 cup red lentils
1 tbsp. sesame oil
1 large onion, diced

Procedure: Wash and drain red lentils. Scrub vegetables and slice in 1/2-inch pieces. Heat oil in soup pot and sauté onion for 5 minutes, stirring frequently with a wooden spoon. Add lentils, water and bay leaves; bring slowly to boil. Place on flame tamer and simmer 1 hour until lentils and vegetables are very soft. Remove bay leaves and discard. Purée vegetables in food mill or blender. Dissolve miso in 1/2 cup water and add to soup. (If soup is too thick, add more water.) Heat soup gently, 5 to 10 minutes. Garnish with croutons and parsley.

2 medium carrots,
 chopped
2 beets, peel ends and
 chop
3 bay leaves
6 cups of water or stock
2 to 3 tbsp. red miso or
 sea salt to taste

Garnish:
 croutons, parsley, broccoli
 flowerettes

Variations:
- Season with a dash of umeboshi vinegar or paste.
- For an Italian flavor, add sautéed garlic, a pinch of oregano, basil and rosemary.
- Add a teaspoon of tarragon for a hint of France.
- Kombu can be added to lentils and cooked together.

Menu Suggestions:

Red Velvet Soup	Red Velvet Soup
Swedish Wheat Balls	Rice or Noodle Salad
Creamed Onions	Broccoli
Dilled Cucumbers	Hijiki with Lemon
Lemon Walnut Cookies	

Florentine White Bean Soup

A bowl of this northern Italian soup steaming in the kitchen makes a soul-satisfying meal in itself. Spinach adds a "Florentine" touch.

Servings: 4 to 6
Time: 1 hour

Equipment:
 pressure cooker or large
 pot, soup pot, strainer

Ingredients:
 1 cup dry (= 2 cups
  cooked) navy beans
 1 strip kombu
 8 ozs. spinach noodles
  (fettucini, elbows)
 1 small zucchini, cut into
  half moons
 1 onion, diced
 1 carrot, cut into matchsticks
 4 to 8 ozs. spinach
 pinch of oregano or other
  herb
 2 to 3 tbsp. (approxi-
  mately) white or light
  miso, or sea salt to
  taste

Procedure: Soak beans 4 to 10 hours. Pressure-cook about 30 to 40 minutes, or boil beans with kombu about 1 to 1 1/2 hours until tender, but not mushy. Reserve beans. Cook noodles in lots of water until *al dente*. Drain noodles and run cold water over them to stop cooking. Slice carrots into matchsticks; dice onion and slice zucchini into half moons. Wash and chop spinach finely; reserve. In a large soup pot, layer all vegetables, except spinach and oregano. Add water to cover and simmer 10 minutes. Add beans and noodles to vegetables. Simmer 10 minutes. Before serving, add miso or sea salt and chopped spinach. Heat until spinach wilts.

Variations:
- Tofu cubes could replace the beans.
- Substitute 1/4 cup fresh basil or parsley for fresh spinach.

Menu Suggestions:

Florentine White Bean Soup	Florentine White Bean Soup
Vegetable "Cacciatore"	Garlic Toast
Risi-Bisi	Mediterranean Salad
Lemon Walnut Cookies	Rice pudding

Creamy Leek and Navy Bean Soup

The simplest of soups: leeks add delicate flavor to navy beans which become creamy the longer they are cooked.

Servings: 4 or more
Time: 1 hour

Equipment:
   2 soup pots or pressure cooker and soup pot or skillet

Ingredients:
   1 cup dried navy beans
   1 or 2 strips kombu or wakame
   2 or 3 large leeks, washed
   1 onion
   2 or 3 bay leaves (optional)
   1 tsp. oil
   1 to 2 tbsp. white or light miso to taste (or sea salt)

Garnish:
   blanched carrot, matchsticks or flowers

Procedure: Wash and soak navy beans 2 to 8 hours. Drain and bring to a boil in 4 cups of water with sea vegetable and bay leaves. Low boil for 1 hour, or pressure-cook 40 minutes until beans are very soft. Slice leeks in half-lengthwise; wash very well to remove all sand and slice finely. Dice onion. Sauté onion and leeks over medium heat until they are soft and clear, 10 to 15 minutes, in soup pot or skillet. When the navy beans are soft, combine with sautéed leeks; add 2 to 3 cups of water if needed for creamy consistency. Simmer 20 to 30 minutes over low heat. Dissolve miso in 1/2 cup boiling water and add to soup during the last 5 minutes of simmering.

Variations:
- Chop fresh herbs (2 to 3 tbsp. of basil or dill) for seasoning soup, along with miso or sea salt.
- Serve as soup or use less water to make "sauce."
- Purée part of the beans to make creamy smooth soup.

Menu Suggestions:

Creamy Leek and Navy Bean Soup	Creamy Leek and Navy Bean Soup
Nice-Dice-Salad	Baked Stuffed Squash
Rice Bread	Cabbage Salad
Umeboshi Pickles	Cranberry Kanten

Golden Nugget Stew

Flashes of autumn colors gleam through this simple dish. Vegetable chunks offer contrasting texture to the smooth split pea base.

Servings: 4 or more
Time: 1 to 1 1/2 hours

Equipment:
   soup pot, blender

Ingredients:
   1 cup yellow split peas
   2 onions, chopped
   2 carrots, chopped

Procedure: Wash split peas carefully and drain. Sauté onions and carrots in oil. Add peas, stock and herbs to vegetables. Simmer 1 hour or until very soft. Blend or purée. Add miso or sea salt to taste. Fry the tofu, seitan or tempeh cubes and add to soup. Sliced raw scallions are a pungent garnish.

Variations:
- Instead of tofu or tempeh, add diced hijiki.

1 tbsp. sesame oil
1/2 tsp. sage or rosemary
(optional)
1 to 2 tbsp. white or
yellow miso or sea salt
to taste
1 to 2 qts. stock
1/4 to 1/2 lb. tofu, seitan
or tempeh cubes, fried
in oil until golden

Garnish:
scallions, thinly sliced

- Leftover baked squash or sweet potatoes may be diced and added to the puréed soup as a sweet and colorful complement.
- Once again, spice the soup to your taste. Cumin, coriander and curry are delicious!

Menu Suggestions:

Golden Nugget Stew	Golden Nugget Stew
Rice Burgers, Sprouts,	Hijiki Noodle Salad
Lettuce	Orange Jewel Cookies
Pecan Pie	

Special Split Pea Soup

My grandfather loved pea soup and my mother served it often. Growing up, I never liked it. Tastes do change. Now split pea soup is a favorite. The peas cook down to a thick base and special ingredients can be added. Crispy croutons are a perfect garnish.

Servings: 6 or more
Time: 1 to 1 1/2 hours

Equipment:
soup pot, lid, flame tamer,
sauté pan, blender
(optional)

Ingredients:
1 tsp. oil (optional)
1 large onion, minced
2 carrots, diced
3 celery stalks, diced
1 to 1 1/2 cups split peas
(green or yellow)
6 cups water
1 strip kombu
pinch of sea salt

Garnish:
parsley, scallions
herbed croutons

Procedure: Dice vegetables. Sauté in oil 3 to 5 minutes or simply layer in soup pot. Sort split peas and wash. Add to vegetables with water and kombu. Bring to boil, skimming foam. Reduce flame. Place on flame tamer and simmer 1 hour until peas are very soft. Remove kombu; dice and return to soup. Season with sea salt. Serve as is or add additional ingredients.

Variations: Make it special with your favorite vegetables.

- Leek and Mushroom: sauté 1 large leek and 1/2 lb. sliced mushrooms; add to creamy base, and cook 20 to 30 minutes.
- Broccoli and Cauliflower: cut 1 cup of each into small flowerettes; add to base and simmer.
- Herbed Split Pea: add 1 tsp. of your favorite dried herb and cook in soup or add a minced fresh herb, basil, dill or tarragon, 10 minutes before serving.
- Spices: sauté preferred spices with vegetables and cook in soup.
- "Dahl": use less water and serve thick as a sauce over grain.

Menu Suggestions:

Special Split Pea Soup	Special Split Pea Soup
Herbed Croutons	Stuffed Peppers
Vegetable Fried Rice	Cauliflower Crown
Salad, Pickles	Apple Crisp
Fruit Smoothie	

Special Split Pea Soup
Corn Bread or Millet
Baked Squash
Greens or Salad

Red Lentil-Squash Soup

Quick-cooking red lentils make a filling soup in the time it takes to cook rice.

Servings: 6 or more
Time: 45 to 60 minutes

Equipment:
  soup pot, strainer

Ingredients:
  1 tsp. sesame oil
  1 onion, diced
  1/2 squash, cubed (2 to 3
    cups)
  pinch of cumin, coriander
    (optional)
  1 cup red lentils, cleaned
    and washed
  6 cups water or stock
  2 bay leaves or strip
    kombu
  sea salt or miso to taste

Garnish:
  roasted chopped walnuts
  fresh parsley or water-
    cress

Procedure: Heat oil; sauté onion and squash 2 to 3 minutes; add pinch of cumin. Pick through red lentils carefully. Rinse in strainer. Add to squash and onions. Pour in water and add bay leaves; bring to boil and simmer 45 minutes until soft and creamy. Remove bay leaves. Season with sea salt or miso. Garnish with greens.

Variations:
• Brown lentils or split peas can be substituted.
• Any type of squash can be used, or yams and carrots.
• Add additional vegetables.
• Vary spices or add herbs.

Menu Suggestions:

Red Lentil-Squash Soup	Red Lentil-Squash Soup
Chinese-Style Vegetables	Stuffed Grape Leaves or
Rice or Noodles	Cabbage Rolls
Stuffed Dates	Wakame Cucumber
	Salad

Brazilian Black (Turtle) Bean Soup

My Brazilian friends favor black beans and cook them long and slow with plenty of hot spices. This is a basic black bean recipe; try it first, then improvise, Brazilian-Style. Don't pressure-cook black beans, because their skins can clog the valve.

Servings: 4 to 6
Time: 1 1/2 to 2 hours

Equipment:
   heavy soup pot with lid,
   blender, skillet

Ingredients:
   1 cup black beans, soaked
      overnight
   1 large onion, diced
   1 large carrot, diced
   2 bay leaves (optional)
   6 cups water

Seasonings:
   1 tsp. oil
   3 cloves garlic, minced
   1 tsp. ginger juice
      (optional)
   pinch of sea salt to taste
      -or-
   hot sauce or salsa to
      taste (optional)

Garnish:
   chopped parsley, scallions,
      or red onions

Procedure: Soak beans overnight; rinse. Combine beans, diced vegetables, bay leaves and water in the pot. Bring to a boil; simmer 1 to 2 hours until very soft. Purée half or all of the beans, depending on your preference for consistency of the soup. Return puréed beans to soup pot. To season: sauté minced garlic in oil for 1 minute; grate ginger and add to soup with sea salt. Simmer 15 minutes. Season with hot sauce or salsa; a little goes a long way, so add it a teaspoon at a time and taste as you go.

Variations:
• Black Beans and Cumin: sauté 1/2 to 1 tsp. cumin with onion and carrots and cook together with beans.
• Potato-Black Bean Soup: dice 2 or 3 potatoes and add them 1/2 hour before soup is ready.
• Black Bean-Corn: cut corn off the cob; purée soup. Then add corn; simmer until soft (10 to 15 minutes).

Menu Suggestions: Corn and black beans are like sisters and brothers. I usually serve them together. Rice and millet are a wonderful combination, too.

Brazilian Black Bean
   Soup
	Brazilian Black Bean
	   Soup

Corn Bread or Polenta	Corn-on-the-Cob
Dandelion Sauté	Baked Garlic
Salad and Pickles	Sautéed Collard Greens
Orange Kanten	Coconut-Date Cake

Chickpea Stew with Winter Vegetables————

A hearty chickpea stew satisfies a family all year round. A large pot cooks enough for two meals. Vary the basic recipe with whatever is handy in the refrigerator or pantry.

Servings: 6 or more
Time: 2 hours

Equipment:
   pressure cooker, soup pot

Ingredients:
   1 cup dry chickpeas, pre-
      soaked
   2 strips kombu
   2 tsp. sesame oil (to
      sauté vegetables)

Procedure: Soak the chickpeas overnight in 3 cups water. Drain off soaking water and rinse; add 3 to 4 cups fresh water and kombu and pressure-cook for 1 hour. The chickpeas should be soft, but not mushy. While the chickpeas cook, wash and cut the vegetables. Heat oil in a large soup pot and sauté vegetables in the order listed. Add the cooked chickpeas, their cooking water and bay leaves. Simmer until vegetables are tender. Season with miso or sea salt and thicken with kuzu if you wish. Garnish with broccoli or green pepper.

2 onions, chopped
2 carrots, chopped
1 burdock root, sliced
  diagonally into thin
  rounds (optional)
2 garlic cloves
1 parsnip, chopped
2 celery stalks, chopped
2 bay leaves (optional,
  for flavor)
2 to 3 tbsp. miso or pinch
  of sea salt
2 to 3 tbsp. kuzu (optional
  to thicken stew and
  give it "body")

Garnish:
  broccoli flowerettes,
    blanched
  green pepper, diced

Variations:
- Almost any winter vegetable can be used in a stew. Remember to cook root vegetables longer. Quicker cooking ones such as broccoli, cauliflower, zucchini and watercress are used toward the end of cooking.
- Shell noodles or potatoes can be added to the stew if you want to stretch the meal.
- Deep-fried tempeh chunks may replace the chickpeas. Add to sautéed vegetables and simmer.

Menu Suggestions:

Chickpea Stew	Chickpea Stew
Millet Mashed Potatoes	Noodles or Corn Muffins
Greens or Salad	Cabbage Salad
	Pear-Cranberry Kanten

Chickpea Stew
Stuffed Peppers or Grape Leaves
Salad
Corn Bread

Minestrone-Escarole Soup

The Italian penchant for adding greens to beans and pasta in making soup distinguishes this traditional recipe. Chickpeas and noodles are a good base for hearty soups.

Servings: 6 to 8
Time: 1 hour

Equipment:
  pressure cooker, soup pot,
  pot, strainer

Ingredients:
  2 cups cooked chickpeas
  strip of kombu or wakame
  6 to 8 ozs. shell or elbow
    noodles
  1 head escarole, chopped
  1 leek, thinly sliced, or
    4 scallions
  1 small cauliflower, cut
    into flowerettes
  chopped parsley
  pinch of sea salt
  herbs (optional)

Procedure: Soak chickpeas overnight. Pressure-cook chickpeas with sea vegetables about 1 hour. Reserve beans. Boil noodles until *al dente*. Drain and rinse in cold water. Reserve. Wash escarole and leek very thoroughly. Chop or slice thinly. Cut cauliflower into flowerettes. Layer vegetables in soup pot. Add chickpeas. Simmer 10 minutes. Add noodles and simmer 5 minutes. Season with herbs if desired. Salt to taste, cook another 10 minutes and garnish with chopped parsley.

Variations:
- Fried tempeh cubes may be substituted for chickpeas.
- Broccoli-rabe or broccoli can replace escarole.
- Carrots, onion, garlic or mushrooms add extra flavor and color.

Menu Suggestions:

Minestrone-Escarole Soup	Minestrone-Escarole Soup
Polenta with Estella's Red Sauce	Pizza or Calzone
Tossed Salad with Oil and Vinegar	Fennel Sticks
	Pears in Lemon Sauce

Mung Bean and Cauliflower Soup (Dahl)

Mung beans have been sprouted and eaten as a vegetable for centuries. Try cooking them as a bean in this traditional Indian recipe. "Dahl" is a thick bean dish, eaten with bread or spooned over rice.

Servings: 4 to 6
Time: 1 1/2 hours

Equipment:
   soup pot, skillet, small pot

Ingredients:
   1 to 1 1/2 cups mung
      beans, dried
   1 strip kombu
   3 bay leaves
   3 to 4 cloves garlic
   1 tsp. sesame oil
   1/2 tsp. cumin
   1 small cauliflower, cut
      into flowerettes
   pinch of sea salt or your
      favorite light miso to
      taste

Garnish:
   fresh parsley or scallions,
      finely chopped

Procedure: Wash and soak mung beans a minimum of 2 hours. Drain soaking water and rinse. Cover with 4 cups water; add kombu and bay leaves. Bring to boil; lower flame and simmer 1 1/2 to 2 hours. Sauté garlic and cumin and add to beans. Add more water as needed. The beans should be very soft. While the beans cook, cut the cauliflower into flowerettes. Blanch cauliflower to retain shape and color. Ten to 15 minutes before serving the dahl, dissolve miso in water; add to beans or add sea salt to taste. Add cooked cauliflower. Keep warm on low heat. Garnish with lots of chopped parsley or scallions.

Variations:
- Add 8 ounces sautéed mushrooms.
- Add favorite spices (*garam masala*, curry).
- Cauliflower may be added to soup raw without blanching if you prefer, and simmer.
- Hot pepper may be added; sauté with spices.

Menu Suggestions:

Mung Bean "Dahl"	Mung Bean "Dahl"
Millet or Rice	Pita Bread
Nice-Dice Salad	Rice Salad or Sweet
Chutney	Barley
	Pickles, Salad
	Peaches and Pears

Scottish Stew

Cabbage, oats and dulse are staples in the British Isles. Add squash for color and sweetness; sauté the ingredients and simmer the stew just until vegetables are tender yet retain their shape and color, or cook on low flame for a long time like a porridge.

Servings: 6 or more
Time: 45 minutes

Equipment:
  soup pot with lid

Ingredients:
  1 tsp. oil
  1 onion, sliced
  1/2 small cabbage, thinly
    sliced
  1 small squash, cubed
    (approximately 3 cups)
  4 to 6 cups water
  1/2 cup oatmeal
  1 handful of dulse
    (approximately 1/2 cup)
  pinch of sea salt
    (optional)

Garnish:
  roasted sunflower seeds
  chopped parsley

Procedure: Heat oil in soup pot; sauté onion and cabbage 2 to 3 minutes. Add squash, sauté another 2 minutes. Pour in water and sprinkle oatmeal over vegetables. Cover and simmer on medium flame for 20 minutes until squash is tender. Rinse dulse in a strainer; it will shrink to a few tablespoons. When the vegetables are soft, add dulse. Chop lots of parsley and stir in before serving. Season to taste.

Variations:
- Add other root vegetables to stew: burdock, carrot, parsnip or rutabaga.
- Sunflower seeds make a good, crunchy garnish for soup, as do toasted croutons.
- Season with a pinch of dried herbs: try sage, rosemary, thyme, basil or dill.

Menu Suggestions:

Scottish Stew	Scottish Stew
Scones	Sautéed String Beans
Braised Greens with	with Mushrooms
Caraway	Sunflower Seeds
Cranberry Relish	Gingery Couscous Cake

Scottish Stew
Tempeh 'n' Potato Cakes (or Fish)
Greens or Salad
Stewed Fruit

Leek and Barley Soup

A simple combination of leeks, carrots and cooked grain, seasoned with miso, provides a warming breakfast cereal or instant soup using leftover cooked barley, or other grain.

Servings: 4 to 6
Time: 30 minutes

Equipment: soup pot

Ingredients:
  1 tsp. sesame oil
  2 to 3 leeks, washed,
    thinly sliced
  1 to 2 carrots, cut into
    matchsticks
  1 strip wakame (optional)
  1 qt. stock or water
  1 to 2 cups cooked barley

Procedure: Heat oil; sauté leeks and carrots 3 to 5 minutes. Soak wakame in 2 cups water until soft; chop into small pieces. Add water and barley. Simmer 15 to 20 minutes. Add sea salt or dissolve miso in water and season to taste.

Variations:
- Cooked rice, whole oats or millet can be used in the recipe.
- Fresh or dried mushrooms could also be added. Sauté 4 to 6 ounces of fresh, sliced mushrooms along with leeks, or soak dried mushrooms; slice caps and add to barley.

2 to 3 tbsp. miso or sea
salt to taste

- Sauté spices with leek and carrots.
- Add pinch of herbs.

Menu Suggestions:

Leek and Barley Soup	Leek and Barley Soup
Hummus or Tofu	Baked Potato, Tempeh
Sandwich	and Carrot Casserole
Pickles	Steamed Green
	Vegetables
	Apple-Pear Crisp

Corn Chowder

Each autumn, golden corn figures prominently in my New England menus. Corn-on-the-cob should be freshly picked and eaten while chowder can use up day-old corn.

Servings: 6 to 8
Time: 45 minutes

Equipment:
large soup pot, bowl, pot,
flame tamer

Ingredients:
6 ears corn, cut off cob
1 strip kombu (optional)
6 to 8 cups water
1 tsp. corn oil
1 green pepper, diced
(optional)
1 red pepper, diced
(optional)
1 large onion, diced
1/2 cup cornmeal
1 to 2 tbsp. white miso or
sea salt to taste

Garnish:
fresh dill or basil, chopped

Procedure: Slice corn off cob. Make stock: place cobs and kombu in pot; add water; simmer 15 minutes. In large soup pot, over medium heat, sauté onion and pepper in oil; add corn. Sprinkle cornmeal in and stir well so vegetables are coated with flour. When it begins to turn golden, strain corn cob from hot stock and add stock to vegetables, stirring quickly to prevent lumps. Place pot on flame tamer; lower flame and simmer for 1/2 hour. Dissolve miso in water and add to soup before serving. Adjust saltiness with miso and garnish with chopped dill or basil.

Variations:
- Instead of cornmeal, soup can be thickened with 1/2 cup of soaked rolled oats or 2 large potatoes, diced.
- Carrots and leeks can be used in place of peppers.
- Tofu cubes, fried or plain, can be added to cooking.
- Garnish with parsley or scallions.
- Season with fresh chopped basil or dill.

Menu Suggestions:

Corn Chowder	Corn Chowder
Tempeh or Tofu	Hijiki-Sweet Potato Pie
Sandwich	String Beans or Salad
Salad	Peach Smoothie
Couscous Cake	

6. Vegetables ———————————————————

What can be pressed, pickled, steamed, sautéed, stewed, boiled, baked, pressure-cooked or just plain sliced into a salad? Cabbage! A versatile vegetable! Let's look at the various culinary incarnations of cabbage: it can be pressed into a salad, pickled for sauerkraut, steamed in a basket, sautéed in braised greens, stewed in soup, boiled in dinners, baked with grain stuffing as cabbage rolls, pressure-cooked plain or with root vegetables or just sliced and enjoyed raw for its peppery flavor. And people say vegetables are boring!

Many people didn't like vegetables when they were kids, but perhaps they only had the frozen or canned kind. Maybe they never planted a garden and watched it grow, never picked and cooked their vegetables fresh from earth to soup pot. Most people know little about cutting and handling vegetables, with the exception of simple salads and steaming. Many new vegetarians have yet to learn the joys of cooking vegetables, as their main diet consists of eggs, dairy, whole wheat products and salad. What delights await them!

There needs to be a balance between cooked and raw foods: if two dishes are cooked for a meal, e.g., soup and grain, then serve vegetables raw or as a lightly cooked salad. Seasonal adjustment calls for a higher proportion of raw to cooked vegetables in summertime. In winter, the reverse is true. Supermarket or ethnic stores stock a wide variety of vegetables; scout for farmer's markets, too. Visit a farm to really get a feeling for the energy of vegetables. Look for an organic farm in your area. If produce is more expensive, consider it an investment in health. Once you've tasted freshly picked organic vegetables, it will be hard to settle for commercially-grown produce again.

Vegetable Cookery—————————————————

Here are seven basic cooking techniques.

Steaming: Bamboo Steamer Baskets: Chinese and other Asian cooks have perfected this method of stacking woven baskets, filled with artfully arranged vegetables, over a boiling pot of soup or grain. Steam from the pot cooks the vegetables in the basket. A sense of timing, which comes from experience, is important so as not to overcook the vegetables. The baskets come in two tiers with a tightly woven lid. One layer, for example, may be filled with squash sliced in thin wedges, the other with broccoli.

These baskets can be purchased in Oriental or department stores. Store them according to directions: dry carefully; keep in a cool, dry place and rinse before using. Steamer baskets make a wonderful gift.

Metal Steamer Baskets: These are gaining popularity with health-conscious folks. Make certain the baskets are stainless steel and not aluminum. They are used by filling a pot with an inch or two of water, placing the basket inside over the water and arranging the vegetables to steam. Cover and cook until they turn bright in color. Remove and serve vegetables hot, or cool for salad. Baskets can be found in groceries and most natural foods stores or kitchen departments. Dry carefully before storing.

The Art of Nabemono: This Japanese method of cooking vegetables is the easiest of all; one pot is taken from stove to table. For a quick meal, vegetables are sliced in a fashion so that several types can be cooked together; softer vegetables are sliced more thickly than firmer root vegetables. In a shallow pan or skillet, a decorative arrangement of groups is made. Tofu or fish can be added. A half inch or so of water is added to the pan. Vegetables are covered and steam-boiled until crisp and tender. Season before serving from the pan.

Sautéing or Stir-frying: All cuisines have a method of cooking vegetables in a large pan over a high heat which is controlled for the desired effect. Oil is heated in a wok, sauté pan or skillet. If spices are used, they are added next, and stirred until a rich, roasted smell arises. Vegetables are added according to their length of cooking time and stirred to prevent burning. A pinch of sea salt will draw out the juices, making their own flavorful sauce; or water is added to cover and vegetables are simmered until soft, then thickened with kuzu.

Boiling-Blanching: Simply bring a large pot of water to a boil. While it's heating, slice vegetables keeping them neatly organized and grouped according to cooking times. Either blanch each group separately, dropping it in cold water immediately after quick-boiling to shock and stop the cooking process. To cook together, drop the vegetables into a pot, starting with those needing the longest cooking. Add the remaining groups so all will be finished at the same time. You will know by their color when vegetables are crisp. Remember, heat will continue to cook vegetables a bit even after they are removed from water.

Stewing: Long cooking of greens makes them more digestible and delicious. In Southern American cookery, collards are boiled first and sautéed; in Italy and Himalayan areas, greens are sautéed, then cooked with stock and oil. Examples of these recipes can be found in this chapter.

Roots can be layered in a pot, covered with stock or water and slowly brought to a boil, allowing each vegetable to retain its shape and color. The broth is thickened and other ingredients added. Stews differ from soups only in that they use less water.

Baking: This method is popular in colder climates where every family has its own stove or hearth. In earlier times, families brought their casseroles to the local baker who would cook them in bread ovens overnight.

All members of the root family and squashes become very sweet when baked with a pinch of sea salt and a drizzle of oil. I found leftover baked vegetables such as carrots or squash made the ultimate in creamy soups. I began to purposely prebake these and other roots before adding them to soups and stews.

The larger the slice, the longer the cooking time that is needed. If in a hurry, cut roots into small 1 1/2 inch pieces; cover with a lid and bake until fork pierces through easily.

Here again, I don't recommend the use of aluminum foil in place of a lid. Cover baking dishes with stainless steel lids or cookie trays. Look for such trays or lids in the kitchen-wares section of a department store or restaurant supply store. Bake in large batches to make the most efficient use of your oven. Store food in meal-sized containers to reheat as needed.

Broiling: This method is used in hot climates where much cooking is done out of doors. Vegetables are marinated, skewered and placed over coals or on the barbecue. Your oven's broiler or toaster oven can substitute. Kebab sticks are needed. This style of cooking is always a hit at parties and cook-outs, as snacks or as a main course if tempeh or tofu on skewers are included.

Final Tips:
- Coordinate shopping trips with cooking ahead sessions to keep fresh produce in the house.
- Onions, garlic and squashes do not need refrigeration in cool weather.
- Salad greens which are washed, spun-dried and stored in sealed containers will keep crisp for days, ready for quick salad making.
- Parsley, watercress, dill and basil can be washed and stored with stems immersed in a container of water, then covered with loose plastic wrap.
- Keep lower drawers and shelves of refrigerator for produce. Organize them according to type of vegetables (e.g., roots, salad, specialty items). This helps you keep an inventory of available produce and makes it easy to see at a glance what there is for supper and what to pick up at the market to complement it.
- Wilted vegetables can be saved and used in stock or soup.
- Remember: sharpen your knife before using it. Wash and allow vegetables to dry before cutting them.
- Don't wash and cut most vegetables until just before cooking time.

Fennel Sticks (Sliced)

Fennel, known as *finocchio* by Italians, is a crunchy vegetable (like celery) with an anise taste. Refreshing fennel sticks are served after a hearty meal to clear the palate for dessert. High in flavor, low in calories, Fennel Sticks are good for snacks or after meals.

Servings: 6 to 8
Time: 5 minutes

Equipment: knife, bowl

Ingredients:
    1 head of fennel

Procedure: Cut off the feathery fennel tops (which can be minced or used to flavor pickles, soups). Slice bottom off bulb; separate stalks of fennel and cut into sticks or bite-sized pieces.

Variations:
- Fennel can be used as a tasty substitute for celery.
- Cook or braise as vegetables.

Bright Green Broccoli

A short plunge into boiling water assures the brightest green color and crispness. Broccoli is a favorite vegetable with children of all ages.

Servings: 4 or more
Time: 10 minutes

Equipment:
  pot, colander, slotted
  spoon

Ingredients:
  1 head broccoli, sliced
    into small "flowerettes"
  pinch of sea salt or shoyu
    to taste (optional)

Procedure: Bring a large pot of water to boil; add a pinch of sea salt and drop in broccoli. After it has come to a full rolling boil again, the broccoli should be crisp and ready. If you prefer it softer, allow to boil for another few minutes. Remove from water and serve immediately, or place in colander and cool under cold running water to prevent overcooking and preserve bright green color. The cooking water can be used for making soup or boiling other vegetables.

Variations:
- Steam in basket until bright green.
- Use in salads or marinade.

Menu Suggestions:
- Broccoli, a quick green to cook, is perfect with any meal.

Kale

Kale's curly, dark green leaves provides one of the richest—and tastiest—sources of calcium.

Servings: 4 or more
Time: 10 minutes

Equipment: pot

Ingredients:
  1 bunch kale, washed,
    sliced into 1-inch pieces
  pinch of sea salt or shoyu
    to taste (optional)

Procedure: Wash the greens well. If leaves are large, slice down the middle along the stalk and chop into 1-inch pieces. If small, leave whole. Drop into boiling water and cook uncovered for 5 to 15 minutes, depending on how soft you like them. Drain. Serve plain or mixed with other vegetables. Reserve water for soup stock.

Variations:
- Whole blanched kale leaves may be used as garnish instead of parsley or watercress.
- Try adding cooked, drained kale to sandwiches instead of lettuce.

Menu Suggestions:
- Harvested mostly in cooler seasons, kale is a wonderful accompaniment to bean and grain dishes.

Collard Greens————————————————

Tender collard greens, picked in the spring, may be cooked like spinach. Larger collards sold in fall or winter require longer cooking. Try preparing them the old-fashioned way: boil uncovered in lots of water; drain and sauté with onions and garlic.

Servings: 4 or more
Time: 20 minutes

Equipment:
  large pot, colander, skillet

Ingredients:
  1 bunch collards, washed
    and sliced
  2 tsp. sesame or olive oil
  1 large onion, sliced
    (optional)
  2 cloves garlic, minced
  pinch sea salt, shoyu or
    umeboshi vinegar

Procedure: Wash and slice collards. If stems are thick, slice thinly so they will cook faster. Bring a large pot of water to boil; add greens and cook uncovered for 15 to 20 minutes, until soft and tender. (Collards should retain green color.) Drain in colander. Heat oil in skillet; add onions and garlic and sauté 2 to 3 minutes. Add drained collards; stir and cook 5 more minutes. Season to taste.

Variations:
- Collards and Carrots: slice 1 large carrot into matchsticks or half moons. Sauté with onion and collards or steam carrots separately and toss into sautéed greens.
- Collards and Mushrooms: add 4 oz. sliced mushrooms to onions and garlic.
- Collard greens can be used in sandwiches with tofu or tempeh.

Menu Suggestions:
- Serve with any meal; try these American classics:

Succotash	"3 Sisters" Casserole
Corn Bread or Muffins	Collard Greens
Collard Greens	Roasted Sunflower Seeds
Pecan Pie	

Stewed Broccoli-Rabe————————————

My Italian friends always have a pot of greens ready when I arrive. While broccoli-rabe is in season I make a pot two to three times a week. Ask for it at your vegetable market or local Italian grocery. This slightly bitter green becomes sweet with long, slow cooking.

Servings: 4 to 6
Time: 1 hour

Equipment:
  heavy pot with cover,
  plate or small lid

Procedure: Wash greens carefully and chop into 1-inch pieces. Pour 2 inches of water into a heavy pot and layer in the greens, onion and garlic. Top with oil and shoyu. Place a plate (or lid that fits inside pot) directly on contents to press down; then cover. Cook on medium heat until bubbling; then lower heat to simmer and cook an hour or more. The greens cook down, making a delicious juice. Serve the

Ingredients:
- 1 to 2 bunches broccoli-rabe
- 2 large onions, sliced
- 4 cloves garlic, minced
- 1 tbsp. olive oil
- 1 tbsp. shoyu or pinch of sea salt

greens in their liquid, or drain to make sandwich filling, saving juice to use elsewhere. Add a squeeze of lemon for extra perk.

Variations:
- Drained broccoli-rabe is used in calzone recipes.

Menu Suggestions:

Red Beans and Rice	Tofu Cacciatore
Stewed Broccoli-Rabe	Stewed Broccoli-Rabe
Corn Bread	Garlic Toast

Hummus Sandwich
Stewed Broccoli-Rabe
Rice Pudding

Braised Greens Caraway

Greens become tender and sweet by sautéing, then adding a little water and caraway seeds.

Servings: 4 to 6
Time: 30 minutes

Equipment:
  pot with cover

Ingredients:
- 1 tsp. sesame oil
- 1 large leek, thinly sliced
- 1/2 head cabbage, shredded (approximately 4 cups)
- 1/2 bunch kale, thinly sliced (approximately 2 to 3 cups)
- 1 cup water
- pinch of sea salt
- 1 tbsp. caraway seeds

Garnish:
  freshly chopped parsley

Procedure: Wash and slice vegetables. Heat oil in pot. Sauté vegetables, beginning with leeks, for 1 or 2 minutes. Add cabbage and kale, sautéing 2 to 3 minutes. Sprinkle with sea salt. Pour water and caraway seeds over greens; stir and cover. Simmer 15 to 20 minutes. Liquid should cook down so greens are not soggy. Be careful not to let them burn.

Variations:
- Prefer not to sauté? I layer leeks, cabbage and kale in pot. Add 2 cups of water, a pinch of sea salt and caraway seeds. Cover and simmer 20 to 30 minutes until cooked down.

Menu Suggestions:

Swedish Wheat Balls with Onion Sauce	Rice Pilaf
	Adzuki Beans
Steamed Carrots	Braised Greens Caraway
Braised Greens Caraway	Pickles
Cookies	Apple Crisp

Dandelion Greens Sauté

My Korean friends take me along on wild food forages in early spring. Once savoring the subtle flavor of the greens, it's no wonder the tradition of gathering wild foods has been passed down through generations and is becoming popular again. Bring an illustrated field guide when foraging, or find an experienced person to take you along.

Servings: 4 or more
Time: 30 minutes

Equipment: pot, skillet

Ingredients:
  1 bunch dandelion greens,
    washed 2 to 3 times,
    chopped
  2 onions, cut in half
    moons
  1 bunch other greens
    (curly dock, lambs
    quarters, collard greens)
  1 tbsp. olive oil
  1 tsp. shoyu, umeboshi
    vinegar or pinch of sea
    salt
  lemon juice

Garnish:
  sesame or sunflower
    seeds, toasted

Procedure: Wash dandelions very carefully; change water until no more sand comes out. Bring a large pot of water to a rolling boil. Add a pinch of sea salt and the dandelions. Boil uncovered for 15 to 20 minutes, depending on how fresh and tender they are. (If cooking other greens, boil separately, then sauté together.) When greens are soft, drain and save cooking liquid. Heat skillet and add a touch of oil. Add onions, pinch of sea salt, and sauté until translucent. Add greens and sauté for 3 minutes. Add more liquid if necessary. Season with shoyu and lemon. (I drink the cooking liquid from greens, if it isn't too bitter. Try it, you may like it!)

Variations:
  • Combine dandelions with fresh kale or collards.
  • Sautéed dandelion greens make a delicious filling for sandwiches.

Menu Suggestions:
  Minestrone Soup
  Pizza or Calzones
  Dandelion Greens Sauté
  Fennel Sticks

  Sweet Potato—Squash Soup or Golden Nugget Stew
  Brown & Wild Rice
  Dandelion Greens Sauté
  Pickles

Chinese Cabbage Rolls

With an eye for color and design, Chinese chefs roll dark green watercress in light green cabbage. They can be cut into rounds as Norimaki for an unusual way to serve greens.

Servings: 4 to 6
Time: 15 minutes

Equipment:
  pot, slotted spoon, bowl
  for water, sushi mat

Ingredients:
  1 chinese cabbage
  small bunch watercress
  pinch of sea salt

Procedure: Bring water to a boil and blanch cabbage until limp. Submerge in cold water; drain. Blanch watercress; drain and squeeze out excess liquid. Overlap 2 or 3 cabbage leaves on sushi mat, covering 2/3 of the mat. Line 1/4 of watercress in the center. Roll up mat tightly. Unroll mat, and slice roll into 1-inch pieces. Turn on side to display color and design of the vegetables.

Variations:
  • Instead of watercress, other green vegetables such as Swiss chard or spinach may be used.

- A blanched carrot strip can be included for extra color.
- Serve with Sweet Soy Sauce or mustard.

Menu Suggestions:

Miso Soup	Arame with Tofu
Adzuki Beans	Chinese Cabbage Rolls
Rice or Barley	Rice Croquettes
Chinese Cabbage Rolls	Fruit Kanten
Umeboshi Pickles	

Fig. 29   Chinese cabbage roll. Leaves of Chinese cabbage are overlapped, watercress is lined across bottom of cabbage, then rolled.

Fig. 30   Sliced Chinese cabbage rolls. Cut into 1-inch pieces.

Himalayan "Creamed" Greens

Lynne found a sure-fire way to make greens creamy and melt-in-the-mouth tender. She adapted this recipe from Himalayan-style sautéed greens to which tofu "yoghurt" is added. It makes an exotic vegetable which gets raves at parties.

Servings: 4 to 6
Time: 30 minutes

Equipment:
   large pot with lid, blender

Ingredients:
   1 large onion, thinly sliced
   1/2 lb. mushrooms, sliced
   1 bunch kale, chopped
   1 tsp. sesame oil

Procedure: Slice onion and mushrooms. Wash greens and chop into 2-inch pieces. Heat oil in large pot. Sauté onions and mushrooms until soft. Add greens plus 2 cups water to steam them. Cover and cook on medium heat until greens wilt and become tender, according to your taste. While greens are cooking, mix tofu "yoghurt" in blender or suribachi. Add "yoghurt" to cooked greens and allow to simmer 3 to 5 minutes to thicken. Adjust seasonings.

Tofu "Yoghurt"
 1/4 lb. tofu
 2 tsp. umeboshi paste*
  (or 1 plum)
 1 tbsp. tahini (optional)
 1 tbsp. kuzu or arrowroot
  dissolved in 1/4 cup
  water

*1 tbsp. lemon juice plus
 pinch of sea salt can be
 substituted for umeboshi

Variations:
- Spices (cumin, coriander or curry) can be added to sautéing onion and mushroom.
- "Creamed" greens will keep 1 or 2 days in the refrigerator.
- Combine collards, Swiss chard or spinach with kale.

Menu Suggestions:
- Himalayan "Creamed" Greens can be served as a light entrée, side dish or sandwich filling.

Golden or Mung Bean Dahl	Leek and Barley Soup
Himalayan "Creamed" Greens	Himalayan "Creamed" Greens
Pita Bread or Rice	Carrots or Baked Squash
Chutney, Pickles	Pecan Pie

Sautéed String Beans with Mushrooms

String beans are a versatile change from leafy greens. They combine well with other kinds of vegetables for a side dish or with tofu, tempeh or almonds as a main course.

Servings: 4
Time: 15 minutes

Equipment: pot, skillet

Ingredients:
 1 lb. string beans (whole
  or diagonally cut)
 1/2 lb. mushrooms, sliced
 1 tsp. sesame or olive oil
 pinch of sea salt
 pinch of herbs: dill,
  oregano or rosemary
  (optional)

Procedure: Blanch string beans in a large pot of boiling water until bright green or steam in steamer basket. Drain; heat oil; sauté mushrooms on high flame to seal in juices. Add string beans and stir to heat. Season with sea salt or herbs.

Variations:
- String Beans with Tofu: add 1/4 lb. golden fried tofu; 1/4 lb. of tempeh cubes can also be used.
- String Beans Almondine: add 1/2 cup toasted almonds slivered or whole, to skillet.

Menu Suggestions:

Corn Chowder	Autumn Stew
String Beans with Mushrooms	Barley or Millet
Hijiki-Sweet Potato Pie	String Beans with Mushrooms
Pickles	Apple Crisp
Peanut Butter Cookies	

Nabemono: One Pot Meal

The preparation of nabemono is simplicity itself. Vegetables are thinly sliced and artfully arranged in a skillet. A little water is added; it is steamed and served in the skillet. This dish can be arranged ahead of time; add water and cook when ready to serve it.

Servings: 2 to 3
Time: 15 minutes

Equipment:
skillet with lid (cast iron preferred)

Ingredients: choose a variety of vegetables:
1 stalk broccoli, sliced into flowerettes
1 small cauliflower, sliced into flowerettes
1 carrot, thinly sliced
1 small yam or squash, thinly sliced (into 4 or 5 pieces)
1 pepper, sliced into rings, for garnish (optional)
1 stalk celery, sliced on diagonal
1 to 2 cups water
4 oz. tofu, cut into cubes (optional)

Seasonings:
1 tsp. miso or 1 tsp. shoyu or pinch of sea salt

Garnish:
sea vegetables: dulse or nori strips

Procedure: Slice vegetables: softer vegetables into larger pieces; harder root vegetables into thinner slices. Arrange vegetables in skillet; group to form a design. Leave space in the center for tofu. Add 1 to 2 cups of water to pan, to a level of about 1/2 inch deep. Cover and steam until vegetables and tofu are tender, about 5 minutes. Season with shoyu and lemon juice.

Variations:
- Instead of sea salt or shoyu, season with chopped fresh dill, basil, oregano or rosemary.
- This dish can use up all the vegetables in your refrigerator, sliced attractively.
- Try snow peas, zucchini or brussel sprouts.
- A small fish fillet can be substituted for tofu.
- Add cooked noodles, ramen, udon or soba, to center of vegetables and steam together.

Menu Suggestions:

Nabemono	Kidney Beans and Corn
Sweet Rice or Barley	Nabemono
Wakame-Cucumber Salad	Fruit Kanten

The Vegetable Batch

The art of "par-boiling" or blanching vegetables requires a sense of timing and color. This is the technique we use in restaurant cooking. Vegetables are dropped into a large pot of boiling water, the longest-cooking vegetables first, followed by those with shorter cooking times. All are finished at the same time, and the cooking is stopped at the peak of color and crunch. They are drained and saved for use in many dishes. Here is another basic recipe for cooking ahead, a good way to use up all vegetables in your refrigerator.

Servings: 4 to 6
Time: 30 minutes

Equipment:
  large pot, colander or
  strainer, bowl

Ingredients:
  2 qts. boiling water
  1 small daikon, cut into
    1/2-inch cubes
  1 large carrot, matchstick
    or half-moon cut
  1/2 lb. pearl onions or
    diced white onions
  1/2 lb. brussel sprouts or
    broccoli
  2 celery stalks, sliced

Procedure: Bring pot of water to boil. Wash and cut vegetables. Drop daikon first into boiling water. Cook 10 minutes. Add carrots, onions and brussel sprouts; cook 5 to 10 minutes (depending on your taste); add celery and continue to cook 2 more minutes. Drain vegetables, saving water for soup stock.

Variations:

- Use different combinations of 5 to 6 vegetables; choose firm vegetables, not soft ones like yellow squash or zucchini. Try lotus root, burdock, parsnips, broccoli, string beans and cauliflower.
- Vegetables-in-Kuzu Sauce: drain vegetables. Thicken 2 cups of cooking "broth" with 1 1/2 tbsp. kuzu. Season with ginger juice and shoyu.
- Add kombu or shiitake mushrooms to pot of water before adding vegetables.

Menu Suggestions: Serve dressed as "salad" in summer. In winter, try it with kuzu sauce. Add blanched vegetables to fried rice, soups or bean dishes.

Succotash or Chili	Grain or Fish
Vegetable Batch	Croquettes
Pickles	Vegetable Batch
Muffins	Apple Pie or Tart

Black Bean Soup
Rice
Vegetable Batch
Tahini Dressing
Chutney

Chinese-Style Vegetables

Another favorite for cooking ahead. Oil-free and quicker than stir-frying, this dish is layered, steam-boiled and finished with sauce. Crisp and delicious!

Servings: 4
Time: 20 minutes

Equipment:
  skillet or pan with lid

Procedure: Layer onions, cabbage, carrot and green beans; add water. Cook until tender, 5 to 10 minutes; then add the squash and peppers and cook until tender (2 minutes). Blend together the sauce ingredients; stir into vegetables until clear and thick. Garnish with cashews.

Ingredients:
- 2 cups water
- 1 large onion, 1/8-inch sliced
- 4 cups cabbage, sliced thinly
- 1 carrot, 1/8-inch half-moon cut
- 4 oz. string beans or broccoli, cut in 1/8-inch pieces
- 1 summer squash, 1/8-inch half-moon cut
- 1 pepper, 1/8-inch matchsticks
- 1/2 cup cashews, roasted

Sauce:
- 1/4 cup water
- 1 tsp. shoyu
- 1 tsp. ginger juice
- 1 tbsp. arrowroot or kuzu

Variations:
- Soybean or mung sprouts, celery, snow peas, water chestnuts, or red pepper may be used also.
- Almonds, walnuts or pecans can stand in for cashews.
- Fried tofu or tempeh cubes can be added.
- Add sautéed garlic and red pepper for authentic Chinese flavor.
- Seitan and Vegetables: add 1/2 lb. seitan to recipe.

Menu Suggestions:

Miso-Watercress Soup	Miso Soup
Chinese-Style Vegetables	Chinese-Style Vegetables
Noodles	"5 Senses" Rice or
Fruit Kanten	Norimaki
	Orange Jewel Cookies

Cauliflower Crown

A regal crown of cauliflower makes an impressive centerpiece. Don't cut it apart: trim leaves but leave whole. Steam and then bake. Surround with steamed kale and carrots.

Servings: 4 to 6
Time: 30 minutes

Equipment:
- pot with lid large enough to fit cauliflower, baking dish, mixing bowl

Ingredients:
- 1 medium cauliflower
- water to steam
- 2 tbsp. olive oil
- 1 cup bread (crumbs) or cracker crumbs
- 1 tsp. herbs (optional)

Garnish:
- parsley, steamed kale or carrots

Procedure: Trim the leaves off cauliflower; slice off "stem" end so the bottom is flat. Place cauliflower in pot with 2 inches of water. Cover. Bring to a boil and steam 5 to 10 minutes until cauliflower is soft when pierced with fork, but not mushy. Remove from pot and place in baking dish. Fifteen minutes before serving, rub with olive oil; sprinkle with bread crumbs and bake 10 to 15 minutes.

Variations:
- Omit bread crumbs; simply steam until tender and serve with your favorite sauce.

• Menu Suggestions:

Dahl or Black Bean Soup	Chili or Baked Beans
Cauliflower Crown	Corn Bread
Carrots and Collards	Cauliflower Crown
Pita Bread, Sprouts	Salad with Croutons
Peach Chutney	Pickles
	Orange Kanten

Beets and Greens

Beets brighten meals year round from winter soups to summer salads. Look for beets with green tops still attached: they're best this way.

Servings: 4 to 6
Time: 30 minutes or more

Equipment: pot with lid

Ingredients:
  1 bunch beets with
    tops, if available
  pinch of sea salt

Procedure: Cut greens off beets, above roots. Scrub beets and wash greens carefully. If beets are large, slice in half or quarters. Place beets in a pot; cover with water. Cover pot and bring to a boil. Cook for 30 minutes or longer until fork pierces easily. Remove beets from liquid and cool. Peel and slice beets. Chop beet greens. "Steam-boil" in pot with water until tender. Add pinch of sea salt or shoyu. Serve beets with greens.

Variations:
- Cold Beet Salad: cube or slice peeled beets; toss in favorite salad dressing.
- Hot Beet Salad: serve beets in a hot ginger-shoyu sauce or with orange-miso sauce.

Menu Suggestions:

Baked Fish	Leek 'n' Barley Soup
Corn or Risi-Bisi	or Dahl
Beets and Greens	Cauliflower Crown
	Beets and Greens

Miso Soup
Broccoli-Corn-Tofu Medley
Beets and Greens
Pear Crunch

The Best Braised Red Cabbage

The bright red color and sweet-tart flavor of this dish mingles with grain and bean entrées for a festive meal with Northern European flair.

Servings: 4 or more
Time: 1 hour

Equipment: large sauté pot,
  baking dish, cover

Ingredients:
  2 large onions, thinly sliced
  1 small red cabbage
    (approximately 6 cups
    thinly sliced)

Procedure: Slice onion and cabbage thinly. In a large pot, heat oil and sauté the onion until it becomes clear and sweet-smelling. Add the red cabbage and sprinkle with sea salt. Stir and sauté until cabbage wilts. More oil may be needed. Mix vinegar (which keeps cabbage red) and water; pour over the red cabbage and mix well. Oil a baking dish and spoon the cabbage into the dish. Cover and bake at 375°F. for 1 hour. Dish will keep 3 to 4 days in refrigerator. Serve warm or cold.

1 tbsp. oil
1/2 tsp. sea salt
2 to 3 tbsp. vinegar
1/2 cup water

Variations:
- Two to 3 apples can be substituted for onions.
- Green cabbage or carrots can be added.
- Caraway seeds or roasted, chopped nuts add extra flavor and crunch.

Menu Suggestions:

Tofu or Tempeh Sandwich	Consommé with Carrot Flowers
Red Cabbage with Caraway	Swedish Wheat Balls with Onion Gravy
Chips, Pickles	Braised Red Cabbage
	String Beans Almondine
	Apple Crisp

Carrots Vichy

In France, "Vichy" is a brand of bottled mineral water. A popular item on French menus, this sparkling water makes carrots even sweeter and take on a sunny glow.

Servings: 4 to 6
Time: 20 minutes

Equipment: pot with lid

Ingredients:
1 to 2 lbs. whole baby or regular carrots, cut into rounds
1 to 2 pts. mineral or spring water
pinch sea salt
1 tsp. arrowroot (optional)

Garnish:
chopped parsley, dill or basil

Procedure: Wash carrots. If using baby carrots, use whole; if large carrots, slice into attractive rounds. Place in pot and cover with mineral water; add pinch of sea salt and slowly bring to a simmer. Cover pot and allow to cook slowly. Reduce liquid until about a cup remains. Serve as is, or thicken by dissolving arrowroot in 1/4 cup water and adding to carrots in water. Stir and simmer 2 to 3 minutes until there is a clear shiny glaze. Garnish with parsley.

Variations:
- Carrots and Celery Vichy: add 2 stalks celery, "triangle cut," after carrots cook 10 minutes. (Celery needs less cooking.)
- Add pearl onions.

Menu Suggestions:

Fish in Mushroom Sauce	Navy Bean with Leek Soup
Rice with Peas	Garlic Toast
Carrots Vichy	Carrots Vichy
Salad	Salad, Olives
	Fruit Kanten

Creamed Onions

Onions are used to flavor other dishes, but not often served by themselves. Pearl or small onions are an elegant (and economical) side dish.

Servings: 4 to 6
Time: 1/2 hour

Equipment: pot, bowl

Ingredients:
 1 to 2 lbs. pearl onions
 pinch of cumin (optional)
 2 tbsp. kuzu or
  arrowroot
 2 tbsp. tahini (optional)
 shoyu or sea salt to taste

Procedure: Peel onions by blanching in boiling water for 60 seconds. Drain them and discard liquid. Onions should slip easily out of their skins. Place peeled onions in heavy saucepan with water to cover. Add cumin. Bring to a boil and simmer 15 to 20 minutes until onions are tender. Dissolve kuzu or arrowroot in 1/2 cup water. Slowly stir into onions, and continue stirring over medium heat until thickened. Lower heat and simmer for 5 minutes. Add tahini if desired, but do not boil. Season to taste. Heat until warm and serve with chopped parsley.

Variations:
• Try adding another vegetable or 2 while onions are cooking, such as small mushrooms.
• "Triangle-cut" celery and roasted walnuts also improve the dish.

Menu Suggestions:
 Tempeh "Turkey"   Fish and Rice Croquettes
 Rice Pilaf   Creamed Onions
 Creamed Onions   Beets and Greens
 Cranberry Relish or Light Pickles
  Braised Red Cabbage

Butternut Squash with Orange

Zesty orange flavor complements the sweetness of squash. We serve this on Thanksgiving and winter holidays. It's sweet enough for dessert.

Servings: 4 to 6
Time: 45 to 60 minutes

Equipment:
 baking dish, cover

Ingredients:
 1 medium butternut
  squash
 1 orange, grated rind and
  juice

Procedure: Slice squash into 1/2-inch to 1-inch rounds. Peel each slice and cut into 1-inch pieces. Remove seeds. Place squash cubes in shallow baking dish (glass pie pan works well). Combine remaining ingredients and pour over squash. Cover and bake in a 375°F. oven for 45 to 60 minutes until tender.

Variations:
• Squash Purée: mash baked squash. Serve as side dish or garnish with nuts for a quick dessert or snack.

2 tbsp. maple syrup
(optional)
1/4 tsp. cloves
1/4 tsp. cinnamon
pinch of sea salt

- Combine carrots, sweet potatoes and squash.
- Squash Pie: make a crust; fill with squash purée.

Menu Suggestions

Chili or Kidney Beans and Corn	Special Split Pea Soup Grain or Noodle
Butternut Squash with Orange	Butternut Squash with Orange
Collards or Salad	Greens or Salad
Pickles	Apple Pie

Baked Root Vegetable Medley

A popular dish in my fall and winter repertoire. While making soups and grain on top of the stove, utilize the oven: bake root vegetables and muffins or roast seeds. Baked root vegetables will keep two to three days. Reheat in oven or add to soups and stews.

Servings: 4 or more
Time: 1 hour

Equipment:
baking dish, cover or lid

Ingredients:
2 large onions, diced
1 small rutabaga, peeled, cut in 1-inch cubes
2 parsnips, cut in chunks
1 turnip, cubed
3 carrots, "roll cut" or chunked
1 tbsp. sesame oil (optional)
pinch of sea salt or shoyu to taste
1/2 to 1 cup water (optional)

Procedure: Cut all vegetables. Place in oiled baking dish; add water and sea salt; cover and bake at 375°F. for 30 to 45 minutes until fork-tender.

Variations:
- Burdock Medley: add 1 burdock; cut into small pieces. Precook with water to cover for 10 minutes. Add burdock and water to roots; bake.
- Add potatoes or sweet potatoes.
- Season with herbs or miso dissolved in water; bake.
- Garnish with lots of chopped parsley or scallions, and roasted seeds.

Menu Suggestions:

Adzuki Beans or Chickpea Stew	Leek–Barley Soup Fried Tofu or Tempeh
Millet or Kasha	Root Vegetable Medley
Root Vegetable Medley	Greens or Salad
Greens or Salad	
Fruit Pie	

Baked Garlic

I first savored baked garlic as an appetizer at the Cafe Venezia in Berkeley, California, run by chef Janice Wilcox, my friend since culinary school days. Baked garlic becomes mellow and spreads like butter on bread. Only serious garlic lovers need venture.

Servings: 4 to 8
Time: 1 1/2 hours

Procedure: Remove the outer layers surrounding the garlic bulb; slice a knife around the base of garlic and peel to reveal cloves. Place bulbs in a small baking

Equipment:
  small baking dish, lid or
    foil

Ingredients:
  4 whole bulbs of garlic,
    or more, allowing 1 bulb
    for 2 to 3 people
  2 to 3 tbsp. olive oil
  pinch of sea salt
  pinch of pepper
  1/2 cup water

dish; pour olive oil over them and sprinkle with sea salt and pepper. Cover and bake 20 minutes at 300°F. Add water and baste bulbs; cover and continue to bake for 1 hour or longer until very soft when pierced with a fork. To serve, place on a small dish with a knife and a loaf of good bread. Squeeze garlic cloves from one end, and the creamy, baked garlic will pop out on bread. Spread with a knife.

Variations:
• Traditionally this recipe uses butter. If you desire, dab each bulb with 1 tablespoon butter before baking.

Menu Suggestions:

Fish, Baked or Fried	Chili, Baked Beans or
Rice Pilaf	Black Beans
Baked Garlic	Corn-on-the-Cob
Bread, Salad	Baked Garlic
Fruit in Sauce	Bread, Salad

Curried Vegetables

Adapted from Indian cuisine, this recipe substitutes oil for "ghee" (clarified butter) and goes easy on the spices. I double the recipe to serve 15 to 20 guests. To transform it into a main dish, simply add chickpeas, tempeh or tofu cubes or cashews.

Servings: 6 or more
Time: 30 minutes

Equipment:
  heavy pot with lid

Ingredients:
  1 onion, sliced
  1 carrot, thinly sliced
  2 stalks celery, diagonally
    sliced
  1 small cauliflower, cut
    into flowerettes
  1 medium zucchini, cut
    into 1/2-inch cubes
  1 tbsp. sesame oil
  1/2 to 1 tsp. curry powder
  2 cups water
  1 to 2 tbsp. kuzu
  1 tsp. ginger juice
    (optional)
  pinch of sea salt or shoyu
    to taste

Procedure: Wash and slice all vegetables. In a large pot, heat oil and begin to sauté onion, carrot and celery. Cook 2 minutes; add cauliflower and zucchini; stir. Add curry powder and stir until vegetables are coated. Pour 2 cups water over vegetables; cover pot and "steam-boil" until vegetables are tender. Dissolve kuzu in 1/4 cup water; add to pot; stir until sauce thickens. Season with sea salt, ginger, and/or shoyu.

Variations:
• Add garlic; for extra flavor: cumin, coriander, dry mustard or white pepper.
• Chickpeas and Curried Vegetables: add 2 cups of cooked chickpeas to vegetables in sauce. Heat and serve.
• Tofu, tempeh or seitan cubes can be added.

Menu Suggestions:

Dahl	Curried Vegetables
Rice or Millet	Himalayan Greens

Garnish:
  diced red pepper
  freshly chopped scallions
    or parsley (optional)

Curried Vegetables
Pita Bread, Salad
Pickles
Carrot Pudding

Rice or Noodles
Pita Bread, Salad
Pickles
Stuffed Dates

Pizza

Homemade pizza: a crisp whole wheat crust spread with sauce, piled high with vegetables, topped with tofu "cheese," served hot from the oven. Sound delicious? Sounds like too much cooking to most of my friends, but this recipe is worth the adventure which pizza making is. Allow plenty of time—2 to 3 hours. I usually make pizza on weekends. The quantities given are enough for 6 to 10 people. Halve the recipe if you have fewer than 4. This dough can also be used for calzones. A pizza stone of clay or brick found in gourmet shops is essential for a thin, crispy crust. I use a jelly roll pan or cookie sheet at home. Sauce and tofu topping can be made a day ahead. Even the kids might actually *want* to get involved in making pizza.

Pizza Dough

I've experimented with many variations of pizza doughs and toppings. My feeling is that the best dough recipe calls for approximately equal parts of whole wheat and white pastry flours.

Equipment:
  large mixing bowl, small
  bowl, pizza stone, jelly
  roll pan or cookie sheet

Ingredients:
  2 tbsp. yeast
  3 cups warm water
  2 tbsp. barley malt
  1/2 cup olive oil
  4 cups white pastry flour
  4 to 6 cups whole wheat
    pastry flour (approx.)
  1/2 tsp. sea salt

Procedure: "Proof" yeast by mixing the first 4 ingredients together and allowing them to ferment for 5 to 10 minutes. This mixture is ready when yeast bubbles. Sift 8 cups of flour into a large mixing bowl add sea salt; add yeast mixture and stir. Form ball and knead, adding more flour if necessary. This dough should resemble *firm* bread dough, feeling very stiff. Continue to knead 3 to 5 minutes. (Dough becomes soft as it rises.) Place it in large oiled bowl. Cover and place in warm spot for 1 hour.

Pizza with Vegetable Topping

Thinly sliced raw vegetables can be used, but I've found lightly sautéed vegetables add extra flavor and reduce baking time.

Ingredients:
   1 recipe pizza dough
   1 qt. Estella's Red Sauce
      (See p. 86), quick
      Tomato Sauce (see page
      87) or store-bought sauce
   1 to 2 lbs. vegetables,
      thinly sliced and lightly
      sautéed (some left raw)
   1 recipe Tofu "Ricotta"
      filling (See p. 131)

Optional Garnishes:
   black olives, anchovies

Procedure: Make dough and begin sauce while it is rising. Slice vegetables and lightly sauté in olive oil for topping. Season with Italian herbs: oregano, thyme, marjoram. Prepare tofu topping. Punch dough down. Oil baking tray and dust with cornmeal. Stretch or gently roll dough to fit pan. Allow to rise 15 minutes. Prebake crust at 350°F. for 10 minutes to "set." Remove from oven and spread with sauce and sautéed vegetables; crumble tofu filling on top. Bake at 375°F. for 15 to 20 minutes, until golden brown on top. Allow to cool 5 minutes before slicing.

Variations for Vegetable Topping:
- Mushroom Pizza: slice 1 lb. mushrooms and sauté lightly in olive oil, adding a pinch of herbs.
- Pepper-Onion Pizza: slice 1 lb. of peppers into thin rings; leave raw. Slice and lightly sauté 1 lb. of onions.
- Zucchini-Summer Squash Pizza: slice 1 to 2 lbs. zucchini and yellow squash; lightly sauté.
- Olive-Anchovy Pizza: top pizza dough with sauce; make design with olives (halves, pitted) and anchovies. Top with tofu.
- Tempeh Pizza: top sauce with 1/4 lb. tempeh, thinly sliced, deep-fried and seasoned with garlic and herbs.

Tofu "Ricotta" Filling

The mild flavor and soft texture of tofu lends itself to recipes calling for ricotta cheese. I use tofu "ricotta" to fill calzones, top pizza or make sandwiches.

Servings: 6
Time: 10 minutes

Equipment:
   pan, suribachi or mixing
   bowl, fork or wooden
   spoon

Ingredients:
   3 to 4 onions, sliced
   1 tsp. olive oil
   2 cloves garlic
   1 lb. tofu, soft, drained
   2 tbsp. tahini
   1 tbsp. miso or pinch of
      sea salt
   pinch of oregano to taste
   1 cup grated mochi(optional)

Procedure: Sauté onions over medium-low flame for 15 to 20 minutes, until sweet-smelling and transparent. Mash tofu in suribachi or mixing bowl. Add tahini, miso and oregano to tofu. Add grated mochi, if available. Add tofu mixture to onions; stir and season to taste.

Variations:
- Tofu "ricotta" can be used in lasagna or manicotti recipes.
- Try filling pita bread with tofu "ricotta" and steamed broccoli or greens.
- Instant "mini-pizzas": split whole wheat English muffins or pita bread in half. Toast lightly. Spread with sauce, vegetables and top with tofu "ricotta." Reheat.

132

Assembling Calzones

A calzone is an Italian vegetable pie or turnover made by rolling out pizza dough, filling with cooked vegetables or tofu "ricotta," folding it over and baking it until golden.

Servings: 6 to 10
Time: 10 to 30 minutes

Equipment:
  cookie sheet, pizza pan or
  large baking dish, rolling
  pin

Ingredients:
  1 recipe Pizza Dough
  filling: Tofu "Ricotta" or
    Italian vegetables
  1 tbsp. oil
  flour

Procedure: Punch dough down. Divide into 4 or 5 balls. Lightly oil baking sheet and dust with flour. Roll dough out to cover pan, 1/4-inch thick, and thicker at edges. Spread filling 1/2-inch thick over half of the dough, leaving 1 inch around edges unfilled. Fold dough over filling until edges meet; pinch edges; lightly brush with oil and bake at 350°F. for 20 minutes. Repeat procedure with remaining dough.

Variations:
• To make individual calzones, roll out pieces of dough into 6-inch to 8-inch circles. Place filling on half of the dough and cover; seal and bake.

Menu Suggestions:

Minestrone Soup	Florentine White Bean
Calzones or Pizza	Soup
Salad, Pickles	Calzones or Pizza
Lemon or Fruit Kanten	Steamed Broccoli
	Sliced Fennel

Italian Vegetable Fillings for Calzone

Calzones are often filled with cooked escarole and dandelion greens which have been drained of excess juices. This recipe is similar to the one for stewed greens. Choose one green or a combination.

Servings: 6 to 10
Time: 1 hour

Equipment:
  large soup pot with cover

Ingredients:
  Choose 2 bunches of
  greens:
  broccoli-rabe
  dandelions
  kale
  mustard greens
  escarole
  2 tbsp. olive oil
  3 cloves garlic
  1 to 2 onions, sliced

Procedure: Wash greens very well to remove sand. Chop leaves and slice stems. Heat oil in large soup pot. Sauté garlic and onions and add greens. Sauté lightly. Add 2 cups water and sea salt; cover and allow greens to "cook down" over low flame for 1/2 hour. Bitter greens will become soft and sweet the longer you cook them, 20 to 30 minutes at least. If you prefer the bitter taste, cook only until wilted. Drain off liquid. This is a delicious broth to drink or add to soup. The greens are ready to fill calzones.

pinch of sea salt or shoyu
   to taste
pinch of each herb:
   oregano, dill, thyme or
   rosemary

"Veggie Rolls"

"Veggie Rolls" are cousins of the Chinese egg roll. Egg roll wrappers can be found in the freezer or refrigerator sections of food stores and supermarkets, or freshly made in Oriental markets. Fillings are limitless and can be prepared a day ahead. Two important tips: the vegetables must be thinly sliced and sautéed; and the filling must be dry. Excess moisture from filling will make wrappers soggy. I store wrappers in the freezer until needed then defrost. This is an easy but impressive dish to make for parties.

Servings: 10 to 12 rolls
Time: 1 hour

Equipment:
   sauté pan, mixing bowl,
   pot for deep-frying

Ingredients:
   1 tsp. oil
   1 onion, thinly sliced
   2 carrots, cut into match-
      sticks
   3 celery stalks, thinly
      sliced
   2 cloves garlic, minced
      (optional)
   1 cup diced mushrooms
   2 to 4 cups cabbage, finely
      sliced
   1 cup mung sprouts
      (optional)

Seasonings:
   pinch of sea salt
   1 tsp. shoyu or umeboshi
      paste
   1 tsp. ginger juice
   12 egg roll wrappers
   2 to 3 cups oil for deep
      frying

Dipping Sauce:
   Teriyaki or Orange-Miso
   Sauce

Procedure: Sauté all vegetables 5 to 10 minutes. Add pinch of sea salt to help "cook down" vegetables to boil off any excess liquid. Season with shoyu and ginger. Allow to cool. (I usually place vegetables in a strainer.) Heat oil. Have wrappers, filling and dish of water to moisten fingers ready. Place wrapper as diamond. Spoon 1/3 cup filling on lower half. Fold up bottom; fold over sides. Moisten edge of top point; roll up. Continue with other rolls. When oil is very hot, drop rolls in gently. Fry 2 to 3 at a time; cook on one side until golden brown; then turn over. Fry 2 to 3 minutes on other side. Drain on paper towels. Serve immediatiely.

Variations:
- Cooked rice, tofu and sea vegetables can all be added to filling.
- Season filling with mustard, horseradish or Chinese spices.

Menu Suggestions:

Tofu-Watercress Soup	Miso Soup
"Veggie Rolls"	"Veggie Rolls"
Quick Teriyaki Sauce	Dipping Sauce
White or Brown Rice	Noodles with Tofu
Mustard Green Pickles	Steamed Vegetables
Fruit Kebabs	Strawberry Kanten

Sea Vegetables————————————————

When I mention eating sea vegetables to friends who are new to them, they imagine eating the sea weeds that wash up on shore. These cannot be eaten. New England's cold waters are abundant with edible sea vegetables, rich in minerals, which are important to a vegetarian diet. Sea vegetables grow on rocks or other surfaces in the ocean. They are "harvested" just as land vegetables are, at certain times of the year; then they are sundried, packaged and stored for future use. I have gone harvesting on Boston's north shore, whose rocky points are covered with plentiful vegetation. We pick them during the low tide of summer solstice when the water recedes enough to gather slippery long kombu, sea lettuce and other vegetables that are exposed. It is advisable to go out with an experienced gatherer or buy a detailed guidebook to do it yourself.

Native Americans were said to to have traveled to the coasts to collect sea vegetables and to return home with a light-weight dried food supply. Sea vegetables are still part of the diet of Oriental and island nations. The long, lustrous hair of island people is attributed to a diet rich in sea vegetables such as black hijiki and arame. Dulse has long been used in the diet of the Scots and Britons. The Maine coast is experiencing a revival of interest in this natural food. These indigenous vegetables are being harvested by small companies and distributed to natural food stores.

Most people eat sea vegetables, but don't know it. They are used as stabilizers in processed foods, ice cream and frozen foods, but it is not required by law to list them as ingredients. When introducing sea vegetables consciously into one's diet, it is best to do so in small amounts. Soup or bean dishes are the best places to start. Don't over-salt them: they are naturally high in minerals and they have their own flavor.

Tips on buying and storage: Sea vegetables can be stored for years; buy in bulk to save money and store them in a cool, dry place. Don't seal them tightly in plastic because any moisture will cause mold. Sea vegetables need to be picked over carefully: there can be tiny shells, stones, etc., caught inside the dried folds. Spread them out on a dish and shake gently to look for these; then soak and rinse.

There are basically seven types used in this book. To learn more about the other varieties of sea vegetables, it is advisable to buy books on sea vegetable cookery.

Agar-agar: This mild-tasting gelatin from the sea is used primarily to thicken desserts. It can be used to make aspics or jellied salads. Simmer agar in stock as in dessert recipes; then add seasonings and diced vegetables; chill and serve.

Arame and Hijiki: These are delicate black threads that need to be soaked first, then sautéed and simmered alone or with land vegetables. While camping, I found that they can be soaked overnight and eaten the next day without cooking. The black strands offer a striking contrast to other foods and are often used as garnishes.

Nori: Imported from Japan or China, sheets of nori are used to roll rice or noodles into norimaki. Nori needs only to be toasted over a flame 1 minute by waving a sheet of it back and forth until it changes color from black to green. It can be cut into strips to wrap around tofu cubes or rice balls. Cut into 1-inch by 3-inch strips or crumble and serve on top of grain dishes. Wrap a strip around a mouthful of rice and eat as sushi. Cut into small shapes with scissors to garnish other foods. Nori is generally liked by all.

Dulse: This purplish vegetable of soft, leafy texture has been part of the diets of Britons, Scandinavians and eastern Canadians for centuries. After thorough washing, it can be added to oat stews and porridge, roasted and eaten as a high energy snack, or dissolved (without precooking) into soups and stews. It goes well with dressings, salads and mixed vegetable dishes.

Kombu: Add this hearty, broad-leafed vegetable to beans for flavor; it also aids in digestion and adds minerals. It will "melt" if cooked long enough.

Wakame: The satiny sea vegetable wakame is loved, or at least liked, once one takes the time to get used to it. Its traditional use is in salads with crisp, marinated vegetables or added to soups, stews or beans in place of kombu. Wakame has a tough spine that is removed after soaking; otherwise, it must be cooked for a long time to soften.

Arame-Stuffed Mushroom Caps

My guests love these marvelous stuffed mushrooms. But they can't guess what the filling is. Arame's sublime flavor is enhanced with saké and lemon to create an unusual appetizer or garnish for meals.

**Servings: 6—2 or 3 mush-
rooms per serving
Time: 1/2 hour**

Equipment:
small pan, skillet, baking
dish

Ingredients:
1 cup arame
12 to 18 fresh mushrooms
1 tsp. sesame oil
1 small onion, minced
1/4 cup saké
1 lemon, juiced
2 tbsp. shoyu
1 tsp. ginger juice

Garnish:
fresh parsley, minced red
pepper or lemon slice

Procedure: Soak arame for 10 minutes. Rinse mushrooms and remove stems. Place in baking dish. Dice stems and set aside. Drain arame and place in small pan, adding enough water to cover. Bring to boil and simmer 15 minutes. Drain. Squeeze out liquid from arame and mince. Heat oil in small pan and sauté onion and mushroom stems for 3 to 5 minutes. Add diced arame to vegetables. Combine saké, shoyu, lemon and ginger juice. Pour half over arame mixture and simmer until liquid evaporates; pour remaining marinade over mushroom caps. Stuff mushroom caps with arame mixture. Cover and bake 15 minutes. Garnish with parsley. Be careful not to overcook: mushrooms will "shrink."

Variations:
- No time to stuff mushrooms? Prepare arame "stuffing" and serve on lettuce leaves.
- Use filling to stuff pita bread with lettuce and tofu dressing.
- Serve as appetizer or garnish for fish.

Menu Suggestions:

Miso Soup
Stir-Fried Vegetables
  with Tofu
Arame-Stuffed
  Mushroom Caps
Cherry Kanten

Pan-Fried Fish
Couscous with Peas
Arame-Stuffed
  Mushroom Caps
Greens or Salad

Arame with Tofu

Golden cubes of fried tofu and feathery black arame are tossed in lemony dressing for a main dish or salad. A dish high in protein and minerals.

Servings: 4
Time: 30 minutes

Equipment:
  small pot, fry pan, mixing
  bowl

Ingredients:
  1/2 lb. tofu, firm
  1 cup dry arame (approxi-
    mately 1 ounce)
  1 cup oil (to fry tofu)
  1 tsp. shoyu or pinch of
    sea salt
  1 lemon, juiced
  2 scallions, sliced

Procedure: Press tofu for 15 minutes or longer. Cut into bite-sized cubes. Sort over arame. Place in bowl with water and soak 10 minutes until it expands. Drain; place in pot and cover with water. Bring to a boil, simmer 15 minutes. While arame cooks, heat oil and fry tofu until golden. Drain on paper towels. Place fried tofu in bowl and sprinkle with shoyu or sea salt, and lemon juice. Drain arame; add to tofu and toss together. Add sliced scallions; mix. Allow flavors to marinate 30 minutes or longer.

Variations:
- Tempeh can be substituted for tofu.
- Hijiki can replace arame.
- Cook sea vegetable fresh or use leftover.
- Umeboshi or 1 to 2 tsp. rice vinegar can be substituted for lemon juice.
- Carrot "flowerettes" or blanched red pepper strips make dramatic garnishes.

Menu Suggestions:

Gingery Miso Broth
Stuffed Cabbage Rolls
Arame with Tofu
Salad
Fruit Smoothie

Rice Pilaf or Millet
Carrot Sauce
Arame with Tofu
Broccoli

Hijiki

Hijiki is a sea vegetable harvested along the coastal areas of Japan. It looks like delicate black spaghetti when it is soaked and cooked. The flavor is mild and slightly salty or "fishy." Hijiki has been sun-dried, steamed and dried again, then packaged and exported to natural food stores. As with all sea vegetables, it is necessary to inspect it for shells, then soak to reconstitute, drain and cook according to directions. When introducing hijiki to family and friends, I tend to dice hijiki (leaving it in long strands doesn't appeal to everyone), then combine it with grain or vegetable dishes. I find as hijiki expands, it becomes sweet and melts in the mouth when simmered at least 30 minutes to one hour.

Servings: 4 to 6
Time: 1 hour

**Equipment: bowl, pot with
    cover**

Ingredients:
    **1 cup dry hijiki (approxi-
        mately 1 oz.)**
    1 large onion, sliced
    1 tsp. sesame oil
    pinch of sea salt or shoyu
    water to cover

Procedure: Sort over hijiki; soak for 15 to 20 minutes. While hijiki is soaking, slice onion and sauté in oil over medium heat. Drain soaked hijiki; chop into 1-inch pieces and add to sautéing onion. Cover with water and simmer 30 minutes to 1 hour (or for a shorter time if the hijiki will be cooked again in strudel or pie). Stir occasionally. Watch carefully and allow liquid to boil down, but not burn. Season with sea salt or shoyu. Drain and serve.

Variations:
- Add matchstick-cut carrots or cubed squash to hijiki. Steam separately and toss together, or add carrots to hijiki and cook together 15 to 20 minutes.
- Season with 1 tsp. lemon juice, rice vinegar, ginger juice or dark sesame oil.
- Add fried tempeh or tofu cubes to simmering hijiki. Garnish with scallions.
- Add blanched snow peas, red peppers, carrots and yellow squash for an "Oriental look."
- Add leftover cooked hijiki to rice or noodle salads.
- Use in strudel or pie.

Menu Suggestions:

Miso-Watercress Soup	Rice and Tofu Burgers
Yellow Rice	Hijiki with Carrots
Vegetables in Curry	Pickles, Salad
Sauce	Fruit Smoothie
Hijiki with Scallions	

Hijiki and Sweet Potato Pie

Delicate black hijiki with a slightly salty flavor, layered with orange sweet potatoes, is a dramatic introduction to a new sea vegetable. Try it for surprising results. For sea vegetable fans it's also a good way to use up leftovers.

Servings: **4 to 6**
Time: **1 hour**

Equipment:
  **bowl, 2 pots, baking dish
  or casserole**

Ingredients:
  **1 to 2 cups cooked hijiki
  1 lb. sweet potatoes,
    mashed or puréed
  pinch of sea salt or 1 tbsp.
    light miso to flavor
    sweet potatoes
  1 tbsp. oil**

Garnish:
  **3 tbsp. roasted sunflower
    seeds
  chopped parsley**

Procedure: Cook hijiki according to basic recipe. Boil sweet potatoes until soft; drain, mash and season with sea salt or miso. Oil baking dish; spread layer of sweet potatoes. Cover with hijiki and top with sweet potatoes. (Make thick layers, or alternate thin layers.) Cover and bake 20 to 30 minutes; allow to set. Garnish with roasted sunflower seeds and chopped parsley.

Variations:
- Puréed squash, carrots or yams can be substituted for sweet potatoes.
- Arame can be used instead of hijiki.
- Season with ginger juice.

Menu Suggestions:

Tempeh "Turkey"	Tofu-Watercress Soup
Rice or Barley	Hijiki and Sweet
Hijiki and Sweet	Potato Pie
Potato Pie	Grain Croquettes
Greens or Salad	Chinese Cabbage Rolls
Applesauce	Pickles, Salad

Dulse and Red Onion Salad

The easiest-to-fix sea vegetable salad. Dulse needs only to be soaked, drained and mixed with red onions. The salt from dulse "wilts" the onions, bringing out their sweet taste.

Servings: **4**
Time: **10 minutes**

Equipment:
  mixing bowl, strainer

Ingredients:
  **1 cup dry dulse
  2 red onions, thinly sliced
  1 tbsp. vinegar
  pinch of sea salt**

Procedure: Clean dulse, removing any tiny shells. Soak in bowl of cool water. Slice red onions, thinly. Place in bowl. Drain dulse, squeezing out liquid. Add dulse to red onions. Mix well; add vinegar and sea salt. Allow salad to set for 1 to 2 hours.

Variations:
- Add radish, celery or cucumber.

Menu Suggestions:

Corn Chowder	Consommé with Carrot
Stuffed Squash or	Flowers
Cabbage	Rice with Primavera
Dulse and Red Onion	Sauce
Salad	Dulse and Red Onion
Apple-Peanut Sauce	Salad
	Couscous Cake

Sautéed Onions with Dulse

Sweet sautéed onions are the base to which dulse is added. A tasty sea vegetable dish to introduce to your family.

Servings: 4
Time: 30 minutes

Equipment:
   heavy pot with cover

Ingredients:
   3 large onions, thinly
      sliced
   1 tbsp. sesame oil
   pinch of sea salt
      (optional)
   1 cup dry dulse
   1/2 cup water

Garnish:
   chopped, blanched,
      watercress or kale

Procedure: Thinly slice onions. Heat oil in a heavy pot and sauté onions until clear, on a medium flame. Add sea salt. Clean dulse, looking for tiny shells; rinse. Add dulse to onions as they cook; stir. Add 1/2 cup water. Cover and let simmer 10 to 15 minutes. Garnish with greens.

Variations:
• Add matchstick-cut carrots to onions and dulse.

Menu Suggestions:
"3 Sisters" Casserole
Greens or Salad
Sautéed Onions with
   Dulse

Jane's All-in-One Meal
Sautéed Onions with
   Dulse
Salad, Pickles

Kombu and Variations

Kombu is a sea vegetable that grows abundantly in cold ocean waters from Maine to Japan. The long (20 to 60 feet), graceful "leaves" are harvested, sun-dried, cut into 6-inch to 12-inch lengths and packaged. It is the most frequently used seaweed.
   Dashi, a basic Japanese cooking stock, derives flavor from it. Kombu is used, too, in bean dishes, with rice and in soups. To serve it as a vegetable, soak and simmer it for 30 minutes; then sauté with onions.

Servings: 4 to 6
Time: 45 minutes to
      1 hour

Equipment:
   pot with lid or pressure
   cooker, skillet

Ingredients:
   5 to 7 strips kombu
      (approximately 1 oz.)
   1 qt. water
   1 tbsp. sesame oil
   1 large onion, thinly sliced
   1 carrot, matchstick-cut
   pinch of sea salt or 1 tsp.
      shoyu

Procedure: Soak kombu in a bowl of water for 10 to 15 minutes (or longer, overnight). Simmer it for 30 to 40 minutes. Remove kombu; reserve "stock" for soups and sauces. Slice into strips 1-inch wide, then cut across into thin pieces. Heat oil in skillet. Sauté onion and carrot for 1 minute; add sliced kombu; stir. Sauté for 10 minutes or longer. By now, the kombu should be tender and sweet. Season with sea salt or shoyu to taste.

Variations:
• Vegetable-Kombu Sauté: add other matchstick-cut vegetables to carrots and onions (e.g., parsnips, cabbage, mushrooms).
• Sweet-Simmered Kombu: add 1 tbsp. mirin to kombu and onions; sauté.

140

Garnish:
   2 sliced scallions

- Onion and Kombu: omit carrots and add extra onions, plus 1 tsp. rice vinegar or 1 tsp. ginger juice.

Menu Suggestions:

Tofu or Tempeh Kebabs	Baked Fish in Sauce
Rice or Couscous	Rice Pilaf or Noodles
Vegetables and Kombu	Onion and Kombu
Salad	Salad

Cucumber-Wakame Salad

Crispy cucumbers combine with the subtle flavor of wakame for a quick, refreshing salad.

Servings: 4 to 6
Time: 30 minutes

Equipment:
   bowl, pot

Ingredients:
   1 to 2 ozs. wakame
   1 large cucumber, cut in thin half slices
   3 to 5 radishes, sliced
   1 to 2 tbsp. vinegar or lemon juice
   1 tsp. shoyu or pinch of sea salt

Garnish:
   3 scallions, sliced diagonally, radish flower

Procedure: Soak wakame (in enough water to cover) for 15 minutes. Remove "stem" and discard the soaking water. Place in the pot with 2 times as much water. Bring to a boil and simmer for 15 minutes. Drain and chop wakame. Then place it in a bowl to cool. Toss wakame in vinegar and shoyu. Add the cucumbers and radish. Garnish with scallions and radish flowerettes.

Variations:
- If the cucumber is large and seeds are not so soft, remove them with a spoon before slicing.

Menu Suggestions:

Autumn Stew	Tofu Kebabs
Millet	Rice Pilaf
Cucumber-Wakame	Cucumber-Wakame
Salad	Salad
Baked Apple	

Salads————————————————————————

Seven Styles of Salads: Salads have a wide variety of uses: as a main course, as lunch at work, or as an appetizing format for cooked grains and beans. Their ingredients reflect changing seasons, weather and activity. A summer garden variety of freshly picked lettuce, radishes, watercress or scallion, is followed in winter by a vegetable salad cooked and marinated, served warm or cool.

Raw Salad: I like this one best in warm weather, when lettuces are fresh and local. Wash greens carefully, spin dry and mix with other thinly sliced vegetables. Add the dressing at serving time, so salad won't wilt. Try mixing different greens: escarole, chicory, red leaf, curly, Bibb, Boston, arugula, chopped, tender watercress or dandelion greens.

Pressed Salad: Cabbage or lettuce and other vegetables are sliced thinly, sprinkled with sea salt and pressed for 1/2 to 1 hour or longer. This method of salad-making is used in the Orient and Europe; it's a cross between pickles and salad.

Boiled or Steamed Salad: In cooler weather, a lightly cooked salad makes a good main dish. A variety of land or sea vegetables are boiled or blanched and tossed with a dressing.

Grain Salad: Rice, barley, corn, wheat berries or rye berries can be used as a basis for a hearty, satisfying salad. Served this way, grains are more flavorful and are visually enhanced by the addition of colorful diced or sliced vegetables. They will keep for a few days this way. Noodles, couscous and bulghur can be used in salad, too. Grain salads are perfect for lunchboxes and picnics, and a good way to use up extra grain.

Bean Salad: Although "three bean" is a salad favorite, I prefer to feature one bean rather than mix them. Chickpeas, white and red beans are the ones that best hold their shape when cooked. An olive oil and lemon or umeboshi dressing works well with bean salad.

Fish Salad: Season and bake a fillet of fish until flaky. Cool and combine with raw or cooked vegetables or with grains; then toss with a lemony or basil dressing.

Fruit Salad: Select fruits in season that are of the same type: apples and pears; a few different melons; or a selection of berries. Toss with lemon juice or thick kuzu glaze for a light breakfast snack or dessert. It is best to eat raw fruits separately from cooked foods.

The Art of Salad Making:

The pleasure of cooking ahead is always having a cooked grain in the refrigerator to make instant all-in-one salads. For a main course, there can be four elements to a salad:
   1. Cooked grain: 2 to 4 cups rice, barley, corn, cracked wheat, couscous—alone or in combination.

2. Beans: 1/2 cup of roasted nuts or seeds; or 1 cup cooked beans, or fried tofu or tempeh.

3. Raw or cooked vegetables: 1 to 2 cups chopped or sliced raw vegetables in any combination of the following: scallions, parsley, mint, dill, basil, watercress, cucumber, radish, red onion, grated carrot, zucchini, onion and celery. With blanched or steamed vegetables: use 2 to 3 cups of string beans, broccoli, peppers, carrots, snow peas, or any combination thereof. Cooked and diced arame, hijiki or dulse can also be incorporated.

4. Salad dressing: a choice of oil and vinegar, basic basil, tahini or tahini-ume-onion—or your own creation.

A Sampling of Salad Combinations:

Raw Vegetable Salad:	*Blanched Vegetable Salad:*	*Sea Vegetable Salad:*
rice	rice or noodles	rice or corn
red onion, diced	broccoli, blanched	hijiki or arame, cooked
scallion, sliced	carrot flowers, blanched	red and green peppers, blanched
parsley, minced	chickpeas or tempeh	lemon-shoyu dressing
sunflower seeds, roasted	basil dressing	
oil and vinegar dressing		
dulse as garnish		

Julienne Salad

"Julienne" is the term used in French cooking to describe finely sliced foods. I make winter and summer versions of this salad, using matchstick-cut seasonal vegetables. Tossed with oil and vinegar dressing, salads will keep two or three days.

Servings: **4 or more**
Time: **10 minutes**

Equipment: mixing bowl

Ingredients:
1 small daikon, matchstick-cut
4 or 5 red radishes (large, if available) matchstick-cut
2 celery stalks, matchstick-cut
2 or 3 scallions, thin, diagonally-cut

Umeboshi Dressing:
2 tbsp. olive or sesame oil
1 tbsp. vinegar or 2 ume-boshi plums (mashed)
2 tbsp. chopped fresh parsley or dill

Procedure: Wash and scrub vegetables. Cut into matchstick pieces. Combine in bowl; add dressing, toss and chill. Serve as salad or light pickle.

Variations:
- In summer: add red onion, peppers and basil.
- In winter: try green or red cabbage.

Menu Suggestions: Here's a refreshing, crunchy salad to complement all meals.

"3 Sisters" Casserole	Bean Soup or Stew
Julienne Salad	Rice or Cracked Wheat
Rolls or Bread	Julienne Salad
	Mocha Pudding

Mediterranean-Style Salad

A Mediterranean-style salad, attractively displayed and garnished on a lettuce-lined platter, is the foundation of an antipasto plate or part of a light meal. You can almost feel the warmth of the southern sun as you tuck into it.

Servings: 4 or more
Time: 15 minutes

Equipment:
strainer, large plate, blender or shaker

Ingredients:
- 1 head Bibb or curly leaf lettuce, washed and drained
- 1 large cucumber, sliced
- 1 small bunch radishes, thinly sliced
- 4 stalks celery, cut diagonally
- 1/2 lb. mushrooms (raw or marinated)
- 1/2 lb. Tofu Cheese, Marinated Tofu or Tempeh "Bacon"

Oil and Vinegar Dressing:
- 2/3 cup olive oil
- 1/3 cup red wine or rice vinegar
- 1 tsp. oregano
- pinch of sea salt
- pinch of pepper
- 3 cloves garlic, minced

Garnish:
- 1/2 lb. black olives
- 1 pt. cherry tomatoes (optional)
- 1 tin anchovies (optional)
- parsley or watercress

Procedure: Wash lettuce and vegetables; drain well. Tear lettuce gently, reserving some whole leaves for garnish. Peel cucumber (if desired) and cut into quarters lengthwise, then into 1/4-inch slices. Slice other vegetables; set aside. Combine dressing ingredients by blending or shaking. At serving time assemble salad. Line large plate or platter with lettuce leaves. Toss lettuce, cucumbers, radishes, celery, mushrooms and tofu cheese with enough dressing to coat vegetables. Arrange salad on lettuce and garnish. Serve with remaining dressing on side.

Variations:
- Fresh basil, dill or chives can be added to dressing.
- Blanched, steamed or marinated cauliflower, broccoli, string beans or carrots could be substituted for raw vegetables.

Menu Suggestions:

Minestrone-Escarole or
   Florentine White
   Bean Soup
Mediterranean-Style
   Salad
Rice Pudding or
   Couscous Cake

Stuffed Grape Leaves
   or Peppers
Mediterranean-Style
   Salad
Fruit Tart

Croquettes with Miso-Tahini Dip
Mediterranean-Style Salad
Lemon Pudding

Dilled Cucumber Salad

A cool, refreshing salad. Prepare first, before your other dishes.

Servings: 4
Time: 10 minutes; press
30 minutes

Equipment:
bowl and plate to fit inside
for pressing

Ingredients:
1 large cucumber, sliced
into rounds
1 medium red onion, sliced
into thin rounds
2 tbsp. fresh dill
vinegar
sea salt
oil or mayonnaise

Garnish:
parsley, black olives,
radish flower

Procedure: Peel cucumber if waxed. Slice into 1/8-inch rounds. Slice onion the same way and pop out onion rings. Layer the onions and cukes. Sprinkle with a dash of sea salt, vinegar and dill. Continue alternating the vegetables and seasonings. Press lightly while preparing remainder of the meal. Before serving, toss in olive oil or mayonnaise to coat the vegetables. Garnish with parsley and olives.

Variations:
• Add radish, cilantro.

Menu Suggestions:

Borscht or Red Velvet Soup	Tempeh-Potato Croquettes
Noodle Kugel	Baked Garlic
Carrots Vichy	Dilled Cucumber Salad
Dilled Cucumber Salad	Rice Bread or Rolls

"Quick" Pressed Cabbage Salad

You won't recognize the usual taste of cabbage in this easy pickled salad. Its sharpness is completely mellowed by light pressing. A large batch will keep three to four days in the refrigerator, ready for lunchboxes or to round out a meal.

Servings: 6
Time: 1 hour

Equipment:
grater, bowl, plate,
weight

Ingredients:
1 small head cabbage,
thinly sliced
1/2 head red cabbage,
thinly sliced

Onion Dill Dressing:
3 tbsp. grated onion (1
small onion)
2 tbsp. vinegar (rice
vinegar is best)
2 tbsp. sesame or olive oil

Procedure: Cut cabbage into wedges and slice paper thin. Save core for soup or stock. Place cabbage in mixing bowl. Grate onion on a ginger or other fine grater and add to cabbage. Pour dressing over salad and toss with spoon or clean hands. Place a plate that fits inside bowl on top of cabbage. Put a weight (heavy jar) on the plate to press salad. Press for 1/2 to 1 hour. The longer cabbage is pressed, the softer and sweeter it becomes. Stir before serving. Water from cabbage will press out, making a "dressing."

Variations:
• Add 1/2 cup roasted sunflower seeds for crunch.
• Grate carrot for color.
• Add 1 tbsp. caraway seeds for flavor.
• Use umeboshi vinegar or paste instead of sea salt and vinegar.

1/4 cup chopped fresh dill
   or parsley
1/2 to 1 tsp. sea salt

Menu Suggestions:

Jane's All-In-One Meal
Cabbage Salad
Date-Nut Squares

Succotash or Chulent
Cabbage Salad
Bread or Muffins

Tempeh-Potatoes-Carrots
Cabbage Salad
Lemon Walnut Cookies

Nice-Dice Vegetable Salad

To save time these diced vegetables are cooked together in one pot. Potatoes and carrots are started in cold water and the remaining vegetables tossed in for a quick boil. Bathed in piquant dressing, this salad improves after one day.

Servings: 4 to 6
Time: 1/2 hour

Equipment:
   large pot with cover,
   strainer, mixing bowl

Ingredients:
   4 potatoes, peeled, cut in
      small cubes
   2 carrots, cut in 1/2-inch
      dice
   1 stalk celery, diced
   1 large onion, diced
   1/2 lb. string beans, cut
      into 1/2-inch pieces
   1/2 lb. fresh peas, shelled

Dijon Dressing:
   1/2 to 3/4 cup mayonnaise
      (safflower or soy)
   2 to 3 tbsp. dijon or stone
      ground mustard
   pinch of white pepper
   2 tbsp. fresh parsley,
      chopped
   1 tbsp. pickle juice
      (optional) or pinch of
      sea salt

Garnish:
   lettuce, parsley, radish or
      tomato

Procedure: Wash vegetables. Dice potatoes and onion into 1/4-inch to 1/2-inch pieces. Cut carrots and celery lengthwise into 1/4-inch strips; then dice across width. Place carrots and potatoes in large pot. Cover with cold water and bring to a boil; turn down heat and simmer 5 minutes. Then add celery, onion, string beans and peas on top of simmering potatoes and carrots. Cover and steam or boil until vegetables are brightly colored and tender, approximately 2 minutes. Strain vegetables and set aside to cool. Save cooking liquid for stock. Mix all dressing ingredients and add to cooled vegetables. Refrigerate and serve on lettuce leaves for garnish. Decorate with parsley, radish or tomato.

Variations:
• Make a simple salad with potatoes, peas or beans.
• If using new red potatoes, leave skins on.

Menu Suggestions:

Black Bean Soup
Croutons or Garlic
   Bread
Nice-Dice Salad
Ginger Couscous Cake

Chili or Baked Beans
Corn Bread or Muffins
Nice-Dice Salad

Broccoli-Corn-Tofu Medley———————————————

This dish combines my favorite summertime grain-bean-green medley tossed with a fresh basil dressing. I make a large batch in the cool of morning and bring it to the beach to enjoy after swimming. It keeps for two days.

Servings: 4 or more
Time: 20 minutes

Equipment:
  pot, mixing bowl

Ingredients:
  4 ears corn
  1/2 lb. firm tofu, cut in
    1/2-inch cubes
  1 head broccoli, cut in
    flowerettes

Basil Dressing:
  1/2 cup olive oil
  juice of 1 lemon
  1/8 cup chopped fresh
    basil (or 1 tsp. dried)
  pinch of sea salt

Garnish:
  1 red pepper or red onion
    sliced into rings

Procedure: Boil corn-on-the-cob for 5 to 8 minutes; save water to blanch broccoli and tofu. Cut corn off cob and place in mixing bowl. Cut off broccoli flowerettes and dice the broccoli stems into 1/2-inch pieces. Bring water to a boil; then drop broccoli in. When the water resumes boiling (about 2 to 3 minutes), the broccoli will be bright green and tender. Remove from the water and let cool. Then drop tofu in the blanching water and simmer 2 to 3 minutes. Drain and cool. Combine dressing ingredients by blending or shaking. Pour over drained vegetables to marinate. Garnish with red pepper or onion rings.

Variations:
• Add blanched cauliflower or carrots, olives or sliced radish.
• Umeboshi vinegar is a delicious replacement for sea salt and lemon.

Menu Suggestions:

Fish Fillet	Sweet Potato Soup
Broccoli-Corn-Tofu	Broccoli-Corn-Tofu
Medley	Medley
Strawberry Crunch	Toasted Nori or Seeds

Millet "Loaf" with
  Estella's Red Sauce
Broccoli-Corn-Tofu Medley
Olives, Pickles

"It's a Meal" Macaroni Salad with Creamy Dill Dressing———————

Try piquant tofu-dill dressing instead of the usual mayonnaise in this macaroni salad for a hot weather main course, or a wonderfully tasty salad in winter.

Servings: 4 or more
Time: 20 minutes

Equipment:
  mixing bowl or blender,
  pot, serving bowl or
  platter

Procedure: Cook noodles *al dente* and toss with oil to prevent them from sticking together; cool. Wash vegetables and slice into 1/8-inch to 1/4-inch matchstick or "julienne" strips. Lightly blanch or steam vegetables only until brightly colored and crisp. Add vegetables to noodles, reserving a few strips of vegetables for garnish. For dressing, press water out of

Ingredients:
  1 lb. macaroni (shell or
    spiral)
  1 tsp. oil
  1 red onion, thinly sliced
  1 medium zucchini,
    matchstick-cut
  1 carrot, matchstick-cut
  2 stalks celery, thinly
    sliced on diagonal

Tofu-Dill Dressing:
  1 small onion, grated or
    minced
  2 cloves garlic, minced
    (optional)
  2 tbsp. dill pickle juice
  1/8 to 1/4 cup fresh dill,
    chopped
  1/2 lb. tofu
  2 tbsp. lemon juice
  pinch of sea salt
  pinch white pepper
    (optional)

Garnish:
  1/2 cup roasted sunflower
    seeds
  red or green leaf lettuce
    (optional)

tofu. In a mixing bowl or blender, combine all dressing ingredients until smooth, similar to the consistency of mayonnaise. If it's too thick, dilute with 1 or 2 tbsp. water. Adjust the seasonings as necessary, adding salt, dill, lemon, etc. Toss salad with dressing and chill. Serve in a bowl or mounded on a platter lined with lettuce. Garnish with parsley and vegetable strips.

Variations:
• String beans, peas, snow peas, broccoli and scallions can be substituted as vegetables.
• Add extra seasonings.
• Substitute basil for dill.
• Garnish with toasted nuts or seeds.
• Try olive and radishes as garnishes.

Menu Suggestions:

Macaroni Salad	Red Lentil and Squash Soup
Tempeh Sandwich	Herbed Croutons
Pickle	Macaroni Salad
Apple Crisp or Pie	Pickles
	Date-Nut Squares

Barbecued Tempeh or Fish
Orange-Miso Sauce
Macaroni Salad
Baked Corn or Corn Muffins
Fruit Kebabs

Hijiki Noodle Salad

Black hijiki, white noodles and bright vegetables make a striking dish. Spiral, shell or ziti noodles work well in this salad. Cut vegetables to harmonize or contrast with the shape of the noodles.

Servings: 6
Time: 20 minutes

Equipment:
  soup pot, mixing bowl

Ingredients:
  2 cups cooked hijiki (1 cup
    dried), chopped into 1-
    inch pieces
  2 cups noodles, cooked

Procedure: Cook hijiki according to directions on package or use leftover hijiki; drain in colander to remove liquid. Chop into 1-inch pieces. Boil noodles. Blanch or steam carrots and celery. Slice scallions. Mix dressing. Combine all ingredients in mixing bowl; pour dressing over and toss. Allow flavors to marinate 1/2 to 1 hour. Serve on lettuce.

Variations:
• Use Umeboshi dressing.

2 carrots, sliced into half
moons
1 stalk celery, sliced
diagonally
2 scallions, thinly sliced

Lemon Dressing:
1/4 cup lemon juice
1 tbsp. oil
pinch of sea salt or shoyu
to taste

- Marinated tofu or tempeh cubes may be added.
- Blanch snow peas or string beans and use whole as garnish, or cut into bite-sized pieces and add to dish.

Menu Suggestions:

Tofu-Watercress Soup	Split Pea Soup
Hijiki Noodle Salad	Hijiki Noodle Salad
Fruit Kanten	Apple Pie

Marinated Chickpea Salad

Lots of parsley and fresh mint enliven this chickpea and vegetable salad with color and flavor. It will keep well for two days and can be prepared ahead for tomorrow's lunchbox or parties.

Servings: 4 or more
Time: 15 minutes

Equipment:
bowl, serving platter

Ingredients:
2 cups cooked chickpeas
4 red radishes, cut in half, sliced
1 small cucumber, cut in quarters, sliced
2 stalks celery, diced
1/2 cup watercress, chopped
1/4 cup fresh parsley, minced
1/4 cup fresh mint, minced, or 1 tbsp. dried

Garnish:
Sprouts or lettuce leaves, black olives, whole watercress

Ume-Oil Marinade:
1/4 cup olive oil
2 tbsp. umeboshi or rice vinegar
pinch of sea salt

Procedure: Toss cooked chickpeas in oil, vinegar and sea salt. Marinate all day or overnight. Vegetables may be cut earlier, but should be added not more than 1 hour before serving time to preserve color and freshness. Slice and dice vegetables the same size as the chickpeas and add to chickpeas. Add finely chopped parsley and mint. On a platter spread a bed of lettuce or sprouts and place chickpea salad over this. Garnish with olives and whole watercress. Serve with pita bread.

Variations:
- Any raw salad vegetables can be substituted.
- Replace chickpeas with cracked wheat for "tabouli" salad.

Menu Suggestions:

Miso-Lemon Soup	Barley-Leek Soup
Stuffed Grape Leaves or Millet Croquettes	Marinated Chickpea Salad
Marinated Chickpea Salad	Pita Bread
	Stuffed Dates

Marinated String Bean Salad

String bean salad is a tangy, colorful complement to grain dishes.

Servings: 4 or more
Time: 20 minutes

Equipment:
   pot, serving platter, mixing
   bowl

Ingredients:
   1 large red or white onion,
      thinly sliced
   pinch of sea salt
   1 lb. string beans,
      snapped

Herbed Marinade:
   2 to 3 tbsp. olive or
      sesame oil
   1 tbsp. rice vinegar
   1/2 tsp. oregano
   1/2 tsp. dill
   1 clove garlic, minced
   pinch of sea salt

Garnish:
   1 head lettuce, washed,
   1/4 pt. black olives
      (optional)   or toasted
      almonds

Procedure: Sprinkle sliced onion with pinch of sea salt; toss and allow onion to "wilt." Snap beans and drop into boiling, salted water for 2 to 3 minutes until bright green. Run under cold water to prevent overcooking. Prepare marinade and mix with beans and onions. Dressing should lightly coat vegetables. Allow to rest at least 1 hour. To serve, place marinated vegetables on a bed of Bibb lettuce and garnish with olives or almonds.

Variations:
- Add yellow "wax" beans to salad.
- Add marinated tofu cubes.
- Tempeh "Bacon" can be added, too.

Menu Suggestions:

Leek and Barley Soup	Corn Chowder
Marinated String Bean Salad	Marinated String Bean Salad
Baked Squash with Orange	Pita Bread
	Sweet and Sour Pickles

Fish Stew
Garlic Toast
Marinated String Bean Salad
Cherries Jubilee

7. Whole Grains, Beans, Tofu and Tempeh————————————

Grains and beans are daily fare year-round, but each one comes from a particular climate and has a distinct growing season. A look at when and where they are grown gives insight into which seasons and culinary forms they are best suited.

Corn, for example, grows as high as an elephant's eye in New England from July to early October. So, for peak freshness, it is featured on summer and fall menus. During the rest of the year, or for those living in perpetually warm climates, corn grits or cornmeal ground fresh from dried corn can be used. Both combine well with red or pinto beans and summer or winter squashes.

Buckwheat, rye and oats are cold winter grains, perfect for frosty falls and blustery, white winters. A bowl of steaming buckwheat or creamy oatmeal keeps cross-country skiers and skaters going all day. Buckwheat croquettes and knishes are strengthening; and whole oats, cooked hours until soft and added to soups and stews, can't be beat for stoking the inner fires. Bean casseroles and root stews make good complementary dishes.

In spring, the green shoots of grains, beans and vegetables that have been slowly germinating through the winter burst forth. Wheat is a good choice for spring, in the form of whole wheat berries, noodles or cracked wheat. Sprouted soy or mung beans, whole fresh peas or dried split peas accompany wheat. Stewed greens and green salads are excellent cleansing foods that give a light feeling after the long, cold months.

Rice, millet and barley are the grains used all year round. Only their cooking methods vary with respect to the season. Rice or barley salads and millet burgers are delightful in summer, while slow-cooked soups, stews, and grain casseroles hit the spot in winter.

Beans are a natural complement to grain. Naturally, the quicker cooking varieties are best in summer—red or brown lentils, split peas, tofu and tempeh. Serve marinated bean salads or hummus sandwiches on warm days. Thick bean soups and stews warm and satisfy in cooler weather.

Shopping, Storing Tips for Grains and Beans: Grains and beans will keep for years in a cool, dark place. Unlike flour and produce which need to be used that week, you can keep a variety of whole grains on hand almost indefinitely. My kitchen is home to over twenty large gallon jars, holding warm-hued grains and beans. We never have to worry about what to make for dinner when shelves are lined with whole grains.

Locate a food co-op and buy quality grains in bulk at considerable savings. Most stores will order 25- to 50-lb. sacks for you. Consider sharing them with friends. But first buy a pound or two of each type of grain and bean to see which ones you prefer. We buy one or two kinds of brown rice, millet and chickpeas or adzuki in bulk.

Keep grains away from heat at all times, especially in summer, when it is advisable to store in a cool place or the refrigerator. Placing bay leaves or a drop of bay oil on a

Q-tip taped to the lid of a container or sack is supposed to discourage moths. If grain becomes infested, throw it away before other grains are affected. In any case, sift and wash them carefully before cooking.

Tips for Cleaning Grains and Beans:

- It is best to sort over whole grains a cup at a time to remove hulls and stones. This may seem like a lot of work, but consider it preventive dental care. Teeth have been known to break on tiny stones.
- Some grains are cleaner than others: millet, for example, is so fine that not much else can pass through while screening it.
- Buckwheat can have black hulls: some dark hulls are wild grains, but often some are stones and need removal. Beans of all types need thorough cleaning, too. Use a large plate or dish; pour out one cup at a time. Sort to one side and you may be surprised at what you will find. Red lentils have many little rocks. Look closely at beans or grains from the bottom of the bag or barrel.

Basic Brown Rice———————————————————————

Procedure:

1. *To boil:*   Cover grain with twice as much water. Add a pinch of sea salt and bring to a boil on a medium-high flame. Place flame tamer beneath the pot (optional). Cover pot and turn flame to medium-low. Simmer until all liquid is absorbed and grains are tender, 45 to 60 minutes. *Never stir cooking grains.* Tiny "vent" holes appear in grain as it boils and are necessary for uniform cooking. If liquid evaporates and grains are still hard, add more water and continue cooking until grains become tender.

2. *To pressure-cook:*   Add sea salt and water to rice (1 1/4 cups liquid to 1 cup grain for dry, fluffy rice; 1 1/2 cups liquid to 1 cup rice for softer grain) in cooker. Cover and seal tightly. Bring up to pressure on medium heat; place on flame tamer and lower heat. Cook 40 minutes. Shut off flame; remove pot from stove and allow pressure to drop naturally (10 minutes). Open pot and transfer grain to bowl.

3. *Transferring rice to bowl:*   Use a wooden rice paddle that is moistened with water. Scoop out the center part of the grain first and place into a bowl. Fluff and spread gently to separate grains. Spoon the remaining rice into bowl. Should the bottom rice burn or brown, remove only the softer rice, leaving the bottom crust in pot. Loosen edges of bottom rice and remove by rolling it up into a log. Slice and let dry for a crunchy treat.

Tips:

- To loosen burnt grain stuck in the pressure cooker: after removing fresh hot rice from the top, return cover to pot and seal. The heat and steam from the pot will "lift" the rice. If the burnt rice is dry, then add 1 cup of water. If the pan is really burnt, add baking powder, a little water and let it sit overnight.

- Avoid all aluminum pots and pans, especially for cooking grains.
- Soaking: for lighter, more digestible grain, wash rice, add water and soak 6 to 8 hours or overnight before cooking.
- "Set-up" (wash and soak) rice in the morning for dinner time or in the evening for next-day cooking. This shortens cooking time.

Variations:
- Wild Rice-Brown Rice: add 1/4 cup wild rice to each cup of rice, use 2 1/2 cup water.
- Nutty Rice: add 1/2 cup roasted nuts or sunflower seeds to rice; cook together.
- Rice with Kombu: add 1 strip of kombu to rice; cook together.
- Rice with Sauerkraut: add 2 to 3 tbsp. chopped sauerkraut to rice, and a teaspoon of caraway seed to each cup of grain; cook together.

Rice and Millet

Combining grains adds variety to menus. Cooked with enough water, the grains will be soft and sticky, perfect for rice balls or croquettes.

Servings: 4 to 6
Time: 1 hour

Equipment:
    pressure cooker or pot
    with lid

Ingredients:
    1 1/2 cups brown rice
    1/2 cup millet
    pinch of sea salt
    4 to 4 1/2 cups water for
        pressure cooking, 5 cups
        water for boiling

Procedure: Wash rice and millet. They can be low-boiled for 40 to 50 minutes or pressure-cooked for 45 minutes.

Variations:
- The grains can be roasted for extra flavor. Follow roasting instructions for grains.
- Roasted walnuts or sunflower seeds can be added to grain before cooking for a richer flavor, or use them as a crunchy garnish.
- While grain is warm, shape into balls and roll in Spicy Walnut or Coconut Condiments. Pack in lunchbox or serve with meal.

Menu Suggestions:

Miso Soup	Black Bean Soup
Rice and Millet	Rice and Millet
Lentils and Squash	Baked Squash with
Broccoli	Orange
Tahini Sauce	Coconut Condiment
	Greens or Salad

Curried Vegetables
Rice and Millet
Umeboshi Pickles

Rice 'n' Rye

If you like the taste of rye bread, try adding rye "berries," the staple grain of Scandinavian countries, for a chewier version of brown rice. Rye berries are whole, unpolished grain, as are whole wheat berries. It's best to pressure-cook them, after soaking overnight.

Servings: 4 or more
Time: soak grains overnight; boil 1 hour

Equipment:
pot with lid or pressure cooker with flame tamer

Ingredients:
1/2 cup rye "berries," soaked overnight
1 cup brown rice
3 to 3 1/2 cups water
pinch of sea salt

Procedure: Wash grains; place in pot with water. Cover and set in cool place to soak overnight. Cook in the soaking water or drain and add an equal amount of fresh water. Add pinch of sea salt. Bring to a boil, or up to pressure, slowly. Simmer 50 to 60 minutes until water is absorbed and grains are separate.

Variations:
- Add 1 tsp. caraway seeds.
- Substitute 2 umcboshi plums or 2 tbsp. chopped sauerkraut for sea salt. Cook together.
- Rice 'n' Rye Ring: add sautéed, minced onion, carrot and celery to rice; cook and spoon while warm into oiled ring mold. Unmold on platter and garnish with steamed greens.
- Raisin Rice 'n' Rye: add 1/4 to 1/2 cup raisins to Rice 'n' Rye and cook together or make a soft breakfast cereal by simmering leftover Rice 'n' Rye with raisins and water or apple juice until it reaches a creamy consistency.

Menu Suggestions:

Red Velvet Soup	Autumn Stew or
Rice 'n' Rye	Chickpea Stew
Braised Greens Caraway	Rice 'n' Rye
Carrots	Braised Red Cabbage or
Baked Apples	Cabbage Salad
	Pickles, Salad

Rice Pilaf

The secret of perfect, fluffy pilaf is in roasting the rice, sautéing the vegetables and adding boiling water. Pilaf can be pressure-cooked, boiled or baked. Try this version on family and friends.

Servings: 4 or more
Time: 1 1/4 hours

Procedure: Wash rice and drain well; roast in pot over low flame, stirring gently back and forth until nutty aroma arises (approximately 5 to 10 minutes).

Equipment:
  pressure cooker, flame
  tamer, pot with lid or
  casserole dish to bake

Ingredients:
  2 cups brown rice
    (medium or long grain)
  1 tsp. oil
  1 medium onion, diced
  1 carrot, diced
  2 celery stalks, diced
  3 cups water for pressure
    cooking: 4 to 4 1/4 cups
    for boiling or baking
  pinch of sea salt

Boil water in separate pot or kettle. Remove roasted rice from pan and reserve. Heat oil in pot; sauté diced vegetables for 2 to 3 minutes. Return rice to pot, stirring to coat grains with oil. Measure boiling water and pour over rice and vegetables. Add pinch of sea salt to pot.

To pressure-cook: Bring pot to pressure; cook 45 minutes.

To boil: Add 1 cup extra water (total: 4 to 4 1/2 cups). Bring to boil; simmer 45 to 50 minutes.

To bake: Place in heavy pot, casserole or baking dish. Add 4 cups of boiling water; bake at 400°F. for 45 minutes.

Variations:
- Omit vegetables and add 1 cup toasted nuts or seeds.
- Add spices to sautéed vegetables: curry, turmeric, cumin, coriander or bay leaves with dried herbs.

Menu Suggestions:

Escarole Soup	Chinese-Style Vegetables
Rice Pilaf	Rice Pilaf
Tofu Kebabs	Pita Bread
Greens or Salad	Cucumber or Raw Salad

Yellow Rice, Indonesian-Style———————————

Indonesians call yellow rice *nasi kuning lengkap*. Traditionally this rice cone, decorated with colorful vegetables, was a ceremonial dish. Now it is served at feasts and parties. Use it as a dramatic centerpiece for an island-style buffet.

Servings: 6 to 10
Time: 1 hour

Equipment:
  2 pots, strainer, large
  round platter, wooden
  spoon

Ingredients:
  3 cups long grain rice
  1 large onion, minced
  1 tsp. oil
  1 tsp. turmeric (for yellow
    color)
  1/2 tsp. coriander

Procedure: Wash rice until water runs clear. Strain. Sauté onion in oil 1 minute; add spices and stir 1 minute longer. Add rice, water, lemon juice and sea salt; bring to a boil. Lower heat and simmer 45 to 50 minutes.

Blanch or steam collard leaves to a bright green color. Wash and cut garnish vegetables into shapes you like such as circles, half moons, or julienne strips, and the broccoli into flowerettes. Blanch to crisp and brighten. (Save vegetable scraps for soup stock using blanching water.)

Assembling "Rice Cone": Gather warm, cooked yellow rice, collard leaves and blanched vegetables. On platter, arrange collard greens in circle. Gently

1/4 tsp. white pepper
5 1/2 cups water
1/4 cup lemon juice

Garnish:
1 bunch of collard greens,
    large leaves
small bunch of radishes
1 each: carrot, zucchini,
    red pepper, broccoli
    (spears)

mound yellow rice in center, on top of leaves. Keeping rice in a neat circle (don't cover entire platter), build it higher into a "cone" shape, using wooden spoon or hands. Rice cone should be approximately 8 to 10 inches across at base and 8 to 10 inches high. At serving time, garnish with vegetables. Ring the base of cone with colorful crisp vegetables. Create a pleasing design with contrasting colors and textures.

Variations:
• Turmeric is needed for yellow color; if you don't have any, make a white cone or add curry powder.
• Vary spices. Try freshly ground cardamon.
• Just use it as a bright rice and vegetable side dish if you don't care to build the cone.

Menu Suggestions:

Yellow Rice Cone	Tofu or Tempeh
Tempeh 'n' Coconut Milk	Kebabs with Peanut Sauce
Coconut Condiment	Yellow Rice Cone
Sweet-Sour Pickles	Tropical Island Fruit Fantasy

Risi-Bisi

Risi-Bisi is a Venetian variation of the rice and bean theme, made by delicately cooking white rice and peas together. Here we cook each separately and toss together.

Servings: 4 to 6
Time: 15 minutes

Equipment:
    pot, steamer, bowl, serv-
    ing bowl

Ingredients:
    2 cups cooked rice
    2 cups fresh peas
        (shelled)
    1 to 2 tbsp. lemon juice
    1 tsp. oil (olive)

Procedure: Cook rice. Shell peas and steam or blanch until tender, but firm. Mix rice, lemon juice and oil together. Add blanched peas. Toss gently and serve.

Variations:
• Fresh Mint Risi-Bisi: add 1 or 2 tbsp. chopped mint.
• Steam leftover rice and mix with peas.
• String Bean Risi-Bisi: substitute string beans for peas; cut in 1/2-inch pieces.
• Risi-Bisi Salad: toss with salad dressing; add sliced radishes and celery; chill.

Menu Suggestions:

Tempeh in Sauce or Tofu Cacciatore	Tofu or Fish in Mushroom Sauce
Risi-Bisi Salad	Risi-Bisi
	Red Onion-Dulse Salad
	Orange Jewels

"5 Senses" Rice (Black Soybeans and Rice)

Black soybeans impart an intriguing hue to rice. This sensually satisfying jewel of a rice dish wins converts to natural foods. It is my favorite filling for norimaki or pita bread—to eat at home or while traveling.

Servings: 4 or more
Time: **soaking overnight;**
   cooking 1 hour

Equipment:
   bowl, heavy skillet,
   strainer, wooden spoon,
   pressure cooker

Ingredients:
   1 cup brown rice
   1/2 cup sweet rice
   1/2 cup black soybeans
   1 to 2 ears corn, cut off
   cob
   1 carrot, diced
   4 cups water (approxi-
   mately)
   pinch of sea salt

Garnish:
   toasted sesame seeds
   scallion, sliced

Procedure: Wash and soak rice and sweet rice. Wash black beans; drain. Dry-roast beans in a heavy skillet until skins "pop," stirring often to prevent burning, for 5 to 10 minutes. Cut corn off cob. Drain rice and combine with beans and vegetables in pressure cooker. Add 4 cups of water and pinch of sea salt. Bring slowly up to pressure, then lower heat and cook for 50 minutes. Spoon into wooden bowl. Garnish with scallions.

Variations:
- Wash rice and roast beans; soak overnight or all day; drain. Add vegetables and cook.
- Try all brown rice or all sweet rice.
- Add other vegetables: onion, burdock, etc.
- "5 Senses" Sushi: make norimaki with sheets of nori, umeboshi paste and scallions.
- Black turtle beans don't give the same results as black soybeans.

Menu Suggestions:

Ginger-Miso Broth	"5 Senses" Rice
"5 Senses" Rice	Cucumber-Wakame
Chinese Cabbage Rolls	Salad
Umeboshi Pickles	Greens, Pickles
Peach Kanten	

Caravan Lentils and Rice

Lentils and rice simmered together in one pot have sustained travelers for centuries. Lightweight and readily available, these foods were carried on caravans and ocean voyages. They lend themselves to seasoning with exotic spices or garden herbs. They are mainstays of quick, hearty meals at home or camping out.

Servings: 4 to 6
Time: **1 1/2 hours**

Equipment:
   pot with lid, skillet, flame
   tamer

Procedure: Wash and rinse rice and lentils. Place in pot with water and bay leaves or kombu. Simmer 1 hour. Sauté vegetables (and spices); add to soft grain. Add sea salt; remove bay leaves. Cook together 20 to 30 minutes. For camping or quick dinner, soak rice and lentils all day or overnight.

Ingredients:
  1 cup brown rice
  1/2 cup lentils
  4 cups water (or more)
  2 bay leaves or 1 strip
    kombu
  1 tsp. olive oil
  1 leek, diced
  1 carrot, diced
  4 oz. mushrooms, sliced
  3 to 4 scallions, sliced
  pinch of sea salt
  herbs or spices of your
    choice

Garnish:
  watercress
  fresh, chopped parsley,
    diced red pepper

Variations: There are endless possibilities.
- Vary the proportion of rice to lentils.
- Try millet with lentils or mung beans with rice.
- Add seasonal vegetables: winter roots such as garlic, burdock, parsnip and pearl onions; celery, tomatoes, peppers or corn in summer.

Menu Suggestions: Serve for a hearty breakfast in winter or for lunch or dinner.

Caravan Lentils and Rice	Caravan Lentils and Rice
Baked Root Vegetables	Pita Bread or Rolls
Greens or Salad	Greens or Salad
Couscous Cake	Fruit Kebabs

Norimaki

Norimaki is to Japan what the sandwich is to America. A quick, portable grain to munch at home, from the lunchbox, or as an Oriental appetizer.

Servings: 2 per roll
Time: 15 minutes

Equipment:
  sushi mat, bowl of water

Ingredients:
  1/2 to 1 cup cooked rice
    for each roll
  1 package nori
  1/4 cup roasted sesame
    seeds (optional)
  1/2 cup chopped parsley
    or scallions
  3 to 4 umeboshi plums or
    paste

Procedure: Toast nori over flame (wave gently until it changes colors lightly and is crisp). Lay sushi mat on table. Place nori sheet on mat. Spoon 1 cup rice on nori. Dip fingers into bowl of water and press rice evenly, very flat, over 3/4 area of nori. Leave 1/4 of the top edge empty. One inch from bottom of nori, spread the flesh of 1 umeboshi plum across rice; sprinkle with 1 tsp. sesame seeds and 1 tsp. parsley. Start from the bottom; lift sushi mat and roll up nori, evenly, pressing ends inward. Moisten uncovered end of nori with water so it will adhere to roll. Roll tightly and allow to rest. When ready to serve, slice 1-inch rounds, wiping knife clean after each slice.

Variations:
- Norimaki can be filled with strips of blanched vegetables, pickles, or roasted chopped nuts.
- Carrot-Scallion: cut carrot in 5-inch strips—1/4 inch × 1/4 inch. Drop in boiling water; cook until tender. Use green of scallion (raw—don't blanch). Flatten rice on nori; spread umeboshi, then press 1 strip of carrot and scallion (1 inch from bottom edge) and roll up. Slice.
- Warm, freshly cooked rice works best.

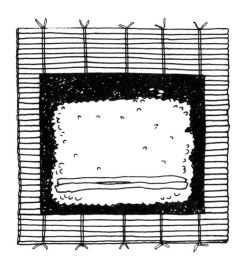

Fig. 31   Norimaki.

Menu Suggestions:
 Party:
Japanese-Marinated   Miso Soup
 Tofu   Norimaki
Norimaki   Adzuki-Squash
Shoyu Almonds   Broccoli
Vegetables with Dip

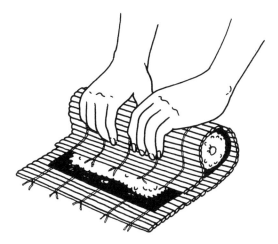

Fig. 32   Rolling norimaki.

Fig. 33   Slicing norimaki.

15-Minute Vegetable Fried Rice for Two

A bowl of plain rice and a few vegetables are transformed into a satisfying meal in minutes. Basic step-by-step instructions follow; ingredients can vary; double quantities for extra servings.

Servings: 2
Time: 15 minutes

Equipment:
skillet, toaster oven or oven, pot, steamer (optional)

Ingredients:
1/2 cup raw cashews (or favorite nut or seed)
2 stalks broccoli (1/2 head, cut into spears) or greens
1 carrot, matchstick-cut
3 or 4 scallions, sliced diagonally
1 cup mushrooms, (4 oz.) sliced
1 tbsp. sesame oil
2 to 3 cups cooked rice
1 tsp. ginger juice
1 tsp. shoyu or sea salt to taste
1 to 2 sheets nori, toasted

Procedure: Toast cashews in toaster oven or oven for 10 to 15 minutes at 325°F. Watch carefully that nuts don't burn. Boil water for broccoli. Slice all vegetables. Heat oil in skillet; sauté carrots 1 to 2 minutes; add scallions and mushrooms; cook 2 minutes. Add rice to vegetables; stir over medium-hot flame. Grate ginger. Blanch or steam broccoli. Season fried rice with ginger juice and shoyu. Toast nori over flame and cut or tear into 2-inch strips. Check cashews. Spoon fried rice on plate; top with cashews. Serve with broccoli and toasted nori.

Variations:
- Vegetable-Spice: add a pinch of spice to sautéing vegetables.
- Vary vegetables: thin cabbage, slivered burdock, sliced onions, celery or pepper can be utilized.
- Kale or other greens can be used.
- Serve dulse or other sea vegetable instead of nori.
- If rice is too dry, add 2 to 3 tbsp. water with seasonings while sautéing with vegetables; cover and steam.

Rice Bread

Rice bread is moist (and heavy) like old-fashioned sourdough bread. This recipe is an excellent way to use up leftover rice or other grains. Slightly soured two to three-day-old grain works best, helping dough ferment. Use an equal amount of grain to flour, adding a little oil and water. If the grain is dry or hard, first pour water over it and heat slowly. If too soft, add extra flour.

Servings: 2 small loaves
Time: 15 minute preparation; overnight rising; 1 1/2 hour baking

Equipment:
mixing bowl, 2 bread pans

Procedure: Rice can be fresh or soured (save grains for 2 to 3 days). Put rice in mixing bowl and add water, oil and sea salt. Mix well. If rice is dry, use more water than if it's soft. It should have the consistency of oatmeal. Add flour a little at a time; stir; work remaining flour in by hand. Dough should be kneaded on floured table for 5 minutes until it resembles stiff bread dough. Adjust liquid or flour for a firm dough.

Ingredients:
  4 cups leftover grain (rice, oatmeal, barley, millet)
  4 cups flour (whole wheat, some corn or rye for flavor)
  1/4 to 1 cup water
  1/4 cup oil (optional)
  pinch of sea salt or 1 tbsp. miso
  herbs, seeds, raisins to taste

Oil 2 bread pans. Shape loaves and place in pans. Cover with a damp cloth and allow to rest overnight in a warm place or inside stove. Bake in oven at 300°F. for 15 minutes, then at 350°F. for 1 1/2 to 2 hours. Allow to cool and enjoy. Keeps well in refrigerator, up to a week.

Secrets: Knead carefully, allow to rise overnight. I usually keep a wooden bowl in the kitchen; all leftover grains from breakfast or dinner are combined until there are enough to make bread.

Variations:
- Herb Bread: 1/4 tsp. basil, 1/2 tsp. dill, 1/2 tsp. oregano.
- Nuts: add 1/2 to 1 cup roasted, chopped sunflower seeds, walnuts or almonds.
- Cinnamon-Raisin: 1 cup raisins, 1/2 tsp. cinnamon.

Menu Suggestions: If crust of bread gets "hard" after 1 or 2 days, moisten a clean towel and wrap bread to soften.

Sweet Rice, Chickpeas and Millet

Nutty chickpeas, mild millet and mellow sweet rice come together for a sticky-soft grain to serve with crunchy sunflower seeds or nuts. This dish can be made into burgers or unusual norimaki. Kids adore it. It fluffs up beautifully with pressure-cooking.

Servings: **4 to 6**
Time: **soak overnight; cook 60 minutes**

Equipment:
  pressure cooker, wooden bowl

Ingredients:
  1 cup sweet rice
  1 cup chickpeas
  1/2 cup millet
  5 to 6 cups water

Procedure: Sort over grains and beans. Wash carefully; place in bowl or pressure cooker and soak in 5 to 6 cups water overnight. Drain and add an equal amount of fresh water. (Do not add salt.) Bring to pressure, cook 50 to 60 minutes, and allow pressure to come down naturally after removing from burner. Sprinkle with sea salt or condiment; stir. If grain seems wet, spoon into wooden bowl and allow to dry.

Variations:
- Rice and chickpeas: substitute regular brown rice for sweet rice.
- Form balls while grain is warm and roll in Spicy Walnut Condiment or toasted seeds.
- Follow recipe for Norimaki.
- Add 1 strip kombu and cook together.

Menu Suggestions:

Sweet Rice, Chickpeas and Millet	Sweet Rice, Chickpeas and Millet
Carrot Sauce	Baked Root Vegetables
Toasted Nori	Greens, Salad
Greens, Salad	Apple-Cranberry Sauce

Basic Barley

Barley soaked overnight cooks quickly. A chewy grain, barley becomes creamy when added to soups and stews.

Servings: 4 cups
Time: 1 hour

Equipment: pot with lid

Ingredients:
1 cup barley
4 cups water
pinch of sea salt

Procedure: Wash barley until water runs clear. Place barley, water and sea salt in a heavy pot. Bring to a boil slowly; then lower flame. Simmer 1 hour. Add more water if needed.

Variations:
- Bay leaves or a strip of kombu may be added while simmering.
- Soak barley all day or overnight to shorten cooking time.
- Add cooked barley to vegetable soups or stews.
- Make a barley salad, following instructions for rice or pasta salads.

Menu Suggestions:

Dinner:	*Breakfast:*
Lentils with Squash	Soft Barley
Barley	Toasted Sunflower Seeds
Cabbage or Nice-Dice Salad	Stewed Fruit
Pecan Pie	

Baked Corn-on-the-Cob

My South American friends showed me how to bake corn in the oven for tender, juicy results. Corn becomes sweeter by baking instead of boiling. I bake up a dozen or so ears and bring them along on summer picnics.

Servings: 6 to 12
Time: 30 to 45 minutes

Equipment: baking tray

Ingredients:
6 to 12 ears of fresh corn

Procedure: Trim the ends off the corn; cut off the corn silk and the stalk end. Remove outer layer of the husk, but leave inner layers covering corn. Place on baking tray, and bake in 325°F. for 30 to 45 minutes. The leaves will brown lightly as they cook. To test if done, remove an ear and peel husk back; corn will be tender and juicy when pricked with a fork. (Or allow to cool and taste it.)

Variations:
- Corn can be placed on a barbecue or grill and roasted.
- Slice baked corn off cob and add to salads or soups.

Menu Suggestions: Baked corn is perfect for picnics or cookouts. Make ahead of time; corn will keep 1 to 2 days, refrigerated. Reheat or eat at room temperature.

Polenta (Basic Cornmeal)

Polenta is the hearty cornmeal Italians have relished for hundreds of years. Dried corn is ground into meal and simmered in water like porridge, then poured into a dish, cooled and sliced. Tangy-Tomato, Basil or Estella's Red Sauce are well-suited accompaniments to polenta. The secret of this simple dish is fresh cornmeal. Grind it yourself or buy it refrigerated to insure quality. Old cornmeal will result in bitter polenta. The ratio of corn to water varies from 1 to 2 to 1 to 4.

Servings: 4 to 6
Time: 1 hour

Equipment:
heavy pot, flame tamer

Ingredients:
3 cups water
1 cup cornmeal, freshly ground
pinch of sea salt

Procedure: Pour 3 cups water into pot. Slowly add meal, stirring to mix without lumping. Bring to a boil over a medium flame, stirring continually, until thickened. Lower flame; stir often; cook for 30 to 45 minutes. After cooking on stove, pour into oiled dish. Allow to cool and slice. Alternatively, once thickened pour into oiled baking dish and bake at 350°F. for 1 hour.

Variations:
- Roast cornmeal in skillet until nutty smell arises; cool; add water and cook.
- Polenta with Onions: add 2 or 3 onions, minced and sautéed; cook together.
- Fresh Corn Polenta: cut kernels off 3 to 4 ears of corn. Add to polenta after it has thickened. Cook 15 to 20 minutes.
- Fried Polenta: leftover polenta can be sliced and pan-fried in oil until golden.

Menu Suggestions:

Polenta
Estella's Red Sauce or Tomato Sauce
Sautéed String Beans with Mushrooms

Marinated Tofu with Fennel
Polenta
Basil Sauce
Julienne Salad
Peaches and Pears

Millet

This tiny, humble component of birdseed mixes holds endless possibilities for creative cooks. Cook millet slowly with 3 or 4 times the amount of water for a creamy grain or roast it and cook with double the amount of water for a light, fluffy grain. Millet is a staple that feeds millions in Asia and India.

Servings: 4 to 6 or more
Time: 30 to 45 minutes

Equipment: pot with lid

Ingredients:
  1 cup millet, washed and drained
  3 cups water
  pinch of sea salt

Procedure: Wash millet and drain in strainer. Millet can be dry-roasted in skillet at this point if you prefer a nutty taste. Place in pot with water and pinch of sea salt. Bring to a boil slowly in a covered pot. Simmer on a low flame for 30 to 40 minutes until water is absorbed.

Variations:
- Umeboshi plums (2 or 3) can be used instead of sea salt.
- Sautéed vegetables and spices can be cooked with millet.
- Cook with butternut or Hokkaido squash and fresh corn for a warming cereal.
- It's great served with toasted sunflower seeds or almonds.

Menu Suggestions: Millet goes with almost any soup, stew or vegetables, and sauce.

Himalayan Greens	Autumn Stew or Adzuki
Millet	Squash
Pita or other Bread	Millet
Pickles or Chutney	Greens or Salad

Millet Croquettes

The fluffy, light nature of millet is perfect for crispy croquettes. My secrets for success are: season millet with "falafel mix" or a blend of herbs and spices; form croquettes while grain is still warm; then cool and deep-fry to golden and serve with a sensuous sauce. Finally, make plenty! One batch is never enough.

Servings: 12 croquettes
Time: 1 hour

Equipment:
  pot with lid for millet, mixing bowl, pan to fry croquettes in, paper towels to drain

Procedure: Wash millet; drain. Place in pot; add water and sea salt. Bring to a boil; lower flame and simmer 30 minutes, until all liquid is absorbed. Spoon hot grain into bowl to cool. Slice scallion and sauté for 1 minute if you desire. (Prepare any optional ingredients.) Add seasonings and mix. When millet is cool enough to handle, form into balls, about walnut-sized. Place on plate and allow to cool. If

Ingredients:
1 cup millet
2 1/2 cups water
pinch of sea salt

Seasonings:
1/4 cup falafel mix
(optional, or 2 tbsp. flour)
3 scallions, sliced, or
chopped parsley
2 tsp. shoyu (if not using
"falafel mix")
2 cups oil for frying

you're in a hurry, place in refrigerator. When croquettes are cold, pour oil into a small pan or wok. The oil should be deep enough to cover croquettes. Heat oil. When it's very hot, gently drop croquettes in, 3 to 4 at a time. Fry until golden. Drain on paper towels. Serve immediately or keep warm in oven.

Variations:
• Spicy Croquettes: if "falafel mix" is not available, add a pinch of favorite spices: cumin, coriander, dill, white pepper.
• Crunchy Croquettes: add 1/2 to 1 cup roasted, chopped sunflower seeds, walnuts, or almonds.
• Vegetable Croquettes: add 1 onion, 1 carrot, and 2 celery stalks, diced finely and sautéed for 2 minutes.
• Millet-Grain Croquettes: mix grains together—rice, couscous, cracked wheat.

Menu Suggestions: Delicious any time of day, in a lunchbox, and at parties.

Lentil Soup	Minestrone Soup
Millet Croquettes	Millet Croquettes
Chinese-Style Vegetables	Estella's Red Sauce
Stuffed Dates	Fennel Sticks
	Broccoli

Millet-Mashed Potatoes with Caraway

Millet cooks up creamy with the addition of potatoes—delicious with sauce or gravy.

Servings: 4 or more
Time: 30 minutes

Equipment: pot with lid

Ingredients:
4 potatoes, peeled and
diced
1 cup millet
2 tsp. caraway seeds
1/2 tsp. sea salt
3 to 3 1/2 cups water

Garnish:
chopped parsley

Procedure: Peel and dice potatoes into 1/2-inch cubes. Place in pot. Wash millet until water runs clear; drain. Pour millet over potatoes and add caraway, sea salt and water. Slowly bring to a boil over a medium flame. Lower flame; simmer 20 to 30 minutes until water is absorbed. Stir before serving; add chopped parsley for garnish.

Variations:
• The dish can be mashed like potatoes in a mixer. Add a little soy milk or 1/4 cup water mixed with 2 tbsp. tahini. Mix until blended.
• Substitute cauliflower for potatoes.
• Omit caraway and add your favorite herb or spice.

Menu Suggestions:

Bean Soup	Tempeh "Turkey"
Millet-Mashed Potatoes	Millet-Mashed Potatoes
Onion or Basil Sauce	Salad, Pickles
Salad	Cranberry Relish

Basic Whole Oats

Oats, the northern grain that has nourished Britons and Europeans for centuries, continue to fortify their New World descendants. Heartier than rolled oats, whole oats must simmer for hours to make a strengthening cereal. Oats can be simmered overnight, ready to warm you on cold mornings.

Servings: 6 or more
Time: 3 hours or longer

Equipment:
  heavy pot with lid, flame tamer

Ingredients:
  1 cup whole oats
  5 to 6 cups water
  pinch of sea salt

Procedure: Wash and soak whole oats overnight in water. Bring to a boil and place on flame tamer; simmer for 3 to 4 hours, or longer. Stir occasionally to prevent sticking. (Whole oats can be simmered overnight in 6 to 7 cups of water on a very low flame with flame tamer and be ready for breakfast.)

Variations:
Breakfast:
- Dry roast whole oats in skillet for extra flavor.
- Breakfast cereal: add 1/2 cup raisins or chopped, dried fruit.
- Orange-Oatmeal: add 1 grated orange peel after oats are soft.
- Serve with roasted nuts or seeds.

Soups:
- Add creamy whole oats to vegetable or bean soups as a thickener, as in Barley-Leek recipe (page 111) or Scottish Stew (page 110).

Buckwheat Croquettes

In cooler weather, I enjoy buckwheat, lightened by the addition of couscous. Buckwheat and cross-country skiing are a favorite winter duo. Croquettes can be deep-fried or rolled in seeds and baked to take along or serve at trail's end.

Servings: 10 to 12 croquettes
Time: 1 hour

Equipment:
  pot for grain, mixing bowl, skillet, slotted spoon or chopsticks, paper towels

Procedure: Bring water to a boil; add grains and sea salt; stir. Lower flame and simmer 20 minutes until water is absorbed. Cover; allow to rest another 10 minutes. Mix in scallions and chopped sunflower seeds. Form into 2-inch croquettes while grain is warm and holds together. Roll in flour. Cool in refrigerator; then fry croquettes in hot oil until golden; drain on paper towels. (If grain is warm, croquettes will fall apart when dropped in hot oil.) Place in serving dish to keep warm.

Ingredients:
- 4 cups water
- 1 cup buckwheat
- 1 cup couscous
- pinch of sea salt
- 3 scallions, sliced
- 1/2 cup sunflower seeds, roasted and chopped
- 1/4 cup arrowroot or pastry flour to roll croquettes
- 1 cup oil for frying

Variations:
- For oil-free croquettes, roll in sesame seeds and place in a baking dish; heat and serve.
- Fill cabbage rolls with this mixture.
- Make a loaf by spooning into oiled bread pan; cool and slice.
- Use pastry dough to make pies or knishes, and fill with buckwheat mixture.

Menu Suggestions:

Red Lentil and Squash Soup	Buckwheat Croquettes
Buckwheat Creamed Onions	Estella's Red Sauce or Carrot Sauce
Greens	Marinated String Bean Salad
Lemon Walnut Cake	Baked Garlic, Bread Applesauce with Crunch

Kasha-Potato Knishes

Kasha (buckwheat) Knishes are savory pastries found in Jewish delicatessens. Adapted from the northern European dish, kasha and potatoes are wrapped in pastry and baked. I usually make it into long "strudel" shapes, and slice; it's quicker than shaping individual knishes. Another favorite I bring skiing.

Servings: 6 or more
Time: 1 hour

Equipment:
pot with lid, mixing bowl, baking tray, rolling pin, waxed paper

Ingredients:
- 1 tsp. oil
- 1 large onion, diced
- 1 1/2 cups kasha (buckwheat)
- 3 or 4 potatoes, cubed
- 2 1/2 to 3 cups hot water or stock
- pinch of sea salt

Procedure: Sauté onion in oil, 2 to 3 minutes. Add kasha, potatoes, boiling water and sea salt. Stir; cover; bring to a boil and simmer 20 to 30 minutes, until water is absorbed. While kasha is cooking, prepare dough; allow to cool. When kasha is cooked, add seasonings, to taste. When dough has cooled, divide it into 3 parts. Roll out between 2 sheets of waxed paper. Lift off top sheet of waxed paper. Trim to approximately an 8-inch × 12-inch rectangle. Spoon 1/3 of kasha along length of dough, 1 inch from edge. Lift bottom sheet of waxed paper to help roll knish. Fold ends under. Lift gently and place on oiled baking dish, "seam side" down. Prick air holes with fork to prevent cracking. Assemble other rolls. Bake at 350°F. for 30 to 45 minutes. Slice carefully. Keep in cool place; heat and serve.

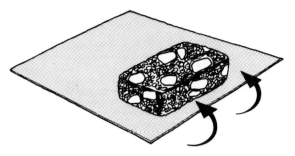

Fig. 34 Kasha knish assembly. Dough is rolled out. Kasha is spread along bottom edge. Dough is lifted to roll filling, ends are turned under and "roll" is placed on oiled baking tray.

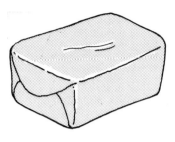

Fig. 35 Finished Kasha knish.

Seasonings:
> 2 to 3 tbsp. dill or parsley, minced
> 1 to 2 tbsp. prepared mustard
> pinch of dill, savory, thyme or marjoram
> pinch of white pepper (optional)
> recipe for puff dough (page 223)

Variations:
- Cook potatoes separately; mash and add to cooked kasha.
- Kasha Pie: instead of "rolls" make a pie. Divide dough in half. Bake in pie dish.
- Individual Knishes: roll dough out; cut into 6-inch × 8-inch rectangles. Place 1/2 to 1 cup kasha inside. Fold edges over.
- Kasha-Vegetable Knishes: add carrots, celery, or parsnips to kasha, instead of potatoes.

Menu Suggestions:

Special Split Pea Soup	Creamy Leek-Navy
Kasha Knishes	Bean Soup
Baked Root Vegetable	Kasha Knishes
Medley	Braised Red Cabbage
Steamed Broccoli	Broccoli or Salad
Apple-Cranberry Sauce	Dill Pickles

"Fluffy" Couscous

Couscous, the quickest of all grain dishes, requires no cooking. A precooked "semolina" made from wheat, couscous fluffs up by merely adding boiling water, covering and waiting 5 minutes. Not a whole grain, this staple of Moroccan and North African cookery has a mild flavor, like other pastas, and is served with tasty vegetable and bean dishes. Couscous helps you get a meal on the table in a hurry!

Servings: 2 to 3
Time: 10 minutes

Equipment:
> small pot with lid

Procedure: Bring water to a boil; add oil; pour couscous in gently. Cover and remove from heat. Allow grains to absorb water another 3 to 5 minutes. Fluff with a fork and serve.

Ingredients:
  1 cup boiling water
  **1 tsp. olive or sesame oil
    (optional)**
  1 cup couscous

Variations:
- Peas and Mint: add 1/2 cup fresh hulled peas to boiling water; simmer 1 minute. Add couscous; cover and remove from heat. Season with fresh mint or dill.
- Golden Seeds and Couscous: add 1/2 cup roasted, chopped nuts or seeds to cooked couscous; garnish with chopped parsley.

Menu Suggestions:

Chinese-Style Vegetables	Fish Filets or Kebabs
Couscous	Couscous
Pickles	Nice-Dice Salad
	Strawberry Kanten with Crunch

Jane's 10-Minute All-in-One Meal

Dedicated to my sister, this quick meal fits into her busy schedule. It's light, tasty and cooked in 1 pot. Bring a container to work, or school. Here is a summer version; winter vegetables can be used in cooler months.

Servings: 4
Time: 10 to 20 minutes

Equipment:
  small pot with lid

Ingredients:
  **1/4 lb. tofu, cut in 1/2-inch
    cubes**
  **1 red or green pepper,
    diced**
  1 small zucchini, diced
  2 scallions, sliced
  **2 tbsp. fresh chopped
    basil or dill**
  1 tbsp. olive or sesame oil
  **pinch of sea salt or 1 tsp.
    shoyu**
  2 cups water
  1 cup couscous

Procedure: Dice tofu, pepper, zucchini; slice scallion and basil. Place all ingredients except couscous in pot. Bring to a boil. When vegetables are boiling, add couscous. Stir, lower flame and simmer 2 to 3 minutes until water is absorbed. Turn off flame and allow to set for a few minutes. Serve at once or fill a container and take to work.

Variations:
- Finely sliced winter (root) vegetables can be used, but cook for a longer time before adding couscous. Try onions, carrots and broccoli.
- Add sautéed spices such as cumin or coriander.
- If you don't have tofu, add chickpeas, or tempeh.
- If couscous dish comes out too dry, serve with a sauce or a salad dressing, such as umeboshi-basil dressing.
- Dice tofu and vegetables even finer and use recipe to stuff cabbage, grape leaves, squash, fish or pita bread.

Menu Suggestions:

Lunch:	*Dinner:*
All-In-One Meal	Pan-Fried Fish
Toasted Sunflower Seeds	All-In-One Meal
Pickles	Arame
	Salad
	Miso-Ginger Broth
	All-in-One Meal
	Kale or Broccoli
	Toasted Nori

Noodle Cookery————————————————————

If your family loves pasta and you rely on noodles for a quick economical meal, be prepared to broaden your culinary horizons. Vegetarian cuisine has elevated noodle cookery to a fine art. To begin with, pasta makers have developed ways to transform grains, beans and even vegetables into tender noodles. Here's a quick run down of what is available in natural food stores or specialty shops: in the whole grain line, look for 100% wheat flour or Japanese udon; buckwheat noodles, which are called soba in Japan; brown rice noodles, usually in the pre-cooked ramen type; and corn noodles. Vegetable pastas include spinach or artichoke noodles; for bean noodles the list includes those made with protein-rich soy flour or exotic mung bean thread noodles, known as cellophane noodles.

Noodles are not considered a whole food since part of the vitamin-packed bran is lost in milling. A digestible form of whole grain, noodles are a good choice for quick meals or snacks that any member of the family can make in minutes.

Noodles combine with beans for a complete protein. Serve them with beans or soybean products. Beans can be mixed together with elbows or shells as the Italian "pasta di faggiole." Or, try serving Japanese soba noodles with a tahini-miso sauce. Pasta can be added to bean soups for a hearty meal. Tofu "ricotta" cheese is a perfect filling for your favorite lasagna or manicotti recipe.

To cook whole grain noodles two methods are used. First, the traditional way: bring a large pot of water to a rolling boil; drop noodles in; stir and boil until noodles are tender. To test, break a noodle in half. It should be cooked through, not white inside. The "shock method" is used to slow-cook noodles, because some whole grain pastas tend to be more delicate and produce a better dish "shocked" and gently boiled.

Boiling Noodles————————————————————

Procedure: Here is the "shock method"* for cooking whole grain noodles: add noodles to the boiling water and stir. When the water returns to a boil, add 1 cup of the cold water to "shock," stop boiling. Repeat. When water comes to a boil for the third time, check noodles to see if they are cooked. They should be *al dente*, tender, but firm. Drain into a colander and run under cool water. Drizzle with a little oil and toss if not used right away.

* This method is not required for all types of grain noodles.

Noodle Kugel————————————————————

Noodle Kugel, a European dish, is traditionally made with lots of eggs and cheese. I serve a lighter version made with blended tofu as a side dish. Extra sweeteners and spices turn it into a dessert kugel.

Servings: 4
Time: 30 minutes

Equipment:
pot, blender or food mill,
oiled baking dish

Ingredients:
8 oz. package artichoke
flat noodles, bows or
elbows
1/2 block tofu (soft is
best)
1/2 cup water
2 tbsp. tahini
1 tbsp. miso or pinch of
sea salt
pinch nutmeg and
cinnamon
1 tsp. vanilla
1/2 cup raisins or currants
1/2 cup roasted, chopped
walnuts
1/2 tsp. grated lemon or
orange rind

Procedure: Boil the noodles in water until *al dente*. Blend the tofu and other ingredients except raisins and nuts in the blender or food mill. Mix noodles with sauce; add raisins and nuts; place in the baking dish and cover with foil. Bake at 350°F. for 15 minutes. Remove foil; bake 5 to 10 minutes.

Variations:
• Any nuts, raisins, dried fruit or other sweet spices (allspice, ginger or coriander) can be added for different flavors.
• Add 2 to 3 tbsp. rice syrup or barley malt and serve for brunch or dessert.

Menu Suggestions:

Cabbage and Corn Soup	Warming Winter Stew
Noodle Kugel	Noodle Kugel
Greens, Salad	Pressed Cabbage Salad
Dill Pickles	Fennel Sticks

Stuffed Grape Leaves

Here's a short cut to preparing this delectable Greek specialty. The usual way of preparing grape leaves involves mixing raw rice with seasonings and steam-boiling them for hours. I precook grain, season it, roll it up in leaves, heat and serve. Look for grape leaves in specialty shops or Greek markets. You can find brands without preservatives. Keep a jar or two on hand for Greek meals in minutes. Soak leaves in fresh water to remove the salt used in preserving them.

Servings: 6 to 8
Time: 45 minutes

Equipment:
pot, bowl, baking dish

Ingredients:
20 to 30 grape leaves
(1 small jar)
3 cups water
1 1/2 cups cracked wheat
or bulghur
pinch of sea salt
1/2 tsp. oregano or dill

Procedure: Remove leaves from jar and rinse. Set aside to drain. Bring water to a boil; add wheat, seasonings and sunflower seeds. Simmer 10 to 15 minutes until excess water has been absorbed. Shut off heat; cover and let stand for 20 minutes. Place leaves vein-side down on a table. Put 1/4 cup of filling on center of leaf. Fold bottom over and sides across; roll away from you. Arrange finished grape leaves in an oiled baking dish. Mix lemon juice and oil; pour over leaves to coat tops. Cover and bake at 300°F. for 20 minutes or until warmed through. Garnish with lemon and serve immediately.

Fig. 36 Stuffed cabbage leaves.

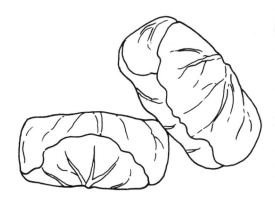

Fig. 37 A stuffed cabbage leaf or grape leaf.

**1/2 cup roasted sunflower
seeds or walnuts
pinch of cumin or cinna-
mon (optional)
2 tbsp. olive oil
2 tbsp. lemon juice**

**Garnish:
lemon slices**

Variations:
- Collard greens or cabbage may be substituted for grape leaves. First simmer in water for 3 to 5 minutes before filling.
- Raisins or currants can be added to grain.
- Couscous or rice can be used.
- Add sautéed onion and garlic.
- Serve with Tahini Sauce.

Menu Suggestions:

Miso-Watercress Soup	Stuffed Grape Leaves
Stuffed Grape Leaves	Chickpea Salad
Creamy Tahini Sauce	Olives, Cucumbers
Mediterranean Salad	Pita Bread
Lemon or Rice Pudding	Fruit Tart

Swedish "Wheat Balls"

Swedish "Wheat Balls" are made from seasoned cracked wheat, rolled in seeds and baked. Serve with your favorite sauce. An alternative to fried croquettes.

**Servings: 20 small "wheat
balls"
Time: 30 minutes**

**Equipment:
pot, bowl, oiled baking
dish, skillet**

Procedure: Bring 3 cups of water to a boil; stir in the wheat and oats. Lower the flame and simmer for 10 to 12 minutes until water is absorbed. Roast seeds; grind or chop. Mix the rest of the ingredients, except the sesame seeds, into the hot grain. Spoon into a bowl and allow to cool enough to handle. Moisten hands with water and form into walnut-sized balls;

Ingredients:
  3 cups water
  1 1/2 cups cracked wheat
  1/2 cup oatmeal
  1/4 cup chopped parsley
  2 tbsp. miso or pinch of
    sea salt
  1/4 tsp. each, nutmeg,
    thyme, basil
  1/2 tsp. sage
  1/2 cup sunflower seeds,
    roasted and ground
  1/4 cup sesame seeds,
    roasted
  1 tsp. oil

roll in sesame seeds. Place in the oiled baking dish. Keep warm in 350°F. oven for 10 to 15 minutes. Serve with sauce.

Variations:
- If grain doesn't hold together easily, add 2 to 3 tbsp. flour or 1/4 cup falafel mix.
- Substitute 1/2 cup couscous for 1/2 cup cracked wheat.
- Vegetable "Wheat Balls": add 1 small carrot and 1 stalk celery, diced finely.
- Omit sunflower seeds or add another type of seed.
- Omit herbs or vary seasoning.
- Tofu "Wheat Balls": add 1/2 cup mashed tofu.

Menu Suggestions:

Swedish "Wheat Balls"	Florentine White Bean
Onion or Mushroom	Soup
Sauce	Swedish "Wheat Balls"
Beets with Greens	Basil Sauce
Salad, Tofu Dressing	Steamed Vegetables or
	Salad
	Apple Pie

Stuffed Peppers with Lemon-Shoyu Sauce

Introduce your family to whole grains by filling bright vegetables with spicy mixtures and serving them with a slightly tart sauce. It's also an appealing way to use up grain cooked earlier.

Servings: 6 or more
Time: 30 minutes

Equipment:
  pot, skillet, mixing bowl,
  and covered baking dish

Ingredients:
  6 peppers

Stuffing:
  2 tbsp. sesame oil
  4 scallions, thinly sliced
  1 carrot, small dice
  1 cup mushrooms, diced
  1/2 cup walnuts, roasted
    and chopped
  1/2 tsp. cumin (optional)

Procedure: Bring a large pot of water to a boil. Cut stem end off peppers and clean the seeds out. Dice vegetables. When water is boiling, drop peppers in; blanch for 3 to 4 minutes until bright green. Remove and drain. Heat oil in skillet; add spices and sauté 1 minute. Add vegetables; stir and cook 3 to 5 minutes. Roast and chop walnuts. Place rice in mixing bowl; mix in sautéed vegetables and walnuts. Fill peppers; place upright in baking dish. Cover with sauce and bake in a covered dish for 20 to 30 minutes.

Sauce: bring apple juice to a boil; add lemon juice and shoyu. Dissolve kuzu in 1/4 cup water and add to juice, stirring until thick and clear.

Variations:
- This stuffing can be used to fill grape leaves or zucchini.

1/2 tsp. coriander
(optional)
1/2 tsp. curry powder
(optional)
3 cups cooked grain: rice,
millet, couscous or
combined grains

Lemon-Shoyu Sauce:
2 cups apple juice or cider
1/4 cup lemon juice
2 tbsp. shoyu or sea salt
to taste
1 1/2 tbsp. kuzu or
arrowroot

- In place of Lemon Sauce, serve with Tomato, Miso-Tahini or Shiitake Mushroom Sauce.
- Make day before, refrigerate and reheat in a low oven for 1 hour.
- Use any leftover grains in this recipe.

Menu Suggestions:

Lunch:	*Dinner:*
Stuffed Peppers (no sauce)	Lentil Soup
	Stuffed Peppers
Tofu Cacciatore	Salad or Greens
Salad	Coconut Orange Jewels

Baked Squash with Bread Stuffing

A tender, sweet squash filled with an herbed bread stuffing is an enticing entrée for parties and pot luck dinners.

Servings: 4 to 6
Time: 1 1/2 to 2 hours

Equipment:
skillet, baking dish,
serving platter

Ingredients:
1 squash: buttercup,
Hokkaido or acorn
2 to 3 tbsp. oil
1 onion, minced
2 celery stalks, minced
2 to 4 garlic cloves,
minced (optional)
2 to 3 tbsp. chopped
parsley
1 tsp. ginger juice
1/2 tsp. dried basil
1 to 2 tsp. shoyu or pinch
sea salt
1/4 to 1/2 loaf of whole
wheat bread
3/4 cup water

Procedure: Wash and dry squash. With a sharp knife cut top off squash. Save lid. Scoop out seeds. Lightly oil outside of the squash; place in a baking dish. (If squash is small, it may fit in a glass pie pan.) Mince vegetables; dice bread. In a skillet heat oil to sauté vegetables, beginning with onion. Add ginger juice, sea salt, and basil, ending with bread cubes. Mix well. If the bread is dry, add 1/4 cup water. Fill the squash with stuffing. Place the lid back on the squash. Pour 1/2 cup water in the pan with squash. (Cover with foil to cook faster.) Place in a hot oven, 400°F. to 425°F., and bake 1 hour; lower oven to 375°F. and continue to bake until knife easily pierces squash. A large squash will take 2 or more hours to bake. Keep warm until serving. Steamed kale can be used as a garnish. Slice and serve 2-inch wedges of squash with a portion of stuffing.

Variations:
- Instead of bread stuffing, add 2 to 3 cups of leftover rice, millet, couscous or bulghur to sautéed vegetables.
- Roasted sunflower seeds or walnuts add a crunchy touch.
- Serve with onion gravy.
- Acorn squash can be cut in half, lengthwise, and filled with stuffing mixture.

Menu Suggestions:

Onion Soup
Baked Stuffed Squash
Kale or Salad
Cranberry Relish

Tempeh in Mushroom
 Sauce
Baked Stuffed Squash
Greens or Salad
Pickles
Pear Parfait

Bean Cookery

A bean by any other name such as peas, legumes, pulses, haricots or grams, are all edible seeds of the Leguminasae family. Some varieties of edible seeds can be eaten whole in the pod, as string beans, snow peas or yellow wax beans. Tender green peas are a summer delicacy hulled, eaten raw or steamed. Dried beans can be sprouted and eaten as a vegetable such as mung or soy sprouts.

The lovely jars of dried beans that grace my kitchen shelves include: adzuki, chickpea, lentils, navy, kidney and black beans. These beans were allowed to mature in the pod, then hulled, dried and stored. Dried beans have the ability to store for years, due to their protective hull. For the best results in cooking, use them within six to twelve months. The older the beans are, the longer it takes to cook them.

Tips for Bean Cuisine: Happy is the slowly cooked bean. Overnight soaking and slow-simmering allow beans to expand gently for delicious results.
- Spread beans out; sort over and pick out stones, twigs and any wrinkled beans.
- Wash carefully until water runs clear.
- Cover with 3 times the volume of water and soak overnight in a cool place, not near stove or heat. In summer or warm weather, place beans in refrigerator to soak, as they will sour at room temperature.
- Drain soaking water; add fresh water and simmer, skimming foam as it forms in cooking. Add sea vegetables or bay leaves at the start of cooking. Add more water as needed.
- Pressure-cook chickpeas to save time; they take the longest to cook.
- Some beans, e.g., split peas, lentils or black turtle beans, should not be pressure-cooked because their foam may clog the steam escape valve. Boil or bake them instead.
- Beans can be slowly cooked in an electric crockpot or clay pot in the oven.
- Cook beans until soft before adding sea salt or salt seasonings, as these prevent the beans from fully absorbing water and cooking through.
- Sauté spices or garlic in oil and add to beans as they begin to soften.
- For salads, cook beans until tender, but still holding their shape.
- For soups, purées and spreads, cook beans until very soft.

Basic Lima or Navy Beans———————————————

Navy beans, small white beans, or limas, which are larger whitish beans, are found in most supermarkets. Features of early American cooking, navy beans were baked in Boston bean pots. A southern stew of limas, corn and molasses was known as "succotash." The mild flavor of these beans combines well with a variety of ingredients in stews or casseroles. I often purée these beans to make "hummus" or bean spreads.

Servings: 4 to 6
Time: 1 to 2 hours

Equipment:
  soup pot, blender
  (optional)

Ingredients:
  1 cup limas or navy beans,
    soaked overnight
  3 to 4 cups water
  1 strip kombu (optional)
  sea salt to taste

Procedure: Soak beans and rinse. Add fresh water and kombu. Simmer 1 1/2 to 2 hours until very soft, adding more water if needed. Season with sea salt. Simmer another 15 minutes.

Variations:
* Beans and Vegetables: add diced root vegetables or squash after 1 hour of cooking.
* Add garlic or onions, sautéed in oil.
* Cream beans for soup (page 105).
* Check recipe for baked beans (page 177), succotash (page 176) or hummus (page 182).

Menu Suggestions:
  Lima Beans
  Corn-on-the-Cob
  Arame or Hijiki with Carrots
  Collards or Kale
  Pumpkin Pie

Savory Succotash———————————————

Another favorite with new-to-natural-food friends! Succotash is a southern dish combining beans and corn. I've substituted tempeh for bacon and added squash to corn and beans for a rich, earthy stew. It's perfect for pot-luck suppers or do-ahead dinners. A large batch will keep two to three days.

Servings: 6 or more
Time: 2 hours

Equipment:
  heavy pot with lid, baking
  dish

Ingredients:
  1 small squash: butternut
    or winter; baked
  2 cups cooked lima beans
  1/2 lb. tempeh, cut in
    1/2-inch cubes

Procedure: Cut squash in half and bake 350°F. for 45 minutes or until cooked (pierce with fork). Meanwhile, cook the lima beans until soft and purée half of them. This purée will thicken the succotash. Reserve. Cut tempeh into cubes and sauté in oil in heavy pot. Add corn kernels, whole limas and puréed beans to tempeh. Cut squash into 1/2-inch cubes. Add to succotash. Add water if needed. Simmer on low flame until corn is cooked. Add herbs and miso or sea salt. Season to taste.

4 to 6 ears corn, cut off
  cob
1 tbsp. oil for sautéing
fresh or dried herbs
2 tbsp. white miso or
  sea salt
4 scallions

Variations:
- If you don't have time to bake squash, either steam it or add to simmering lima beans.
- Replace squash with carrots.
- Fresh dill or basil is delicious seasoning.

Menu Suggestions:
Savory Succotash
Arame-Stuffed Mushroom Caps
Mustard Greens or Collards
Peanut Butter Cookies

Basic Baked Beans

Stove-top-simmered or baked, this version is similar to the tinned beans that are popular in the British Isles. One pound of beans expands to 6 or 7 cups. Make plenty, as the flavor improves after two to three days.

Servings: 8
Time: 2 to 3 hours

Equipment:
  heavy pot, bean pot or
  covered baking dish,
  mixing bowl

Ingredients:
  1 lb. dry navy beans,
    soaked overnight
  2 strips kombu
  6 to 8 cups water
  1 cup tomato sauce
    (optional)
  1/4 cup barley malt
  2 tbsp. mustard, prepared
  2 tbsp. miso or pinch of
    sea salt

Procedure: Soak beans overnight; drain water and rinse beans. Place them in pot with water and kombu. Cook on the stove until beans are soft, about 1 1/2 hours. Add water as needed. Water should reduce to level of beans. Mix last 4 ingredients and stir into beans. Simmer them on the stove for another hour; or place in a bean pot or covered baking dish and bake in a 325°F. oven for 1 to 2 hours. If I'm not using the oven for anything else, I'll simmer the beans on the stove. A crock pot can be used, also. The beans should be soft before adding the seasonings, so they will expand slowly and cook thoroughly.

Variations:
- Sautéed onions, garlic, peppers and/or carrots can be added once beans are soft.
- Seitan is a "meaty" addition to beans that adds extra protein.

Menu Suggestions:

Baked Beans	Baked Beans
Baked Corn-on-the-Cob or Corn Bread	Stuffed Peppers or Cabbage Rolls
Sautéed Collards	Salad
Bread or Rolls	Pickles
Pickles	
Cherries Jubilee	

Bean and Barley Chulent

Adapted from Jewish cooking, this bean and barley casserole was placed in an oven Friday evening. It gently baked all night and was served on the Sabbath. A nourishing one-pot dinner, to slow simmer in a crock pot or bake as "baked beans."

Servings: 6 or more
Time: all day or overnight

Equipment:
crock pot, covered clay or enamel pot, bean pot

Ingredients:
1/2 to 1 cup barley
1/2 cup adzuki beans
1/2 cup lima or navy beans
2 strips kombu
4 shiitake mushrooms (optional)
2 bay leaves
1 large onion, cut in large chunks
4 carrots, cut in large pieces
5 to 7 cups water
2 to 3 tbsp. red or kome miso or sea salt to taste

Procedure: Sort over barley and beans before washing and soak overnight; drain. Wash thoroughly. Place in a cooking pot. For oven baking use a clay pot, bean crock, or heavy covered pot (enameled cast iron). Cut kombu into 1/2-inch strips with a pair of kitchen scissors. Soak mushrooms and cut into quarters. Cut carrots and onion into large 1-inch pieces. Place all ingredients in pot, except miso. Cover and place in 325°F. oven for 2 hours; then lower to 250°F. for 4 to 6 hours, or simmer in electric crock pot or low flame on stove for 3 to 4 hours. Check and add more water after 2 to 3 hours. One-half hour before serving, add miso dissolved in 1/4 cup water or sea salt. This dish should not be soupy, but similar in consistency to baked beans.

Variations:
• Add seitan to chulent at the end of cooking, especially if seitan is salty. Salt will prevent the beans from expanding and lengthen cooking time.
• Vary proportions of barley to beans.
• Other red beans, such as rositas or kidney beans, may be used in place of adzuki beans.

Menu Suggestions:

Chulent	Chulent
Buckwheat-Potato	Noodle Kugel
Knishes	Dilled Cucumber
Braised Cabbage	Salad
Caraway	Lemon Kanten
Pear Parfait	

Pinto, Kidney or Black Beans

Native Americans and settlers depended on these beans to complement corn and rice. In chili, refried in corn tortillas or simply simmered, these beans should be in your kitchen for delicious dinners.

Servings: 4 to 6
Time: soak overnight, simmer 2 hours

Procedure: Sort over beans; wash and soak overnight. Drain. Add fresh water; bring to boil and simmer for 1 1/2 to 2 hours, or pressure cook for

Equipment:
   **heavy pot with lid, flame
tamer, crock pot, or
pressure cooker**

Ingredients:
   **1 cup beans, soaked
     overnight
3 to 4 cups fresh water
1 strip kombu or
   2 bay leaves
pinch of sea salt to taste**

45 minutes. (Don't pressure-cook black beans, as their skins may clog the valve.) When beans are tender, season and cook 15 to 20 minutes.

Variations:
- Corn and Beans: add 2 to 3 cups fresh corn, cut off cob, to beans.
- Spicy Bean Dip: purée or mash beans; add salsa or hot sauce to taste.
- Pinto or Kidney Bean Salad: drain beans and toss in dressing (umeboshi or basil).
- "Creamy Beans": purée half of beans and return to pot for saucy consistency.
- Refried Beans: heat 1 tbsp. oil in skillet. Sauté 1 minced onion, 2 garlic cloves and any spices. Add beans (drain cooking liquid); stir. Mash gently with a wooden spoon. Add some bean liquid if needed to prevent sticking.

Menu Suggestions:

Sweet Potato-Squash Soup	Gingery Miso Broth
Beans	Spicy Bean Dip
Rice or Corn	Corn Bread or Chips

Collards or Kale	Red Onion-Cucumber
	  Salad or Julienne
	  Salad

Chili

Some like chili hot. I go easy on the pepper. Serve salsa or hot sauce on the side, so each one can season his own dish. Corn bread or tortillas with a garden salad are the classic accompaniments.

Servings: **6 to 8**
Time: **2 to 3 hours**

Equipment:
   **heavy pot with lid,
pressure cooker or crock
pot, skillet**

Ingredients:
   **2 cups kidney beans,
     soaked overnight
2 strips kombu (optional)
1 tbsp. oil
1 large onion, minced
1 pepper, minced**

Procedure: Soak beans; pressure-cook or simmer with kombu until very soft. Sauté vegetables in skillet; add seitan and spices. Cook 3 to 5 minutes. Stir vegetables into beans. Add more water if needed. Remove kombu strips and dice; return to pot and slowly simmer for 1 hour. Adjust seasonings.

Variations:
- Tomatoes add color and flavor. Add 1 pint of tomato sauce or 1/4 cup tomato paste to beans and vegetables.
- Rositas (little red beans) or pinto beans can be used in chili.
- Sautéed garlic and mushrooms can be added, too.

1 hot pepper (optional)
1/2 lb. seitan (optional)
1/2 to 1 tsp. chili powder,
   to taste
pinch of sea salt or 1 to
   2 tbsp. miso

Menu Suggestions:

Chili
Corn Bread or Polenta
Salad, Raw Sliced
   Vegetables
Olives, Pickles

Chili
Corn-on-the-Cob
Greens or Salad
Coconut-Orange-Date
   Cake

Rositas and Rice

This is a simple (not spicy) variation of Caribbean fare. Feel free to add hot chilis or serve with salsa, and make a meal of it with greens or salad.

Servings: 4 or more
Time: 1 1/2 to 2 hours

Equipment:
   pot, cast-iron skillet or
   heavy saucepan

Ingredients:
   1 cup red beans (rositas)
      soaked overnight
   1 strip of kombu
   1 tsp. oil, for sautéing
      vegetables
   1 carrot, diced
   2 stalks celery, diced
   1 yellow squash, half-
      moon cut
   1 zucchini, half-moon cut
   2 to 4 cloves garlic
   1 to 2 tbsp. kome or red
      miso or sea salt
   1 tbsp. arrowroot or kuzu,
      to thicken (optional)
   fresh pot of rice

Garnish:
   collards, kale or
   fresh chopped parsley

Procedure: Wash and soak red beans for 2 hours or longer. Place beans in pot with 3 cups water and kombu and bring to boil; lower flame slightly. Low boil for 1 to 1 1/2 hours until beans are soft. Add more water if needed. The beans should be covered with 1 inch of water at all times. While beans simmer, put on rice to cook. Wash vegetables. Dice celery; cut carrot, zucchini, and yellow squash into half moons. Mince garlic. In a heavy saucepan or cast-iron skillet, heat oil and sauté vegetables starting with celery, adding carrots, zucchini, squash and garlic. Sauté 2 to 3 minutes; turn off flame and cover. When beans are soft, strain off the liquid and reserve. Add beans to vegetables. Dissolve arrowroot or kuzu into bean liquid. Add miso or sea salt to liquid. Pour bean liquid over vegetables and beans. Turn flame back on low. Stir until it thickens. Adjust seasonings. Serve beans over rice.

Variations:
- Instead of summer vegetables like zucchini and yellow squash, use root vegetables such as onion, burdock and parsnip in the cooler seasons.
- Add your favorite herbs or spices.
- Mix rice with beans; it is often eaten this way in the Caribbean Islands.

Menu Suggestions:

Rositas and Rice
Sautéed Collard Greens
Sweet and Sour Pickles
Mocha Pudding

Rositas and Rice
Wakame Cucumber
   Salad
Corn Bread

"3 Sisters" Casserole

Native Americans honored their staples—corn, beans and squash—by calling them "3 Sisters." This do-ahead dish of rich colors, red, orange and gold, is sure to please.

Servings: 4 to 6
Time: 1 1/2 hours

Equipment:
   heavy pot with lid

Ingredients:
   1 cup pinto or kidney
      beans, soaked overnight
   1 strip kombu (optional)
   1 small squash, approxi-
      mately 2 to 3 cups,
      diced
   2 to 3 ears corn, cut off
      the cob
   1 tbsp. miso, mellow white,
      or kome or pinch of
      sea salt

Procedure: Soak beans overnight or all day. Drain water; rinse; add 3 to 4 cups of fresh water and kombu strip. Bring to a boil and simmer 1 hour until beans are soft. Skim foam as it forms. Dice squash and cut corn off the cob. When beans are soft, add squash on top and cook until tender, 15 to 20 minutes. Add corn; cook 5 to 10 more minutes. Dissolve miso in water; add to beans. Season to taste. This dish should not be soupy, but thick like a casserole. Use only enough water to steam-cook squash and corn: they will make the dish thick. The leftovers will make a delicious soup.

Variations:
- Red beans, kidneys or adzukis can be used in place of pintos.
- Use up leftover beans in this recipe by steaming squash and corn on the side, adding them to cooked beans and heating in a casserole dish.
- Garnish with lots of chopped parsley or scallions.
- Salsa, peppers or onions can be added for extra flavor. Add a pinch of chili powder to the simmering beans.

Menu Suggestions:

"3 Sisters" Casserole	"3 Sisters" Casserole
Steamed Greens	Tortillas
or Salad	Greens, Salad
Blueberry Couscous	Toasted Pumkin Seeds
Cake	

Chickpeas

Chickpeas are known by many names worldwide. They are called *garbanzos* in Spain and Mexico, *ceci* in Italy and *chana dal* in India. By whatever name they are called, these beans are a treasure. They require the longest cooking time of all beans used in this book. I prefer to pressure-cook chickpeas. They are used to make hummus, delicious in soups, stews or marinated in salads, or, pressure-cooked with brown or sweet rice.

Servings: 2 to 2 1/2 cups
Time: soak overnight,
   cook 1 to 2 hours

Procedure: Soak beans overnight; drain soaking water. Cover with fresh water in pressure cooker; add kombu. Bring to pressure; cook 1 hour for soups

Equipment:
   pressure cooker, crock
   pot or heavy pot with lid

Ingredients:
   1 cup dried chickpeas,
      soaked overnight in 3
      cups water
   4 to 5 cups cooking water
   1 strip kombu (optional)

and salads or longer if beans are to be used for hummus. Allow pressure to come down, slowly. Once beans are cooked, season with sea salt or herbs. Serve plain or add to other recipes.

Variations:
- Garnish with chopped parsley, dill or scallions.
- Chickpeas can be added to soups and stews.
- Marinate them for salads.
- Mix with cooked grains to form "patties."
- Mash and season for dip or spread.

Menu Suggestions:

Fried Rice	Autumn Stew
Chickpeas with	Millet
Scallions	Chickpeas with Dill
Salad	Arame Mushroom Caps
Date-Nut Bars	Salad, Pickles

Hummus

Chickpeas are the main ingredient of this Middle Eastern bean dip. Garlic, tahini and olive oil are blended with mashed chickpeas and counterpointed with lemon for a toothsome sandwich spread or party dip served with crackers and sliced vegetables. This recipe makes 4 to 5 cups, enough for a party. You may want to halve the recipe. Hummus will keep 2 to 4 days refrigerated.

Servings: 4 to 5 cups
Time: soak overnight;
   cook 2 hours

Equipment:
   pressure cooker, blender
   or food processor, mixing
   bowl

Ingredients:
   2 cups dried chickpeas
      (soaked overnight)
   1 strip kombu
   5 to 6 cups fresh water

Seasonings:
   1/4 cup tahini
   3 to 5 cloves garlic,
      minced
   1/4 cup lemon juice (or
      more)

Procedure: Rinse and soak chickpeas overnight. Drain soaking water; place in pressure cooker; add fresh water and kombu. Bring to pressure; cook 1 to 1 1/2 hours until the beans are very soft. While the beans are cooking, prepare the seasonings. (Tahini and garlic may be roasted for 1 minute to bring out their flavors, as an option.) When the beans are cooked, drain off the cooking liquid and reserve. Pour seasonings over beans and mix. Purée the bean mixture in small batches in a blender or food processor. Add liquid the beans were cooked in, if needed, for a smooth purée. Adjust flavorings. (Don't taste with finger or lick spoon and return to beans as the enzymes from saliva can ferment and turn beans sour quickly.) Add more seasonings or olive oil, if necessary, for a smooth texture. The flavors will improve after chilling 6 to 8 hours.

1/8 to 1/4 cup olive oil
(optional)
sea salt to taste
pinch of cumin (optional)

Variations:
- Hummus Spread: for a sandwich spread, use a small amount of liquid to purée or simply mash beans and add seasonings.
- Hummus Party Dip: for a creamy dip, add more liquid to reach desired consistency.
- Tofu-Hummus: substitute 1 cup mashed tofu for 1 cup chickpeas; add seasonings and purée.
- Spicy Hummus: add 1/4 cup or more salsa to basic recipe. Be careful adding hot spices. Serve with chips. This is a hit at parties.

Menu Suggestions:

Party or dinner:	*Lunch:*
Hummus with Pita Bread	Miso Soup
	Hummus Sandwich
Millet or Falafel Croquettes	Sprouts
	Pickles
Stuffed Grape Leaves	Rice Pudding
Olives, Cucumbers, Radish, Pickles	
Stuffed Dates or Cherries Jubilee	

Lentils and Squash

Orange squash adds color and sweetness to basically brown lentils. An easy way to use up leftover lentils in a filling stew.

Servings: 4 or more
Time: 30 to 60 minutes

Equipment: soup pot, lid

Ingredients:
1 large onion, diced
1 small squash or 1/2 large squash
water or stock to cover
1 to 3 cups lentils
1 tbsp. miso or pinch of sea salt to taste

Garnish:
2 tbsp. chopped parsley, dill or scallions

Procedure: Place onion and squash in soup pot; cover with water or stock. Cover pot and bring to a boil; lower flame and simmer until squash is soft. Add lentils; heat thoroughly. Season with miso or sea salt. Garnish with chopped parsley.

Variations:
- Add root vegetables: carrots, burdock, pearl onions.
- Sautéed mushrooms and garlic can be added to soup.
- Sauté curry spices with onion; continue with recipe.

Menu Suggestions:

Lentils and Squash	Lentils and Squash
Barley with Seeds	Corn Bread or Muffins
Arame with Lemon, Scallions	Greens or Salad
Salad or Greens	Pickles

Adzuki-Squash-Kombu

A classic combination from macrobiotic and Japanese cuisine. Slow simmering is the secret of this sweet and satisfying casserole.

Servings: 6 or more
Time: 1 to 1 1/2 hours

Equipment:
pot with lid, wooden spoon

Ingredients:
(For 6 to 8 servings; if you are a small family, use 1/2 proportions.)
1 to 2 cups adzuki beans (Japanese beans are worth the extra cost.)
2 strips kombu
1 small butternut or Hokkaido squash, cubed
pinch of sea salt or 1 to 2 tsp. shoyu

Procedure: Place washed adzuki beans in a heavy pot with kombu; cover with water and simmer. When level of water reduces, add a little water at a time. Cover and cook for 1 hour, adding water as needed. Cut squash into 1-inch cubes. When beans are soft, but not mushy, place the cut-up squash on top of beans; water should come to bottom of squash, but doesn't have to cover it. Cover and simmer until squash is soft, about 1/2 hour. Season with sea salt or shoyu; stir to blend ingredients. Squash should remain bright orange and beans will be soft and creamy, but not soupy. Enjoy!

Variations:
- Onions and carrots can be used instead of squash.
- Try adding 1 tsp. ginger juice.

Menu Suggestions:

Miso Broth	Adzuki-Squash-Kombu
Adzuki-Squash-Kombu	Millet Croquettes or
Corn-on-the-Cob or	Cabbage Rolls
Corn Muffins	Greens, Salad
Greens, Salad	Fruit in Lemon Sauce

Tofu Cookery

Tofu is called "soy cheese" or "meat without the bone" in the Orient. A soy food that looks like a block of soft cheese, tofu is an ancient "processed" food. Whole soybeans are transformed into soy milk by cooking and crushing, after the bran and hull are removed. A coagulant is added and the milk becomes a curd when pressed inside a square box. (Nigari, a natural coagulant derived from sea salt, is preferable to tofu processed with chemical coagulants. Read the label on the package.)

Tofu is high in protein and low in fat, has no cholesterol and is easily digested by everyone from babies to grandparents. Its very mild flavor, milder than ricotta or cottage cheese, baffles some cooks who feel it is tasteless. For the creative cook, however, this quality is an advantage. Tofu's ability to be transformed into various tastes, shapes and textures makes it a delightful addition to meals of all kinds. Its rich protein and mineral balance make it very satisfying to those accustomed to meat and dairy-centered cuisine.

When introducing tofu into your diet, it is wise to make dishes which are in some way familiar. My sister-in-law has perfected this approach admirably. She makes a zippy "blue cheese" spread, tofu cacciatore, tofu parmesan, tofu egg salad—and the list goes on. By adding a little strong-flavored cheese such as roquefort or romano, tofu appeals to even the stubbornest of palates.

Many natural food chefs delight in creating tofu cheesecake, sweet puddings and other desserts. Tofu is best not used in combination with sweets; I avoid this mixture as much as possible. Why? Because tofu desserts can be difficult to digest. But, I do add tofu to cakes and pies in small quantities to replace eggs.

Tofu can be purchased fresh, by the block (usually 1/2 to 1 lb.) at natural food stores or Oriental markets. Unpasteurized tofu has a short shelf life, three to four days at most. This tofu must be kept refrigerated in clean water, changed every day and used up within two to three days at home. It has a delicate, almost sweet flavor when fresh or homemade that must be tasted to be appreciated. Packaged tofu is usually pasteurized and has a longer shelf life—three to four weeks, if unopened. Once a package is opened, the water must be drained and changed daily. It will last two to four days. Tofu can be frozen in the package, but the texture changes and becomes chewy. Many like this texture in dishes.

Tofu is the most misunderstood natural food. Americans feel that if something is packaged, it is ready to eat. A few serious health nuts eat tofu straight from the package, but I don't recommend this practice. It needs flavor and cooking of some sort. In the Orient, it is primarily used as a garnish in miso soup or it is skewered and broiled, marinated or added to stews.

Tofu is made in both firm and soft styles, depending on how much liquid is pressed out in processing. Both have unique flavors and textures and lend themselves to different kinds of preparations. I press the liquid out of tofu at home again before sautéing or frying as any residual water will cause oil to splatter or interfere with the ability of tofu to absorb flavors in marinade.

Here are seven different ways to prepare tofu:
- *Marinated:* firm tofu is pressed, cut into cubes and marinated in ginger, shoyu or garlic with fennel. Use it as an appetizer, snack, party food or add it to salads.

- *Tofu Cheese:* firm tofu is pressed and layered with miso to absorb flavor. Slice or crumble it and add to other dishes.
- *Scrambled Tofu:* soft or medium-firm tofu is pressed and sautéed with diced vegetables, herbs or spices. Serve for breakfast or as sandwich filling.
- *Mashed Tofu:* soft tofu is pressed and mashed with a fork to make salad or tofu "ricotta" filling. Add your favorite seasonings.
- *Puréed Tofu:* soft or medium-firm tofu is buzzed in the blender with water for a smooth, creamy sauce or dressing. Examples: tofu-tahini, tofu-poppyseed, tofu-avocado dressings.
- *Pan-fried Tofu:* firm, pressed tofu is sliced into "cutlets" and pan-fried (they can be marinated first) until crispy; add sauce or serve plain.
- *Deep-fried Tofu:* firm tofu is pressed, cut into cubes or other shapes, deep-fried in hot oil until it puffs up and turns golden brown. Drain on paper towels and serve with dipping sauce or add it to other dishes.

Marinated Tofu with Shoyu and Fennel

Fennel seeds give marinated tofu an Italian twist. Serve as an appetizer, on the antipasto plate or with rice or noodle salad. Make marinated tofu in the evening to have ready for breakfast or lunchboxes the next day.

Servings: 4
Time: 10 minutes preparation; 4 hours marination

Equipment:
2 plates, suribachi or spice mill, saucepan, jar or bowl

Ingredients:
1/2 lb. tofu (firm)

Marinade:
1 cup water
2 to 3 tsp. fennel seeds, crushed
2 to 3 cloves of garlic, sliced
1 medium onion, sliced
1 to 2 tbsp. shoyu

Procedure: Drain tofu and press between 2 plates to squeeze out excess liquid. Cut into 1-inch cubes. Crush fennel seeds in suribachi or spice mill. Slice garlic cloves. Cut onion in half, then slice in 3 or 4 half-moon slices. Blend marinade ingredients, adjusting shoyu for desired saltiness. Bring to a boil in a saucepan. Place tofu cubes in a jar or bowl. Pour boiling marinade over tofu. Allow to cool several hours or overnight.

Variations:
- This is an excellent marinade for slices of fried or boiled tempeh, too.
- Add dill or oregano.

Menu Suggestions:
Rice or Noodle Salad
Marinated Tofu with Shoyu and Fennel
Cucumber-Red Onion Salad

"Tofu Cheese" (Tofu Pickled in Miso)

Tofu "pickled" in miso overnight results in a creamy consistency and cheese-like flavor. Slice and eat as cheese with crackers or add to other dishes. It makes such a great sandwich no one can believe it is tofu.

187

Fig. 38   Pressed tofu is cut into cubes.

Fig. 39   Pressing tofu. Place tofu on a plate, with another plate on top and weight. Tofu is pressed 1/2–1 hour before slicing to fry, marinate or make into "cheese."

Servings: 6 or more
Time: 10 minute pre-
   paration; overnight
   "pickling"

Equipment:
   small ceramic or stainless
   dish, spatula

Ingredients:
   1 lb. tofu (firm)
   1/4 to 1/2 cup miso
      (darker miso makes
      saltier "cheese";
      lighter makes milder)

Procedure: Firm tofu is a must. Press it for at least 1 hour (preferably longer) to remove water. Slice tofu into 1-inch slabs, lengthwise. Spread a thin layer of miso in dish, covering bottom and sides. (I use a small 6-inch × 6-inch Pyrex glass dish that just fits a 1 lb. block of tofu). Begin to layer it as a sandwich: place a slab of tofu in dish, spread with 1/4-inch miso. Place another tofu slab on top; spread miso. Continue alternating until you end up with a thin layer of miso over the top and sides of tofu. Cover dish with clean cloth or sushi mat. Leave on counter or pantry overnight. To serve, carefully scrape miso off tofu. (Save miso to reuse in soups or dressings.) Slice tofu and serve with crackers, in salads or sandwiches.

Variations:
• Garlic-Tofu Cheese: add 2 to 3 cloves minced garlic to miso: spread over tofu.
• Herbed Cheese Spread: mash tofu cheese; add dried herbs: basil, oregano, thyme, marjoram or chives.

Menu Suggestions:
Vegetable Soup   Corn Chowder
Tofu Cheese Sandwich   Tofu Cheese with
Pickles   Crackers or Rice Bread
                         Salad
                         Applesauce with
                            Crunch

Lorraine's Tofu Salad

My sister-in-law Lorraine's delicious tofu salad recipe is perfect to fill sandwiches for work and school.

Servings: 4 sandwiches
Time: 10 minutes

Equipment:
bowl, fork

Ingredients:
1/2 lb. tofu (press out
    water)
3 tbsp. soy mayonnaise
2 tbsp. prepared mustard
2 to 3 tbsp. chopped pickle
    relish
1 tbsp. parsley, minced
3 scallions, finely chopped
1/2 green or red pepper,
    finely chopped

Fresh Herbs:
dill, rosemary, thyme or
    chives (optional)

Procedure: Drain tofu and mash to soft consistency with fork. Mix the rest of the ingredients until smooth. Refrigerate until use.

Variations:
- Turmeric adds yellow color for "egg salad" style.
- Add chopped olives instead of relish.
- Sauté vegetables, peppers, onion, etc. Cool; then mix.
- If you prefer to "cook" tofu, slice it into 4 pieces and drop into a small pot of boiling water. Boil for 2 to 3 minutes. Drain. Press out water. When cool, crumble into mixing bowl.

Menu Suggestions:

Lunch:
Tofu Salad on Lettuce
    with Sprouts, Olive
Corn Chips

Noodles-in-Broth
Tofu Salad Sandwich
Fruit Kanten

Dinner:
Stewed Broccoli-Rabe
    or Escarole
Tofu Salad Sandwich on
    Garlic Toast
Rice Pudding

Spicy Tofu and Rice Burgers

Falafel mix is my secret seasoning. There are many brands on the market. Basically, it's a mixture of ground beans, seeds and spices. Add as much falafel mix as needed to satisfy your taste. The mix also helps bind tofu and rice croquettes. The burgers can be pan-fried or baked in an oiled baking dish.

Servings: 5 to 6 burgers
Time: 20 minutes

Equipment:
mixing bowl, sauté pan,
    skillet or baking dish.

Ingredients:
1/2 lb. tofu, pressed
1 tbsp. sesame oil
1 onion, diced
1 carrot, diced

Procedure: Press tofu while preparing vegetables. Dice vegetables and sauté in oil for 3 to 4 minutes. Place rice in mixing bowl and crumble tofu over rice. Add sautéed vegetables, mustard, miso and falafel mix; stir to combine all ingredients. Form into burgers or croquettes. Allow to cool completely before frying. Pan-fry or bake until golden.

Variations:
- Add sautéed scallions, garlic or mushrooms to burgers.

2 celery stalks, diced
2 cups cooked rice
1 tbsp. mustard
1 tbsp. miso
1/2 to 1 cup falafel mix

- Fresh minced parsley, dill or basil can be added.
- Millet, cracked wheat or couscous can be added to or substituted for rice.

Menu Suggestions:

Rice Burgers	Rice Burgers
Gingery-Carrot Sauce	Tahini Sauce
Greens or Salad	Dulse-Red Onion Salad
Pickle, Bread	Pita Bread, Sprouts
Peanut-Granola Cookies	

10-Minute Tofu with Swiss Chard

Pink tofu? Try using red chard. Swiss or red chard placed over sautéing tofu cooks down like spinach. The juices add color and flavor. A light fast meal any time of day.

Servings: 4
Time: 10 minutes

Equipment:
skillet with lid, spatula

Ingredients:
1/2 lb. firm tofu, pressed
  and cut into 1/4-inch
  cutlets
1 tbsp. sesame or olive oil
pinch of sea salt or shoyu
  to taste
1 small bunch Swiss or red
  chard, washed and
  chopped
1 tbsp. fresh basil or dill
  (optional)

Procedure: Press tofu 15 minutes; slice. Heat oil and pan-fry tofu on one side until golden. Gently turn tofu with spatula. Sprinkle with sea salt or shoyu. Place chopped chard and herbs on top of tofu. Cover and reduce flame. The greens will cook down in 5 minutes. Add 1/4 cup water if needed to steam greens. Serve cutlets of tofu with greens on the side.

Variations:
- Greens and Garlic: add 2 to 3 cloves of minced garlic to oil and tofu.
- Marinate tofu cutlets in equal parts of mustard, shoyu and water, then pan-fry.
- Tofu and Spice: add pinch of a favorite spice to oil and tofu.
- Spinach can be substituted for chard.
- Add sliced mushrooms or zucchini.

Menu Suggestions:
Quick Light Meals:

Tofu with Swiss Chard	Tofu with Swiss Chard
Corn-on-the-Cob	Couscous with Seeds
Pumpkin Pie	Radishes, Olives

Tofu Cacciatore

Italian-style cacciatore is a family-pleasing way to introduce tofu at home. A do-ahead dinner, its flavors improve next day.

Servings: 4 to 6
Time: 30 to 40 minutes

Equipment:
  casserole dish, sauté or
  saucepan, 2 plates for
  pressing tofu

Ingredients:
  1 lb. tofu, pressed
  1/2 cup oil for frying
  1 tsp. olive oil
  1 large onion, sliced
  1 green pepper, sliced
  1 small zucchini, sliced
  1 small yellow squash,
    sliced
  2 cloves garlic, minced
  2 tbsp. fresh or 1/2 tbsp.
    dry basil
  1 pt. tomato sauce, fresh
    or store-bought
  pinch of sea salt or 1 tbsp.
    miso

Garnish:
  chopped parsley, fennel
    sticks
  1 tbsp. capers (optional)

Procedure: Place tofu on plate. Place other plate on top and press with weight for 30 minutes. Sauté vegetables and garlic in olive oil for 5 to 10 minutes. Add tomato sauce, herbs and capers; simmer for 10 minutes. Cut pressed tofu into bite-sized pieces; deep-fry until golden. Drain on paper towels. Place in baking dish. Cover with sauce. Bake covered at 350°F. for 15 to 20 minutes. Garnish with parsley.

Variations:
- Tempeh or chickpeas can be substituted for tofu.
- To use less oil, try tofu cubes plain; don't deep-fry them.
- Vary vegetables and herbs. Add fresh oregano or dill if possible.

Menu Suggestions:

Escarole Italian-Style
Tofu Cacciatore
Pasta or Rice
Salad, Olives

Tofu Cacciatore
Garlic Toast
Sautéed Dandelions or
  Steamed Greens
Salad
Rice Pudding

Stir-Fried Vegetables with Tofu

Everyone loves stir-fried vegetables and marinated tofu. The tofu can be prepared ahead of time and the vegetables sliced well before dinner. The tofu marinade is thickened before serving to make a sauce. Someone always volunteers to stir-fry the vegetables while I get the rest of the dinner on the table.

Servings: 8 to 10 (to feed a family of 4, cut this recipe in half)
Time: 30 to 45 minutes

Equipment:
2 plates for pressing tofu, wok or large pot, wooden spoons, lid

Ingredients:
1 lb. firm tofu
1 to 2 cups oil for deep-frying tofu

Tofu Marinade:
1 cup saké or white wine
2 tbsp. shoyu
2 tsp. ginger juice

Vegetables:
1 onion, thinly sliced
1 carrot, cut in thin matchsticks
1 green or red pepper, thinly sliced
1/2 head chinese cabbage, thinly sliced
6 oz. mushrooms, sliced
6 oz. snow peas or string beans
4 oz. mung bean sprouts
2 tbsp. sesame oil for frying
1 tbsp. kuzu or arrowroot (to thicken marinade for rich sauce)

Garnish:
1 cup Spicy Cashews or toasted sunflower seeds

Procedure: Rinse tofu; press 1/2 hour between plates to remove water. Cut into 1-inch cubes. Heat oil in wok and fry tofu cubes until golden brown. Drain on paper towels; place in small bowl and cover with marinade. (This step can be done a day ahead or the morning before the meal.) Pour off excess oil in wok so 1 tbsp. remains. Wash all vegetables; slice thinly for stir-frying. Roast seeds in oven. Stir-fry vegetables in order listed. (Remember to start sautéing the root vegetables first.) Remove tofu from marinade; add the cubes to vegetables. Dissolve kuzu in tofu marinade; pour over vegetables and tofu; stir until thickened. Cover and cook on low flame for 2 to 3 minutes. Serve immediately. Garnish with toasted nuts or seeds and sliced scallions.

Variations:
- Fried tempeh, seitan or shrimp can be used in place of tofu.
- Any vegetables can be included if thinly sliced; use up vegetables in your refrigerator or make a trip to an Oriental market for authentic vegetables.

Menu Suggestions:

Consommé with
  Carrot Flowers
Stir-Fried Vegetables
  with Tofu
Rice
Toasted Nori or Arame
  Mushrooms Caps
Lemon or Orange
  Kanten

Miso Broth with
  Watercress
Stir-Fried Vegetables
  over Noodles (whole
  wheat or or buckwheat)
Wakame-Cucumber
  Salad
Orange Jewel Cookies

Tempeh

Tempeh originated in Indonesia and is important in vegetarian diets as a source of protein and vitamin B_{12}. It is made from whole soybeans cooked and gently crushed to "split" the beans in half and remove hulls. The beans are then dried out a bit to remove excess liquid. A spore culture is added and stirred into the beans, with a touch of vinegar. Beans are spooned into plastic bags (in traditional times, leaves were used as containers); the bags are sealed and punched with holes. They are then placed in temperature-controlled boxes or rooms and aged one to two days. The culture becomes active, creating a fine white mold which covers the cake and holds the beans together. The result: a sliceable cake with a distinctive taste and texture.

Tempeh is cooked in a myriad of ways in Indonesia, but primarily in coconut milk which increases its protein value and makes a rich sauce. It is also marinated, broiled or fried. To be properly cooked, tempeh has to simmer at least 10 to 30 minutes in broth or savory gravy before frying, broiling or baking. This imparts flavor and increases digestibility.

Basic Methods of Preparation:
- Slice thinly and deep-fry as Tempeh "Chips."
- Marinate in broth, then fry or broil, as Tempeh "Bacon."
- Fry, then boil in broth or stew, as Tempeh "Turkey."
- Chop, then fry and mash as in "Tempeh-Potato Croquettes."

Tips:
- Tempeh is kept refrigerated or frozen in food stores. Refrigerated tempeh can be frozen in its package at home.
- It will keep approximately one week in the refrigerator after purchase.
- Be careful not to leave unrefrigerated once it is defrosted.
- Black "mold" on tempeh is safe to eat; if any other color appears—red, green or yellow—throw it away.
- Tempeh adapts to traditional seasonings for meat and poultry dishes, e.g., sage, oregano, thyme, basil.

Glazed Tempeh Jardiniere

The French term "Jardiniere" accurately describes this tempeh dish that honors the best produce available in season.

Servings: 4 to 6
Time: 45 minutes

Equipment:
  pot with lid, skillet

Procedure: Prepare vegetables; slice tempeh and ginger. Place onions, carrots and ginger in a heavy pot. Add water to cover. Simmer 20 minutes until carrots are tender. Meanwhile, deep-fry tempeh in oil until golden brown; drain on paper towels. Add string beans, tempeh and sea salt to pot, cover and simmer until beans are cooked. Remove ginger pieces. Adjust seasonings. Serve immediately.

Ingredients:
  10 pearl onions, blanched
      and peeled
  2 large carrots, cut into
      large 1-inch matchsticks
  2 cups string beans, sliced
      diagonally in 1-inch
      pieces
  1 package tempeh, cut
      into 1-inch triangles
  2 "quarter-sized" ginger
      pieces
  water to cover
  oil for frying
  pinch of sea salt to taste

Garnish:
  chopped parsley, water-
      cress

Variations:
- Thicken sauce with 1 tbsp. arrowroot or kuzu dissolved in 1/4 cup water.
- Mince ginger root slices and return to dish for extra flavor.
- Chickpeas or tofu pieces can be substituted for tempeh.

Menu Suggestions:

Glazed Tempeh Jardiniere	Glazed Tempeh Jardiniere
Pasta or Grain Salad, Pickles	Rice Salad with Basil Radishes or Pickles
	Cranberry or Blueberry Kanten

Tempeh "Turkey" with Savory Gravy

Slow simmering for 30 minutes or longer results in tender, delectable tempeh. Savory herbs add holiday flavor any time of year. Tempeh "Turkey" is the basis for tasty sandwiches.

Servings: 4 to 6
Time: 1 hour

Equipment: skillet, saucepan

Ingredients:
  1 lb. tempeh
  1 cup oil for frying

Savory Stock:
  2 to 3 cups water or stock
  1 to 2 tbsp. miso or sea
      salt to taste
  1 tbsp. prepared mustard
  1/2 tsp. sage
  1/4 tsp. rosemary
  1/2 tsp. thyme
  1/2 tsp. marjoram
  2 tbsp. kuzu or arrowroot,
      dissolved in 1/4 cup
      water

Procedure: Cut tempeh into thin, bite-sized triangles. Heat oil in heavy pan; fry tempeh until golden brown and drain on paper towels. Place fried tempeh in a saucepan. Mix savory stock ingredients and pour over tempeh. Bring stock to a boil; lower flame and simmer 20 to 30 minutes. When tempeh is tender, dissolve kuzu in water; pour into stock with tempeh and stir until sauce thickens. Adjust seasonings. Turn off flame and cover. Reheat slowly when ready to serve.

Variations:
- Add onions or mushrooms to sauce.
- Omit herbs and add 1 tbsp. sauerkraut.

Menu Suggestions:

Tempeh "Turkey" with Gravy	Cabbage Corn Soup
Millet Mashed Potatoes	Tempeh "Turkey" Sandwiches
Braised Red Cabbage	Cranberry Kanten
Greens or Salad	

Baked Potato-Tempeh-Carrot Casserole

Golden cubes of fried tempeh, potatoes and carrots are baked in a savory broth. Easy to fix (bakes in 45 minutes). Make a large batch and use the extra for lunch.

Servings: 4 to 6
Time: 1 hour

Equipment:
  pan, bowl, casserole dish

Ingredients:
  1/2 lb. tempeh, cut into
    1-inch cubes
  1/2 cup oil
  4 carrots, "roll" cut
  2 onions, large diced
  3 to 4 potatoes, peeled
    and cubed

Savory Broth:
  1 cup water
  2 tbsp. miso or pinch of
    sea salt
  2 tbsp. prepared mustard
  1/2 tsp. thyme
  1/2 tsp. sage
  1/4 tsp. white pepper
    (optional)

Garnish:
  parsley or scallions

Procedure: Fry tempeh cubes until golden brown. Drain on paper towels. Prepare vegetables. Place in casserole dish with tempeh. Mix Savory Broth. Pour over vegetables. Cover and bake for 45 minutes until potatoes are fork-tender. Garnish with chopped parsley or scallions.

Variations:
- Fried seitan cubes can be added.
- Vary herbs: try caraway or fennel seeds.
- Squash can be substituted for potatoes.
- Serve with Kuzu Sauce.

Menu Suggestions:

Casserole	Casserole
Sea Vegetable or	Stewed Greens
Cabbage Salad	or Salad
Corn Muffins	Garlic Toast
	Pear Crisp

Old-Fashioned Potato and Tempeh Croquettes

My mother's fish and potato cakes were the inspiration for this recipe. Make small croquettes and serve with mustard and horseradish as an appetizer at parties. Add to lunchboxes for an unusual treat.

Servings: 12 to 14 cakes
Time: 1 hour

Equipment:
  pot, skillet

Ingredients:
  5 to 6 potatoes, peeled
    and cubed
  1/2 lb. tempeh, diced in
    1/4-inch pieces

Procedure: Peel and dice potatoes; place in pan; cover with water and boil until soft. Dice tempeh in small pieces. First cut in thin strips lengthwise; then mince. Dice onion and mince garlic. Heat oil in skillet and sauté tempeh until slightly golden; add onion and continue to sauté until soft. Add garlic; stir. Dissolve miso in water; add mustard. Pour over tempeh and onion; lower flame and cover; simmer 5 to 10 minutes to allow tempeh to absorb miso flavor. Drain cooking water off potatoes and mash to smooth texture. Add tempeh and parsley; mix. Allow

2 onions, minced
1 tsp. oil
3 cloves garlic, minced
1 to 2 tbsp. miso, dissolved
  in 1/2 cup water (potato
  water is fine) or 1/2 tsp.
  sea salt
1 tbsp. mustard (optional)
1/4 cup chopped parsley
1/4 cup flour for rolling
  cakes in
1/2 cup oil for frying

the potatoes and tempeh to cool; then shape large spoonfuls into cakes. Dust in flour. Heat oil and fry cakes on both sides until crisp and golden. Drain on paper towels. Serve with mustard, horseradish or pickles.

Variations:

- This easy-to-make filling can be adapted to many other recipes.
- Knishes or vegetable pies can be created with this base. Use recipe as is or add other sautéed vegetables: carrots, burdock, leeks or even seitan.
- Don't like frying? Spoon potatoes and tempeh mixture into an oiled loaf pan; allow to set. Turn onto platter and slice. Serve with onion gravy or stew.

Menu Suggestions:

Scottish Stew	Potato and Tempeh
Potato and Tempeh	Croquettes
Croquettes	Onion Gravy or
Mustard or Sauerkraut	Mushroom Sauce
Salad or Greens	Braised Red Cabbage or
	Cabbage Salad
	Greens or Salad
	Apple Crisp or Rice
	Pudding

Barbecued Tempeh

Succulent barbecued tempeh, served on a bun is the star of a summer cookout for soy food fans. After experimenting with various methods, I found tempeh needs to be precooked in broth, then cooked on a grill and basted with a favorite marinade.

Servings: 4 to 6
Time: 20 minutes

Equipment: pot, grill

Ingredients:
  1 lb. tempeh
  2 tbsp. mustard
  2 tbsp. miso
  water to cover

Barbecue Sauce:
  1 recipe Orange-Miso
    Barbecue Sauce or
    Teriyaki Sauce (page 91)

Procedure: Cut tempeh in "burger-size" portions. Place in a pot and cover with water. Dissolve miso and mustard in 1/4 cup water; add to tempeh and bring to a boil. Lower flame and simmer for 20 minutes. Remove from liquid; cool; then store in portable container to take to barbecue. While grill is heating, pour barbecue or teriyaki sauce over boiled tempeh; place on hot grill and use sauce to baste. Cook 5 to 10 minutes on each side. Serve on bun or roll, with sliced onion, lettuce and sprouts.

Sesame-Onion Rolls (page 76)

Variations:
- Tofu or seitan can be substituted for tempeh.
- Add favorite seasonings to broth.

Menu Suggestions:

Barbecued Tempeh and Rolls	Barbecued Tempeh
Corn-on-the-Cob	Rice Salad with Basil Dressing or Hijiki
Baked Sweet Potatoes	Noodle Salad
Salad, Sauerkraut	Pickles, Olives
Cookies	Fruit Kebabs

Tempeh Kebabs

Tempting kebabs: skewered broiled morsels of tender, marinated foods are found from Japan to Java. Keep kebab sticks on hand for sudden inspirations. Kebabs can be made with tofu and seitan, too.

Servings: 6 to 8 kebabs
Time: 30 minutes

Equipment:
  pot, 2 bowls, skewers or kebab sticks

Ingredients:
  1 lb. tempeh, cut into 1-inch squares
  Savory Gravy (see page 193)
  1 red pepper, cut in 1-inch squares
  1 green pepper, cut in 1-inch squares
  1/2 lb. mushrooms, stems removed
  1 tbsp. shoyu (optional)
  2 tbsp. water

Marinade:
  1/4 cup olive oil
  4 cloves garlic, minced

Procedure: Cut tempeh; cook in Savory Gravy from Tempeh "Turkey" recipe, for 15 minutes. Drain. Pour the marinade over cubes and toss to coat well. Cover bowl and allow to rest 2 to 3 hours. Before assembling, add mushrooms and peppers to the tempeh. Mix well and let sit 10 minutes. To assemble: put pepper pieces on the end of the kebab sticks to secure tempeh and mushrooms. Alternate pepper, tempeh and mushrooms. Save marinade; add 2 tbsp. water and 1 tbsp. shoyu (optional) and use for basting. Twenty minutes before dinner, heat broiler. Arrange kebabs on oiled tray and place under broiler. After 10 minutes, lightly brush with marinade. Turn over and brush other side. When vegetables are tender (about 10 minutes), kebabs are done.

Variations:
- Barbecue Kebabs: follow recipe; baste kebabs with Orange-Miso Barbecue Sauce (page 89).
- Vegetable Kebabs: omit peppers; use cherry tomatoes, pearl onions, zucchini or yellow squash cubes instead.

Menu Suggestions:

Tempeh Kebabs	Tempeh Kebabs
Rice Pilaf or Stuffed Grape Leaves	Couscous
Mediterranean Salad	Spicy Peanut Sauce
Basil Dressing	Sweet and Sour Pickles
Lemon Pudding	Tropical Fruit Fantasy

Tempeh and Vegetables in Coconut Milk

Try tempeh the traditional way. Coconut milk is commonly used in Indonesia to cook tempeh in a rich, creamy sauce. The hot spices are optional; use as much as you like.

Servings: **4 or more**
Time: **30 minutes**

Equipment: **pot with lid, wooden spoon**

Ingredients:
- **2 tbsp. sesame oil**
- **1/2 lb. tempeh, cut into pieces**
- **1/2 tsp. chili powder**
- **1/2 tsp. cumin**
- **1/2 tsp. coriander**
- **2 cups coconut milk (fresh or bottled)**
- **1 small zucchini, sliced in 1/4-inch rounds**
- **1 small yellow squash, sliced in 1/4-inch rounds**
- **1 pepper, sliced in 1-inch strips**
- **1 carrot, sliced on diagonal in thin rounds**
- **1 1/2 tbsp. kuzu (optional), dissolved in 1/4 cup water**
- **2 to 3 tsp. shoyu or sea salt to taste**
- **1 tsp. rice vinegar**

Garnish:
- **3 scallions, finely sliced**

Procedure: Heat oil in pot. Sauté tempeh until golden. Add spices and stir for 1 minute; then add coconut milk. Lower flame and simmer. Prepare vegetables; add to simmering tempeh; cover. Vegetables will steam. Stir occasionally. When vegetables are tender, add kuzu and shoyu or sea salt to taste. Garnish with scallions.

Variations:
- For an authentic "hot" Indonesian dish, use 1 tbsp. shrimp paste (trassi) and 1 tbsp. red pepper paste (sambal ulek) instead of spices listed.

Menu Suggestions:

Lunch:
Tempeh in Coconut Milk
Couscous
Umeboshi Radish Pickle
Fruit Kebabs

Dinner:
Tempeh in Coconut Milk
Basmati or Yellow Rice
Coconut Condiment
Sweet-Sour Pickles
Fruit Kanten

8. Fish————————————————

The bounty of the cold Atlantic Ocean has been an important part of my diet. Growing up, I could never understand why everyone didn't love fish as my family did. Buying it fresh from the market and grilling swordfish or tuna steak on the barbecue was a highlight of every summer vacation.

If you choose to eat fish, my advice is, Go Fishing! Catching your own is the only way to be certain of quality. Once you savor fresh fish, store-bought will pale in comparison. If you can't fish, buy small whole ones from the market. Get to know your fish markets; the busy ones will have the fastest turnover. Supermarkets often have high quality if they do a brisk business. Jewish or kosher fish markets are good bets. Don't buy fish on sale, unless it's during the peak of the season. It doesn't usually get delivered on Sunday. Ask what delivery days are at the market you frequent and plan your meals accordingly.

Tips on Purchasing Fish:
- Fish should be odor-free, "sweet"-smelling, not salty or sour. They should be firm, not flaky.
- Each fish has a particular season in which it tastes best and is a better value. Read up on this.
- Buy the proper cut of fish called for in your recipe. Use fish head and bones for stock; scraps for stews or croquettes; firm, large fillets for kebabs or grilling (swordfish, pollock, salmon); flaky textured fish for salads, fishcakes, baking; whole fish for stuffing.
- Never buy fish that is "swimming" in liquid; the juices collect the longer the fish sits in the case.

Cooking and Storage:
- Don't overcook fish. This is the most common mistake. It is best to lightly undercook fish, as the heat carried over from the oven will continue to cook it. Fish should change color from opaque to white or a darker shade. To test for doneness, push it with a fork; it should flake easily.
- Always rinse fish under cold running water before using or marinating. It is best to cook it the day it is bought, even if you plan to use it the next day. Make a salad, croquettes or stew out of it. It will keep one to two days.
- Store fish in the coldest section of your refrigerator.

Equipment: Most cuts are ready to use and need no special knives. But, if you plan to buy a whole fish to fillet or cut for sushi, fillet and sushi knives are needed. Read a book for careful instructions on techniques for filleting or ask your fish vendor to demonstrate filleting for you.

Making Fish Stock

Cultures, around the world, have used all parts of the fish from fillet to head and bones. My culinary training taught me their value in flavoring and now I know their nutritional importance. Fish bones and heads can be purchased at markets or bought as part of the whole and cut up at home. Salmon heads are noted for a delicate, oily flavor, pink flesh and strengthening ability.

Servings: 2 to 3 qts.
Time: 45 minutes

Equipment:
  soup pot, strainer

Ingredients:
  1 or 2 fish heads (salmon or white-fleshed fish) or bones of haddock or cod
  2 to 3 strips kombu or wakame
  3 or 4 shiitake mushrooms (optional)
  vegetables (optional): onion, celery, fresh mushrooms, parsley
  2 to 3 qts. water

Procedure: Rinse fish bones; place in pot with remaining ingredients and bring to a boil; simmer for 20 to 30 minutes. Skim any foam that forms on stock. Pour through strainer. Slice and add kombu and shiitake mushrooms to soup or fish stew. Allow fish bones to cool; then remove flesh from the bones. There should be about 1 to 2 cups of fish. If it's not overcooked, save and add to fish recipes or feed to pets. Use stock in stew or soups, or reduce by boiling down. Thicken with kuzu and use as a sauce over fish.

Fish and Potato Chowder

In half an hour, you can make a leek, potato and fish stew that will warm the cockles of your heart.

Servings: 4 or more
Time: 30 minutes

Equipment:
  soup pot

Ingredients:
  2 large leeks, washed and thinly sliced
  1 tsp. oil
  4 or 5 potatoes, peeled and cubed
  1 to 1 1/2 qts. water or stock
  1 to 1 1/2 lb. fish, cut into bite-sized pieces
  pinch of sea salt or shoyu to taste

Procedure: Wash leeks carefully and slice thinly. Heat oil in pot. Sauté leeks, sprinkling a pinch of sea salt over them. Salt helps the leeks to cook down. Peel and cube potatoes. Add potatoes and water to leeks. Cover. Boil until potatoes are soft, about 15 to 20 minutes. Rinse fish and cut into 1-inch pieces. Just before serving, add fish to stew; stir and cover. Lower flame. Fish will cook in 5 minutes. Season with sea salt or shoyu. Serve.

Variations:
- Add other vegetables: carrots, celery, onions or corn.
- Add herbs or seasonings of your choice: thyme, parsley, sage, basil are excellent enhancers.

Garnish:
    parsley or scallion, diced
        carrot

Menu Suggestions:

Fish and Potato Chowder	Fish and Potato Chowder
Broccoli or Greens	Nice-Dice Salad or
Garlic Toast	Broccoli-Corn-Tofu
Dill Pickles	Medley
Apple Pie	Olives or Pickles
	Peaches 'n' Pears

Savory Fish Stew

Savory Fish Stew combines sautéed vegetables, rice cooked to a soft cream and chunks of fresh fish. This technique can be used all year using fresh, seasonal produce. For a special occasion I may steam in a separate pot shrimp, mussels and clams in a broth of stock, saké and lemon, and serve with the fish stew.

Servings: **6 or more**
Time: **1 hour**

Equipment:
    heavy pot

Ingredients:
    1 tbsp. sesame oil
    1 medium onion, minced
    1 carrot, minced
    1 large celery stalk,
        minced
    2 to 3 cups cooked rice
    6 cups water or fish stock
    6 to 12 oz. white fish
    1 tsp. grated ginger juice
    sea salt or shoyu to taste
    2 tbsp. minced parsley
        or dill

Procedure: Heat oil in pot; sauté vegetables for 5 minutes. Add rice, water or stock, and sea salt. Simmer for 30 to 45 minutes. Rice should get very soft. Cut fish into 1-inch pieces; add to stew and stir. Cover, allowing fish to cook 10 to 15 minutes on medium heat. Add ginger juice and minced parsley.

Variations:
• Finely sliced burdock can be added.
• In warmer weather, add green and red peppers, mushrooms, corn, fresh dill or basil.
• Make fish stock with fish bones or head.

Menu Suggestions:

Savory Fish Stew	Savory Fish Stew
Croutons	Nabemono or Baked
Salad or Greens	Vegetables
Pumpkin Pie	Salad
	Mocha Pudding

Quick Cornmeal-Fried Fish

A simple dish is often the best. Fish fillets are dusted in cornmeal and fried until crispy.

Servings: **4 or more**
Time: **10 minutes**

Equipment:
    heavy fry pan or
    iron skillet, plate, spatula

Procedure: Heat oil in heavy fry pan (I use my black cast-iron skillet). While oil is heating, rinse fillet and sprinkle with sea salt. Spread cornmeal on plate and dip portion-size fillet into cornmeal to coat lightly on all sides. Keep flame moderate so the oil doesn't get too hot while you are doing this. Place coated fish in pan; it should sizzle and get a crisp crust on each side.

Ingredients:
  1 to 2 lbs. fresh fish,
    white-fleshed (cod,
    haddock, sole, cusk)
  2 tbsp. sesame oil or good
    frying oil
  pinch of sea salt
  1/2 cup cornmeal

Garnish:
  lemon wedge or tartar
    sauce

Cook about 2 minutes on each side. Turn over. If fish is thick, it may take 5 minutes on each side. (Flounder or sole need about 2 minutes per side.) Cover the fry pan if the fish is thick so it will cook faster. Serve with lemon and/or tartar sauce.

Variations:
- Sauté 1 large diced onion on high flame so it gets crispy. Remove onions and then cook fish in pan. Spoon onion over cooked fish to serve.
- Pan-fried fish with lettuce, sprouts and pickle makes a delectable sandwich.

Menu Suggestions:

Quick Cornmeal-Fried Fish	Quick Cornmeal-Fried
Corn-on-the-Cob	Fish
String Beans with	20-Minute Tomato Sauce
Mushrooms	Noodles or Rice
Blueberry Couscous Cake	Green Salad or Broccoli

Fish-and-Potato Cakes

My mom could never make enough of these crispy fish cakes. I've adapted her simple recipe.

Servings: 4 to 6
Time: 30 minutes

Equipment:
  pot, mixing bowl, skillet,
    paper towels

Ingredients:
  1/2 to 1 lb. white-fleshed
    fish
  1 large onion, minced
  4 to 6 potatoes, peeled
    and cubed
  pinch of sea salt
  pinch of white pepper
  1 tbsp. mustard
  1/2 tsp. herbs (optional)
  2 tbsp. parsley, finely
    minced
  1 cup cornmeal
  oil for frying

Procedure: Place fish and onion in pot and cover with water. Boil for 5 to 10 minutes until fish is firm (don't overcook). Remove fish from water and save fish "stock." Cook potatoes in fish stock for extra flavor, adding more water if needed. Simmer potatoes until very soft. Drain. Place in mixing bowl; mash. Add fish (break apart with fingers to feel for bones). Add parsley, sea salt, mustard and any seasonings; mix together. Form balls or "cakes" and roll in cornmeal. Allow to cool before frying. Heat 1/4 inch of oil in skillet. Fry on both sides until golden brown. Drain on paper towels.

Variations:
- Use up leftover fish in croquettes.
- Add sautéed vegetables to fish cakes: garlic, celery, carrots, scallions.
- Instead of pan-frying, place in oiled baking dish; bake at 325°F. for 20 minutes until warmed through.

Menu Suggestions:
- Serve with Tartar Sauce, Estella's Red Sauce, or Onion Sauce.

Corn Chowder	Fish-and-Potato Cakes
Fish-and-Potato Cakes	Broccoli-Corn-Tofu
Pickles, Salad	Medley
Cherry or Peach Kanten	Pickles
	Coconut-Orange Jewels

Fish and Rice Croquettes

Fried until golden or simply baked, fish croquettes are a marvelous way to use up rice and stretch a pound of fish. Serve accompanied with a favorite sauce.

Servings: 4 to 6
Time: 30 to 45 minutes

Equipment:
baking dish for fish,
mixing bowl, plate
with paper towels

Ingredients:
1 lb. fish
1 tbsp. mustard (optional)
1 tsp. ginger juice
1 tbsp. shoyu or sea salt
  to taste
1 onion, diced
1 stalk celery, diced
2 cups cooked rice
3 scallions, minced
oil for frying (optional)
pinch of thyme (optional)
pinch of pepper (optional)

Garnish:
parsley and tomato wedges

Procedure: Place fish in baking dish. Combine ginger juice, shoyu, water, mustard and herbs. Pour over fish and top with onions. Bake covered 15 minutes, until fish flakes. Drain liquid from fish. Place in a bowl with rice and scallions. Mix well and adjust seasonings. You may need to add pan juices from fish. Form 2-oz. balls and roll in cornmeal. Pan-fry or deep-fry until golden; drain. Arrange attractively on platter with parsley and tomato wedges.

Variations:
- No need to deep-fry, croquettes can be baked in oiled pan, in 350°F. oven for 20 minutes.
- Add diced vegetables: carrot, mushroom, pepper.
- Use leftover millet, couscous or bulghur wheat instead of rice.

Menu Suggestions:

Fish Croquettes	Baked Fish Croquettes
Tomato or Mushroom	Tartar Sauce
Sauce	Beets with Greens
Greens, Salad	Salad
Pear Parfait	Fruit Smoothy

Baked Fish with Mushroom Sauce

A delicate mushroom sauce poured over marinated, flaky white fish, baked in an oven-to-table dish, is an easy and elegant time-saver. Sauce can be prepared ahead of time.

Servings: 4 to 6
Time: 20 minutes

Procedure: Rinse fish; place in oiled baking dish. Mix marinade; spread over fish. Allow to marinate in refrigerator until guests arrive, no longer than 1 hour.

Equipment:
baking dish, saucepan

Ingredients:
1 large fish fillet (1 1/2
to 2 lbs.), haddock, scrod
or halibut

Marinade:
1 tbsp. mustard (optional)
1 tbsp. mirin or saké
1 tsp. shoyu or pinch sea
salt
1 tbsp. lemon juice
1/2 tsp. dill, oregano or
basil leaves
1 tsp. oil
1 recipe Mushroom Sauce

Garnish:
lemon, thinly sliced
fresh chopped parsley

Cover and bake at 350°F. for 15 to 20 minutes, depending on thickness of fish. When fish flakes easily, it's ready. Don't overcook. Pour sauce over fish and garnish; serve immediately.

Variations:
• Garnish with blanched broccoli, tender kale leaves or snow peas for green color.
• Red pepper or radish flowers for red color.
• Fish with Tofu: extend your fish dinners by adding 1/4 to 1/2 lb. tofu, cut into bite-sized pieces. Place around fish in baking dish. Cover with marinade; bake and serve with sauce.

Menu Suggestions:

Baked Fish with	Baked Fish with
Mushroom Sauce	Mushroom Sauce
Wild & Brown Rice	Couscous or Noodles
Carrots Vichy	Chinese Cabbage Rolls
Greens, Salad	Cherries Jubilee

Orange-Spiced Blue Fish

Lynne Davis's fabulous fish recipe was inspired by Caribbean cuisine. An orange and spice marinade is a perfect foil for the dark oily flesh of blue fish.

Servings: 4 or more
Time: 1 hour

Equipment:
baking dish, mixing bowl

Ingredients:
1 to 1 1/2 lbs. blue fish,
filleted

Marinade:
2 cloves garlic, minced
(optional)
1/2 cup orange juice,
freshly squeezed
pinch of ginger powder or
1/2 tsp. ginger juice
pinch of white pepper
pinch of sea salt

Garnish:
lime and orange slices
parsley

Procedure: Rinse fish and place in baking dish, skin side down. Combine marinade and pour over fish. Let sit for 1/2 hour. Bake at 375°F. for 15 minutes, until flaky. Garnish with lime or orange slices and parsley.

Variations:
• If there is a lot of liquid left after cooking fish, pour into saucepan and thicken with 1 tsp. kuzu.
• Substitute other large flaked, filleted fish.
• Use marinade on fish kebabs.
• Add onion slices; layer on fish; bake.
• Add additional garlic and "island" spices.

Menu Suggestions:

Orange-Spiced Blue Fish	Orange-Spiced Blue Fish
Basmati or Brown Rice	Noodle Salad
Chinese-Style Vegetables	Nabemono or Steamed
Pickles or Salad	Vegetables
	Melon Kebabs

Mediterranean-Style Fish Salad——————

The fruits of the sun-drenched groves and turquoise waters of the Mediterranean marry in this oregano-scented fish salad. A do-ahead dinner for lazy summer days.

Servings: **4 or more**
Time: **20 to 30 minutes**

Equipment:
baking dish, mixing bowl, serving dish

Ingredients:
1 lb. white-fleshed fish (haddock, cod, cusk)
1 tsp. olive oil
1 tbsp. lemon juice
1 tsp. oregano
1 tsp. shoyu, or pinch of sea salt
1 red onion, diced
1 cucumber, diced
1 pepper, diced
2 tbsp. chopped parsley
1 tbsp. or more olive oil
1 tsp. vinegar
1 tbsp. lemon juice for dressing

Garnish:
lettuce, black olives, sliced tomatoes, parsley, sliced scallions

Procedure: Rinse fish under running water and pat dry. Place fish on oiled baking dish. Spread lemon juice, shoyu and oregano over fish. Cover and bake at 350°F. for 10 to 15 minutes until flaky and moist, but not dry. Dice vegetables; place in mixing bowl. When fish cools, break into pieces over vegetables. Feel for delicate bones when you do this and remove. Add olive oil, vinegar, lemon juice and any liquid from baking pan to fish and vegetables; mix together. Adjust seasonings. To serve, arrange on platter lined with lettuce. Garnish with olives and tomatoes, parsley and scallions.

Variations:
• Try perch or salmon for their pink color.
• This recipe is a good way to use up leftover baked fish for a quick meal.
• Create a Fish-Rice Salad: add 1 to 2 cups cooked rice or couscous and extra olive oil dressing.
• Add fresh herbs: tarragon, dill, basil or oregano.
• Instead of raw vegetables, blanch zucchini, celery and red pepper before adding to cooked fish.

Menu Suggestions:

Mediterranean-Style	Miso-Lemon Soup
Fish Salad	Mediterranean-Style
Pita Bread and Sprouts	Fish Salad
Corn-on-the-Cob	Stuffed Grape Leaves or
Strawberry Kanten	Cabbage Rolls
	Fruit Tart

Fish Kebabs——————

Fish and vegetables are marinated, skewered then baked or broiled. One pound of fish can feed six people elegantly. Kebabs make every occasion special.

Servings: **6 kebabs**
Time: **15 minutes prep., 15 minutes cook**

Equipment:
mixing bowl, baking dish, skewers

Procedure: Rinse fish; cut into cubes and place in mixing bowl with cut vegetables. Mix marinade, pour over fish and vegetables; stir to coat evenly. Cover bowl and place in refrigerator. Marinate for 1 hour minimum. Skewer ingredients, alternating vegetables and fish. Lay in baking dish; pour extra marinade over kebabs. Bake at 350°F. for 10 to 15 minutes until

Ingredients:
- 1 lb. fish, (large flake fish, cut into 1-inch cubes)
- 1 red pepper, cut into 1-inch pieces
- 3 scallions, or 1 green pepper cut into 1-inch pieces
- 12 to 18 small mushrooms

Marinade:
- 1/4 cup mirin or saké
- 1 tbsp. shoyu or pinch of sea salt
- 1 tbsp. sesame oil
- 1 tbsp. fresh rosemary or tarragon, or 1/2 tsp. dried herbs

fish is firm to the touch and changes color. Turn kebabs over after 7 minutes. Careful not to overcook. Kebabs can be cooked in the broiler or on a grill outdoors. Watch after 5 minutes on each side; baste with marinade.

Variations:
- Cherry tomatoes can be used in place of red pepper.
- Scallops or shrimp can be added to fish kebabs.
- Add your favorite herbs or minced garlic to marinade.

Menu Suggestions:

Fish Kebabs	Fish Kebabs
Couscous or Noodle Salad	Rice Pilaf
Broccoli or Salad	Marinated String Bean Salad
Strawberry Kanten	

9. Desserts————————————————

The sweet aroma of Mom's desserts lured me into the kitchen at an early age. She gave me a chair to stand on and let me help. My mother has a special touch with desserts, and I learned by watching her how to transform the bushels of apples from New England orchards into pies, crisps, sauces and muffins. I always delighted in the first strawberries of the season we picked at a local farm. Homemade strawberry short-cake was the only birthday cake I wanted.

I progressed to making sugary cookies, cheesecakes and chocolate mousse in my teens. Culinary school seemed a promising place to continue my search for richer, more exotic desserts. But the long complicated techniques required to make classic pastries in the Culinary Institute's bake shops began to dampen my interest in desserts. The time, energy and variety of ingredients needed were overwhelming. It seemed not only wasteful to indulge in baking these hyper-rich dessert fantasies, but eating them brought un-desirable changes in my own health—notably weight gain!

Sugar Blues by William Dufty opened my eyes to the ill effects of my culinary confec-tions. Recognizing the high-low blood sugar cycle he described, I continued my baking classes with a new direction: to adapt desserts to sugar- and dairy-free variations that are both sensual and sensible.

This chapter offers basic techniques for making simple, healthful desserts. You will learn to make fruit kantens, a jelled dessert with limitless possibilities, fruit sauces, pies, tarts and crunchy cookies.

Desserts in restaurants are usually too sweet and too expensive. Better keep loved ones (and yourself) supplied with fresh goodies at home. If the cookie jar is empty for too long, you may feel compelled to rush out and buy poorer quality goodies. Generally, I make desserts two or three times a week.

Basic Techniques and Ingredients————————————————

Changing Over: Taste is so individual; one person's "salty" is another's "bland." The same is true of sweetness in desserts. When I began compiling recipes for this book four or five years ago, I used maple syrup in everything. Gradually, I switched to rice syrup. My tastebuds needed a chance to catch up with my ideas. Now, the natural sweetness of fruits alone are enough for me—most of the time, anyway.

When making desserts for those used to rich dairy delights, offer an alternative: fruit desserts. Pies, kantens, kebabs or fruit salad are always well received.

As you experiment with baking, use your own tastebuds as your "sweetness guide." It's good to introduce baked desserts that are made with half white and half whole-wheat flour. Later you can reduce the amount of white flour. When adopting a new whole foods style of eating, it is necessary to have a large variety of food on hand to ease the change-over.

Ingredients: There are seven groups of ingredients to become familiar with in dairy- and sugar-free baking: flours, sweeteners, oils, thickeners, leaveners, fruits and nuts, and flavorings:

Flours: Grind your own flour for the greatest nutritional value and best taste. Or buy only the amount of flour you'll use in a week and keep it in a cool spot or in the refrigerator to prevent the germ in whole grain flour from spoiling. The properties of the various whole grain flours are important to learn:

Whole Wheat Pastry Flour: It is light enough for cakes, pies and pastries. There is less bran than in whole wheat flour as it is made from softer wheat.

Whole Wheat Flour: Ground from a different type of wheat, this flour has more bran and gluten than pastry flour. It is best for bread and muffins. Sift it if you want to substitute it for pastry flour.

Unbleached White Flour: This flour makes the lightest desserts and contains little bran.

Cornmeal: "Meal" is made from ground whole corn, complete with the corn bran and germ. Corn germ has a high quantity of oil, so it spoils easily and can turn bitter. Make sure when you purchase freshly ground cornmeal, that it has been stored in a cooler in the store.

Corn Flour: This is lighter than cornmeal because the bran has been partially sifted out. It can be substituted for whole wheat flour in many recipes. Corn flour makes delicious breads and muffins.

Oatmeal "Flour": Rolled oats or oatmeal make a nutty, light flour. "Buzz" oats in food processor or blender into a coarse flour or meal. This flour is used in my cookie recipes and pie crusts.

Sweeteners: Check the label for those that are 100% pure. They should contain no sorbitol, molasses, honey or sugar in any form: dextrose, fructose, maltose or sucrose. Buy pure maple syrup in gallon containers to save money. Sweeteners will keep for months in a cool place. I use four types in baking:

Maple Syrup: 100% pure is the best and the sweetest. Grade A is the lightest, most refined syrup, usually poured over pancakes. It is also the most expensive grade of syrup. Grades B and C are less refined, and less costly; they are fine for baking. Store in a cool area or in the refrigerator.

Barley Malt: Similar to molasses in color and aroma, barley malt is thicker and less sweet than maple syrup. It is too heavy for use in cakes, but its distinctive flavor is well-suited to muffins and cookies.

Rice Syrup: Rice is the source of this thick syrup that resembles honey. Rice syrup has a mildly sweet taste. Because of its thickness, it is too heavy to use alone in cakes, but can be mixed with maple syrup. It becomes creamy when melted over hot cereal, pancakes or waffles. Try it on bread or rice cakes instead of jam, or mix with roasted tahini for a spread. If you can't find it in your natural foodstore, it is available by mail order.

Fruit: Many types of dried fruit can be used as sweeteners: dates, raisins, apples, apricots and figs, to name a few. They can be used in place of syrups by "stewing" and puréeing them with their juice. Chopped and added to cakes, cookies, pies and kantens, they add natural sweetness and unique flavor.

Fruit Concentrates: These can be used in most dessert recipes, especially cookies and pies. They also add wonderful flavor to glazes. Be sure to buy unsweetened brands.

Fruit Juices: Apple juice and cider are the base for many of my kantens, pies and baked desserts. Try different fruit juices (e.g., pear, cranberry, apricot) for a variety of tastes.

Oils: There is a wide divergence of views, even within the world of natural foods, as to which oils are best for flavor and health. After experimenting with many types, I have narrowed my choices to a few good quality cold-pressed oils, or unrefined oils.

Corn Oil: This is a very popular oil in dairy-free baking. I find the taste too strong for cakes although it is fine for corn bread and muffins.

Safflower Oil: Another popular oil in baking or frying. with a distinctive flavor.

All-blend Oil: A light mixture of several oils. There are a few brands of cold-pressed all-blends in natural foods stores. The taste is lighter and appeals to most people used to rich dairy desserts.

Sesame Oil: Used in small quantities, sesame oil can give delicate flavor to cookies, crusts or muffins. There are many types of sesame oil. Look for unroasted, cold-pressed sesame oil (dark or roasted oil is for cooking).

Thickeners: These ingredients may have an exotic ring, but once you gain experience with them, making desserts is a joy. Kuzu, arrowroot and agar-agar are staples in my kitchen.

Kuzu: Kuzu, sometimes spelled "kuzu," looks like crushed chalk. It is a starchy powder derived from the root of a hardy vine native to Japan and Asian countries.

Kuzu thickens sauces to clear, smooth perfection. It must be completely dissolved in cold water first, then added to sauce or soup. It will remain set after cooking in puddings, pies and sauces. The price per pound may seem high, but once incorporated into cooking, it is indispensable. Available in Oriental groceries as well as natural foods stores.

Arrowroot Flour: This flour made from the arrowroot plant has qualities similar to kuzu and can be substituted for it in most cases. However, arrowroot is not as strong as kuzu and may require more than the amount of kuzu given in recipes. It will thicken cooking liquids or stews, but may not "set" after cooking as in pudding or kanten recipes.

Agar-agar: This is a sea vegetable imported from Japan. It is a flavorless natural gelatin used primarily in making kanten, a Jello-type dessert. Agar comes in flakes, bars or powder form. I prefer the flakes and use them in recipes in this book. Agar powder is very concentrated. Use 1 tbsp. per 1 quart of liquid. Agar bars are common in Oriental stores (buy only the clear, uncolored ones). Bars vary in strength, so follow suggestions on the package.

Leaveners: Baking powder and baking soda are the only leaveners I use (except for yeast on occasion to make bread or pizza dough).

It is necessary to use a leavener to make light, fluffy cakes or muffins. Yeast, whipped egg whites, baking powder or soda are the most commonly used. If you wish to avoid these products, then use only recipes for cookies, pies, tarts and fruit kanten that don't call for leavening.

Baking Powder: Look for aluminum-free baking powder at natural food stores or supermarkets. Alum is an ingredient of most commercially-made baking powders and is considered harmful. Baking powder loses its leavening ability after a few months. To check if powder is still fresh, dissolve a teaspoon of it in a cup of warm water. It should bubble.

Yeast: Only two recipes in this book call for yeast: pizza dough and sesame rolls. Yeast are organisms that feed on "sugars" and give off carbon dioxide during rising and baking, causing the dough to rise. High-quality dried yeast can be found in the refrigerator section.

Fruits and Nuts: Fruits and nuts have replaced sugar and dairy foods as the main ingredients in my desserts. Growing up near orchards, my family had luscious fruits in every season. It is best to eat fruit from your local area, at its peak of freshness. Peaches, plums, apples and pears are abundant in late summer and fall; spring and summer bring a flow of berries: strawberries, raspberries, blackberries, blueberries and cherries. Then there are the wondrous melons available in summer, all begging to be made into light fruit kantens or sliced and added to kuzu sauce. Fruits, from kantens to pies to kebabs, have limitless possibilities.

Almonds, walnuts, cashews and pecans can often be interchanged in recipes. Nuts must be kept in a sealed jar or plastic container in the refrigerator or in a very cool spot. The oils of nuts go rancid very quickly, especially those of walnuts and pecans. Raw almonds and cashews seem to keep well without refrigeration. Always buy nuts raw; then roast them yourself to save money and for best flavor. Buy walnut and cashew pieces; they are less expensive and easier to use in recipes calling for chopped nuts. Hazelnuts (filberts) and pine nuts are delicious, too, preferably as garnishes rather than ingredients in pastries.

Tahini paste is made of raw, ground sesame seeds; it is used in spreads, or as an ingredient in crusts or cookies. It gives a creamy consistency to mocha or rice puddings and mixes well with fruit purée as a sweet spread.

Peanut or other nut butters are too rich in oil to be used daily, but when you want a treat, they make great cookies and are good in pie crusts or spreads.

Flavorings: These provide the special touch that accents the dessert or brings all the elements together. Use only pure natural extracts, not artificial flavors.

Vanilla Extract: It's very expensive, but blends and sweetens recipes like few other flavorings, as does vanilla bean.

Vanilla Bean: The ultimate in true vanilla flavors. Soak or simmer bean in the liquid that is called for in the recipe. When bean is soft, slit it and scrape the inside into the cooking liquid.

Orange and Lemon: The juice and grated peel of these fruits are classic flavorings. Use organic or low-spray citrus fruit, especially if you are grating peels.

A tip from professional bakers: when using the juice of a fruit in one recipe, grate the peels first and store them in a plastic bag in the freezer or refrigerator for later use. Then they're always on hand to add zest to desserts, dressings, breads and cereals.

When using lemon juice, orange juice or vanilla in sauces or kanten, remember to add them at the end of cooking time, if possible, so their flavor will not boil off.

Spices: Use whole spices when possible and grind them yourself for optimal freshness and flavor: cinnamon sticks, whole nutmeg, cardamon pods (open them first), whole cloves and coriander seeds. Freshly ground spices make your house smell like the holidays at any time of the year.

Tips for Successful Baking:
- Assemble all ingredients and equipment before beginning. Read recipe twice to be sure you understand it before proceeding.
- Refrigerate flour and oil for freshness, but remove 2 to 3 hours before baking. Have all ingredients at room temperature, unless recipe indicates otherwise.
- Always sift flour (with dried ingredients, sea salt, spices, etc.)
- Preheat oven before mixing batters.
- Mix only enough to incorporate all ingredients. Do not overmix.
- Oven temperatures make a big difference. Read directions carefully: high for lighter cakes and pie crusts (375°F.); low for heavier fruit cakes (300° to 350°F.).
- Oil baking pans to prevent sticking. Optional: dust with flour or line with oiled parchment paper cut to size of pan.

Tests for Doneness of Cakes:
- Golden brown color.
- Sides pull away from pan.
- Inserted toothpick comes out "clean."
- Surface springs back when gently pressed with finger.
- Bottoms of cookies are golden brown.
- The smell of freshly baked desserts fills your kitchen.
- Cool 10 minutes in pan before turning onto racks or plate to avoid breakage.

Fig. 40   Cake decorated with glaze, nuts and orange slices.

Fig. 41   Piece of cake.

Fig. 42 Assembling an apple tart. A pie crust is prebaked. Apple-kuzu or fruit purée is spread in bottom of baked pie crust. Apples or other fruits are sliced very thin. The fruit slices are overlapped, beginning at outer edge and filling into center. The fruit is covered with a thin glaze. The tart can be baked for a few moments or served as is.

Fig. 43 A finished apple tart.

Cake Decorating: The colors, textures and flavors of fruit sauces and purées make interesting bases, icings or fillings for cakes. Roasted nuts, seeds and sliced fresh or dried fruits can be used to garnish in appealing patterns and designs.

1. *Cake:* 1 or 2 layers of Basic Cake Recipe or a variation.
2. *Icing:* Raisin Purée, fruit (juice) glaze, thinned jelly.
3. *Garnish:* toasted coconut; ground, toasted nuts; sliced fruits; whole roasted nuts; fruit slices dipped in glaze: strawberries, grapes, apricots, cherries, orange segments, kiwi fruit or apple slices.
4. *Garnish for the Platter:* flowers, greens, leaves, dried flowers, doilies.

The Art of Assembling Tarts and Pies:

Fruit Tarts: Open-faced fruit tarts are a visual banquet with their delicate crusts, pastry cream, colorful sliced fruit and glazes. In European bakeries, you can tell the season by the type of tarts are on display: strawberry in spring; apple or pear in fall, etc.

Simple to make and elegant, these tarts use a small amount of flour and oil. Of course, fruit is the only sweetener. Make 1 large or several small ones with the same recipe.

Couscous Fruit Tarts: In place of a baked pie crust, try a couscous crust. For 1 pie, bring 3 cups of apple juice to a boil; add 1 1/2 cups couscous and stir until liquid is absorbed. Add any seasonings or roasted chopped nuts. Spoon couscous into pie pan. Allow to cool; then arrange fresh sliced fruits on top. Coat with fruit juice glaze.

1. *1 Recipe Pie Dough*, for 1 or 2 crusts, prebaked in 1 large or smaller individual tarts.
2. *"Cream,"* 1 to 2 cups of thick applesauce (kuzu can be added) or puréed dried fruits (apple, pear, date or apricot will do).
3. *Fresh fruit*, sliced. Use what is in season: peaches, pears, berries, apples or grapes.
4. *Glaze:* apple or other fruit juice glaze or thinned jelly are good.
5. *Garnish:* mint leaves, roasted nuts.
   Bake tart for 5 to 7 minutes to soften fruits, if you desire. Garnish.

The Glaze

This basic recipe is "icing-on-the-cake." Use it to glaze fruit tarts, cakes, sliced fruits.

Servings: 1 cup—enough
  for 1 cake or 2 tarts.
Time: 5 minutes

Equipment: saucepan

Ingredients:
  1 cup apple juice
  2 tsp. arrowroot or kuzu
  1 tbsp. sweetener
    (optional)
  pinch of sea salt

Procedure: Dissolve arrowroot with juice in saucepan. Heat over low flame, stirring constantly until juice bubbles, thickens and becomes clear. Cool and "frost" cake or pour over tarts.

Variations:
- Substitute orange, pear or cranberry juice for apple juice.
- Add lemon peel, vanilla or almond extract.

Raisin (Fruit) Purée

Sweet, rich and the color of dark chocolate, Raisin Purée is used to "ice" cakes or spread on muffins.

Servings: 1 1/2 cups
Time: 20 minutes

Equipment:
  saucepan, blender

Ingredients:
  1 cup raisins
  1 cup + 2 tbsp. apple juice
  1 tbsp. arrowroot or kuzu
  pinch of sea salt
  1 tsp. vanilla extract
  pinch of cinnamon

Procedure: Simmer raisins in 1 cup juice for 15 minutes in a saucepan. Dissolve arrowroot in 2 tbsp. juice; add to raisins and stir until thick. Simmer 2 to 3 minutes. Add flavorings; pureé in blender. Cool and "frost" cake or spread on muffins.

Variations:
- Dried apricots, dates and/or peaches can replace raisins.
- Substitute your favorite spices or extracts.

Lemon Pudding

For those who love the tang of fresh lemon, this creamy pudding is a refreshing end to any meal. It is also a delicious sauce over cake or sliced fruit.

Servings: 4 to 6
Time: 20 minutes

Equipment:
  saucepan, serving dish

Ingredients:
  1 qt. apple juice
  1/3 cup agar flakes
  2 tbsp. kuzu, dissolved in
    1/4 cup cold juice
  pinch of sea salt
  1/4 cup lemon juice
  1 tsp. lemon rind, grated
  1/8 to 1/4 cup maple or
    rice syrup (to taste)

Procedure: Combine juice and agar in saucepan. Simmer for 15 minutes. Add dissolved kuzu and stir until thick. Blend lemon juice and syrup into pudding; stir. Remove from flame and pour into a serving dish. Cool to room temperature; then refrigerate.

Variations:
• Serve over blueberries, strawberries or raspberries.
• Slice cake and top with pudding; garnish with toasted almonds or walnuts.

Strawberry Kanten and Friends

A smooth gelled dessert, thickened with agar-agar, nature's gelatin from the sea. The basic recipe inspires endless variations. Kanten keeps two to three days in the refrigerator.

Servings: 4 to 6
Time: 30 minutes cook-
  ing; 2 hours cooling

Equipment:
  saucepan, serving bowl

Ingredients:

For Basic Kanten Recipe:
  1 qt. apple juice or cider
  1/3 cup agar-agar flakes
  1 tbsp. kuzu (or arrowroot)
    dissolved in 1/4 cup
    juice
  pinch of sea salt

Fruit and Flavorings:
  1 pt. fresh strawberries
  1 tbsp. lemon juice
  1 tsp. vanilla (optional)
  2 to 3 tbsp. maple syrup
    (optional for extra
    sweetness)

Procedure: In a soup pot, pour juice and stir in agar. Set on medium flame; stir. Dissolve kuzu in water to make a smooth paste and add it to boiling apple juice and agar. Stir to avoid lumps. Lower flame; simmer 10 minutes until liquid is clear and smooth. Wash and halve strawberries. Add berries and lemon juice (and optional sweeteners) to hot kanten. Remove from stove. Heat will "cook" berries gently. (Strawberries turn brown if overcooked.) Pour into a heatproof glass or ceramic bowl or individual dishes. (Shallow bowls cool faster.) Cool to room temperature; refrigerate 2 to 3 hours. Serve alone; garnish with chopped nuts or serve with cookies or cake.

Variations: Almost all fruits make sweet kantens. Try your favorite.
• Simmer blueberries, cherries, pineapple, oranges, apples, peaches, pears, or grapes (strain grape seeds), etc., for 2 to 3 minutes before cooling kanten.
• Add spices—cinnamon, nutmeg, ginger, cloves—at the start and cook to develop full flavor.
• Add extracts, lemon, lime or orange juice/rind at the end. Cooking makes them bitter.

Garnish:
chopped nuts, mint leaves

- Fruit Sauce: 1/8 cup agar flakes plus 2 tbsp. kuzu. Follow basic recipe. Great over cake and corn bread.
- Agar powder is very concentrated. Substitute 1 to 2 tbsp. for 1/4 cup flakes.
- Agar bars are less concentrated. One bar will thicken 1 quart or more.

Note: Kanten should set at room temperature. Chilling will speed setting time.
- If kanten is too hard, reboil with additional juice and chill.
- If kanten is too soft, reboil with additional agar and chill.

Fabulous "Fruit Smoothy"

There is no dairy in this dessert, yet it is creamery-smooth. (Kanten is made only with juice, allowed to cool; then buzzed in blender with ripe fruit.)

Servings: 4 to 6
Time: 30 minutes

Equipment:
bowl, blender

Ingredients:
1 recipe for Basic Kanten
2 cups ripe fruit: bananas, peaches, berries

Procedure: Follow basic recipe, but place ripe fruit with cooled kanten in a blender. Blend until smooth; refrigerate.

Variations:
- Strawberries and blueberries also work wonders.

"Tropical Island" Fruit Fantasy

Tropical fruits float in a creamy kanten sea of pina colada juice, looking like cool islands. Sweet and refreshing in hot weather, this fantasy dessert caps summer picnics and cookouts. My friends and family can't believe it is sugar-free. I "forget" to tell them it's made with sea vegetables (agar). They wouldn't believe me anyway.

Servings: 6 or more
Time: 20 minutes; cool
**   2 hours**

Equipment:
pot, large shallow serving dish

Procedure: Combine juice with agar in pot. Bring to a boil slowly; simmer 15 minutes on low flame, stirring occasionally. Add kuzu dissolved in water. Stir until clear; add pinch of sea salt. Peel and slice fruit. Place fruit in serving dish. Pour hot fruit kanten over it. (The heat of the juice will cook fruit.) Fruit should float to the top. Allow to cool. When dessert is "set," garnish with kiwi, almonds or toasted coconut. Chill and serve.

Ingredients:
1 qt. pina colada
  juice or other tropical
  fruit juice
1/3 to 1/2 cup agar flakes
1 tbsp. kuzu, dissolved in
  1/2 cup water (optional)
1 mango, peeled and cubed
2 oranges, sliced into
  sections
1 cup pineapple, peeled
  and cubed (optional)
pinch of sea salt

Garnish:
1 kiwi fruit, peeled and
  thinly sliced
1/4 cup slivered almonds
  or toasted coconut

Variations:
- Melons, cut in cubes or scooped into balls, can be added.
- Flavor with lemon juice or vanilla.
- If using local fruit such as apples or pears, don't mix them with tropical fruit.

Cranberry Kanten

Cranberry Kanten is more of a dessert than a condiment, but it can be used either way. It's a sweet and tart complement to a meal.

Servings: 6 or more
Time: 20 minutes; cool
  2 hours

Equipment:
  pot, serving dish

Ingredients:
1 qt. apple juice
1/3 cup agar flakes
1 tbsp. kuzu
2 apples, diced
2 cups cranberries
1/2 cup roasted, chopped
  walnuts
1/2 cup raisins
1 orange, grated and
  juiced
1/4 tsp. cinnamon
  (optional)
1/4 cup maple or barley
  malt syrup (optional
  for extra sweetness)

Procedure: Pour juice into a saucepan. Add agar and stir; bring to a low boil; then simmer for 20 minutes until agar is completely dissolved. While kanten is cooking, dice apples, wash cranberries, roast and chop walnuts and grate orange. When kanten has cooked for 20 minutes, dissolve kuzu in 1/4 cup water. Stir kuzu into kanten; continue to stir until the kuzu cooks and becomes clear. Now add the remaining ingredients. Simmer 2 to 3 minutes until the cranberries "pop." Pour into a serving dish (low or shallow dishes work best). Allow to cool to room temperature; then place in the refrigerator. Serve with the meal or as a dessert. This dish should be made the day before if possible.

Variations:
- Pear-Cranberry: substitute pears for apples.
- Omit orange; add 1 tsp. grated lemon peel.
- Omit nuts or use another type.
- Garnish with sliced orange.
- Festive Cranberry Ring: to "mold" kanten, omit kuzu; add 2 extra tbsp. agar to recipe. Follow directions. Rinse mold with cold water; pour in kanten and chill. To unmold: dip in water. Place plate on top. Flip. Garnish with orange slices.

Pear Parfait

Delicate pear sauce is layered with dark Raisin Purée. Light, sweet and rich.

Servings: 4 to 6
Time: 1 hour, plus
  cooling

Equipment:
  saucepan, blender

Ingredients:
  4 to 5 pears, sliced and
    seeded
  1 qt. pear or apple juice
  1/3 cup agar flakes or
    1 bar agar
  pinch of sea salt
  1 tsp. vanilla (optional)
  1 recipe Raisin Purée
    (page 213)

Garnish:
  mint leaves or toasted
    almonds

Procedure: Place diced pears, juice, agar and sea salt in saucepan. Bring to a boil; simmer 30 minutes. Purée in blender, mash or leave chunky. Cool. Make Raisin Purée and cool. Spoon golden pear sauce into individual serving bowls. Layer with dark Raisin Purée. Chill and serve.

Variations:
- Pear-Amazake: substitute 1 qt. amazake for apple juice.
- Serve as pear sauce, plain or with crunch.
- Add lemon juice for flavor.

Cherries Jubilee

The first cherries of summer are cause for celebration. Serve alone or crown your sweet creations.

Servings: 4 to 6
Time: 30 minutes

Equipment:
  pot, shallow serving dish

Ingredients:
  1 qt. apple juice or cherry
    juice
  1/3 cup agar flakes
  1 lb. cherries, halved and
    pitted
  1 tsp. vanilla
  pinch of sea salt

Procedure: Pour apple juice into pot and add agar. Stir and bring to boil over medium flame. Lower flame and simmer 15 to 20 minutes until agar is completely dissolved. While sauce is cooking, halve and pit cherries. After 20 minutes, add vanilla and cherries. Simmer 5 minutes; remove from heat. Pour into baking dish or bowls. Cool and place in refrigerator.

Variations:
- Cherries Jubilee is delicious with lemon cake or corn bread.
- Add 1 tbsp. kuzu for a creamier sauce.
- Try 1/2 lb. cherries and 1/2 lb. seedless green grapes, sliced in half.

Fruit and Melon Kebabs

Fanciful fruit kebabs are fun to make and share on sunny summer days. Luscious ripe melons of pastel colors can be scooped into balls or cubed for a "jewel" of a snack.

Servings: 16 to 20 kebabs
Time: 15 minutes

Equipment:
   melon scoop, bowl,
   kebab sticks, platter

Ingredients:
   1 small cantaloupe
   1 green melon
   1/4 small watermelon
   1 pt. apple juice
   juice of 1 lemon

Procedure: Slice melons in half; remove seeds. Using the melon scoop, press into flesh of melon; twirl handle of scoop to form perfectly round melon ball. Scoop balls close to each other. Place melon balls in bowl and cover with apple and lemon juice; continue with other melons. Keep fruits in juice until ready to serve. Skewer fruits, alternating colors. Serve immediately or keep covered and refrigerated.

Variations:
- Strawberry-Grape Kebabs: combine strawberries with red and green seedless grapes.
- Tropical Fruit Kebabs: cube mango and pineapple and alternate with rounds of banana. Marinate in orange juice in place of apple juice.

Fig. 44   Fruit kebabs.

Old-Fashioned Applesauce

Store-bought can't begin to compare with homemade applesauce. The art of applesauce making is my dad's autumn pastime. He scouts out the pick of the crop in fall, stores a few bushels in the basement and makes a steaming pot of apples each week. Pink-and-rose-colored sauce comes from cooking apples unpeeled, then puréeing.

Servings: 4 or more
Time: 30 to 45 minutes

Equipment:
  pot, lid, food
  mill or blender

Ingredients:
  1 to 2 lbs. apples, sliced
  1 to 2 cups water
  pinch of sea salt
  cinnamon, stick or ground

Procedure: Quarter apples and remove seeds. Slice apples or cut in chunks. Place in pot; add water, sea salt and ground or stick cinnamon. Cover; bring to boil; simmer 15 minutes until apples are very soft. Cool. Purée in blender, skins and all, or pass through food mill to remove skins. Place in bowl or glass jars. Keep refrigerated.

Variations:
- Apple-Cranberry Sauce: add 1/2 cup washed cranberries to apples; cook and purée.
- Add vanilla or lemon juice for flavor.
- Apple-Crunch: top with granola or crunch recipe.
- Apple-Kuzu: add 1 to 2 tbsp. kuzu dissolved in 1/2 cup juice to 4 cups hot apple sauce. Stir over low flame until clear and thick. Use as filling for tart.
- Apple-Peanut Sauce: add 1/4 cup peanut butter to 3 cups hot apple sauce.

Grated Carrot Pudding with Cardamon

Carrot pudding is a sensuous dessert from India called *gaijar ka halwa*. The original recipe calls for milk and ghee (clarified butter), but I've substituted soymilk and oil. Long, slow simmering is called for. Start this dessert first, then continue with other dishes on your menu. The kids can pitch in to grate carrots and stir this pudding.

Servings: 6 or more
Time: 2 hours

Equipment:
  heavy pan, sauté pan,
  wooden spoon, grater

Ingredients:
  1 lb. carrots, grated
  3 cups soy milk
  6 or 7 cardamon pods or
    1/2 tsp. ground
    cardamon
  pinch of sea salt
  1 tsp. oil
  1/2 cup raisins

Garnish:
  1/2 cup pistachios or
    walnuts, chopped

Procedure: Grate carrots and place in heavy pot with soy milk and cardamon pods. (If using cardamon powder, add later while sautéing.) Cover and simmer on very low flame 1 to 1 1/2 hours. Stir occasionally until liquid evaporates. Heat oil in skillet; spoon carrot mixture into pan. Remove cardamon pods. Sauté carrots with raisins and nuts. The mixture is "wet," but will dry out as it sautés. Stir to prevent sticking. Cook 5 to 10 minutes. (Add the ground cardamon at this stage.) Pour into serving dish. Smooth the surface. Garnish with nuts.

Variations:
- Substitute cinnamon or ginger powder for cardamon.

220

Easy and Elegant Baked Apples

This dessert can easily become the apple of your eye. A sweet, light ending to a hearty meal, the apples can be made early and reheated. Kids are delighted to core and fill the apples.

Servings: 4 to 6
Time: 1 hour

Equipment:
  mixing bowl, baking dish

Ingredients:
  4 to 6 apples, (McIntosh, Macoun, Rome, Cortland) 1 per person

Filling:
  1 cup raisins
  1/2 cup walnuts, roasted and chopped
  2 tbsp. tahini or peanut butter
  1 orange, grated and juiced (reserve for baking dish)
  1/4 tsp. cinnamon
  1/2 tsp. vanilla (optional)
  pinch of sea salt

Procedure: Core apples and peel a 1-inch strip around center of apple or pierce skin with a fork to prevent bursting. Place apples in baking dish. (I use a glass pie pan.) Mix filling ingredients in a bowl. Fill center of each apple. Pour orange juice into baking dish. Cover with foil; bake at 375°F. for 30 minutes. Test with fork to see if tender. Continue baking if needed.

Variations:
- Substitute chopped dates or other dried fruit for raisins.
- Try almonds or pecans instead of walnuts.
- Add a pinch of powdered ginger or allspice.

Mocha Pudding

Mocha pudding is made in two steps: first, grain coffee is simmered with the ingredients for kanten and allowed to cool. Next, tahini is blended in for a pudding consistency.

Servings: 6
Time: 20 minutes;
  2 hours cooling

Equipment:
  pan, bowl, whisk, blender

Ingredients:
  1 qt. apple juice
  1 tbsp. grain coffee powder (Cafix or Pero)
  1/4 cup rice or maple syrup (optional)
  1/2 cup agar flakes

Procedure: Bring apple juice, grain coffee, sweetener and agar flakes to boil in pan; then simmer 10 minutes until agar dissolves. Add kuzu dissolved in cold water and pinch of sea salt; stir until clear. Add vanilla. Pour into bowl; allow to cool. Refrigerate for 1/2 hour. Blend the entire mixture with the tahini in blender. When smooth, refrigerate until ready to eat. Garnish with lemon slices.

Variations:
- 1 tbsp. carob powder can be added.
- Serve with crunch or roasted nuts.
- Blend in 1 ripe banana; garnish with coconut.

2 tbsp. kuzu or arrowroot,
  dissolved in 1/4 cup
  water
pinch of sea salt
1 tsp. vanilla
2 tbsp. tahini

Garnish:
6 round slices of lemon

Raisin and Rice Pudding

The Greeks have mastered the art of making rice pudding, simmering white rice in milk until soft and serving with a dash of cinnamon. This creamy texture can be created by blending one cup of soft-cooked brown rice with roasted tahini until smooth, then returning this cream to the simmering rice. It is almost impossible to give exact proportions: it depends on the amount of ingredients you have. Here is a basic recipe.

Servings: 6 or more
Time: 3 to 4 hours

Equipment:
  soup pot, flame tamer,
  blender or food processor,
  skillet

Ingredients:
  2 to 3 cups cooked brown
    rice
  6 to 7 cups apple juice
  1/4 cup golden raisins
  1/2 cup dark raisins
  1 cinnamon stick
  1 vanilla bean
  pinch of sea salt
  2 tbsp. roasted tahini
  1/2 tsp. grated lemon rind

Garnish:
  1/2 cup toasted walnuts
    or almonds for garnish
    (optional)

Procedure: Mix rice, juice, raisins, cinnamon stick, vanilla bean and a pinch of sea salt in a heavy pot; stir; place on flame tamer. Barely simmer for 3 to 4 hours, stirring occasionally. If rice absorbs all the liquid and starts to look dry, add more liquid. Once rice is very soft, roast tahini in pan and place in blender with 1 cup of rice. Blend until smooth; return to rice and stir. Continue to simmer for 15 to 20 minutes. Add lemon peel for flavor. Garnish with toasted nuts.

Variations: Serve warm with roasted chopped nuts.
• If you don't have a vanilla bean and cinnamon stick, add vanilla extract and a pinch of ground cinnamon when the pudding is soft and ready to serve.
• Vary the flavorings: cardamon pods give a unique flavor when cooked with the rice.
• Leftover barley or millet could be added to rice.

Menu Suggestions: I usually serve rice pudding after a light meal of soup and vegetables. Rice pudding provides a sweet morning start-up as well as a nourishing snack. It is a good way to get kids of all ages to eat their grains.

Note: Raisin and Rice Pudding can be baked in the oven, once the rice has thickened; pour grain into an oiled baking dish; sprinkle with cinnamon and bake at 350°F. for 20 minutes. Reheat rice pudding this way, for a warming dessert, breakfast or snack.

Good Crunch

To make good crunch, flour is needed to hold oats and nuts together. Bake in a low 325°F. oven, stirring occasionally. Vary the ingredients: dried fruit or raisins may be added once crunch has cooled. I bring crunch along on hiking and skiing trips for breakfast or snacks.

Servings: 6 or more
Time: 1 hour

Equipment:
   mixing bowl, baking tray

Ingredients:
   1 1/2 cups rolled oats
   1/2 cup whole wheat
      pastry flour
   1/4 cup sunflower seeds
   1/4 cup almonds, chopped
   1/3 cup maple syrup
   1/3 cup oil
   1 tsp. vanilla
   pinch of sea salt
   1/2 tsp. cinnamon

Procedure: Mix all ingredients in a bowl until well-coated. Spread on a lightly oiled cookie sheet. Bake at 325°F. for 1/2 to 1 hour. Stir 2 or 3 times to turn crunch over and bake evenly. Allow to cool; store in sealed container. Keeps for 1 week.

Variations:
- Add chopped walnuts or cashews, sesame seeds or coconut in place of almonds.
- Add 1 cup raisins or chopped dried fruit to cool granola.
- Top applesauce or stewed fruit with crunch.
- Serve with soy milk.
- Add crunch to cookies or muffins.

"No-Bake" Blueberry Couscous Cake

Here's a welcome change in the dessert department: a fast stove-top cake that even kids can make. It's easily digestible. A basic recipe to adapt to other fruits; garnish with sliced fruits and top with glistening glazes.

Servings: 4 or more
Time: 15 minutes

Equipment:
   saucepan, ceramic or
   glass baking dish

Dry Ingredients:
   2 cups couscous
   pinch of sea salt

Liquid Ingredients:
   5 cups apple juice
   1 lemon, grated rind and
      juice
   1 pt. blueberries

Procedure: Bring apple juice and sea salt to a boil in saucepan; then add lemon rind and juice. Add 2 cups couscous; lower flame; stir couscous until almost thick. Remove from stove; stir in washed berries. Some berries will burst, giving blue streaks. Rinse a ceramic or glass baking dish; pour cake into it. Allow to cool and cut into squares. Garnish with roasted nuts or fruit sauce.

Variations:
- Apple-Raisin: substitute 1 cup chopped apples, plus 1 cup raisins for blueberries. Add raisins to boiling apple juice to soften before adding couscous and chopped apple.
- Raspberry: substitute raspberries for blueberries.
- Basic Couscous Cake: omit blueberries; add chopped dried or fresh fruit. Top with glaze.

Puff Dough

A versatile, workable dough which can be used for knishes, pies and strudel. This basic recipe calls for boiling the liquid ingredients and mixing them into the dry. Knead quickly and let rest.

Servings: 2 pie crusts
Time: 10 minutes; cool, 30 minutes

Equipment:
 small pot, mixing bowl, sifter, rolling pin, whisk, waxed paper or baker's cloth

Ingredients:
 1 cup water
 1/4 tsp. sea salt
 1/3 to 1/2 cup oil (corn, safflower or sesame)
 1 1/2 cup, whole wheat pastry flour, sifted
 1 cup unbleached white flour, sifted
 1 cup cornmeal or corn flour, sifted

Procedure: Boil water; add pinch of sea salt. Whip in the corn oil; pour this mixture into the flours. Mix well. Work quickly to form a smooth dough. Knead 1 minute; place in bowl. Allow to cool before rolling dough out. Divide dough in half for pie crusts. Roll out between floured sheets of waxed paper.

Variations:
- Try different combinations of flours. Keep the ratio of 3 cups flour to 1 cup water.
- If making a single pie crust or small strudel, halve the recipe.

Pie-in-the-Sky Crust

Lynne developed this foolproof recipe.

Servings: 1 9-inch double crust or 2 9-inch single crust pies
Time: 10 minutes

Equipment:
 mixing bowl, rolling pin, waxed paper, pie pans

Ingredients:
 1 1/2 cups whole wheat pastry flour
 1 1/2 cups unbleached white flour
 1/2 tsp. sea salt
 1/2 cup corn oil
 4 to 6 tbsp. apple juice, cold

Procedure: Sift flours and sea salt. Rub in oil until flour forms pea-sized balls. Dribble cold juice over flour. Press with a fork, until dough forms 1 ball. Knead gently 1 to 2 minutes to smooth texture. Divide dough in half. Refrigerate 1/2 hour. Roll out between waxed paper 2-inches larger than pie pan. For 2 pies: fit crusts into oiled, floured pie pans. Tuck over-hanging edges in and crimp. For 1 Pie: fit 1 crust as described and fill. Wet edges and fit top crust in place. Press to seal; trim excess dough and crimp edges. Prick vent hole in top crust. Bake as directed in various pie recipes.

Variations:
- Substitute 1/2 cup rolled oats buzzed in blender for 1/2 cup flour.

Note: Pie doughs roll out best when cool. They may be prebaked (10 minutes at 325°F.).

Autumn Apple Pie

Quintessential American apple pie never lets you down. With only the natural flavors of cooked fruit, this pie fills the craving for a sweet indulgence.

Servings: 1 pie
Time: 1 hour

Equipment:
  mixing bowl, pie pan

Ingredients:
  1 recipe pie crust
  5 to 6 cups chunked apples
    (preferably 2 or more
    varieties)
  pinch of sea salt
  1/2 cup raisins (optional)
  2 tbsp. whole wheat
    pastry or white flour
  1 tsp. cinnamon

Glaze:
  1 tbsp. maple syrup, 1 tsp.
    water (optional)

Procedure: Make pie crust. Cool. Roll out into 2 circles. Toss ingredients together. Fill shell. Fit top crust. Bake at 425°F. for 15 minutes, then 350°F. for 30 minutes. Glaze with 1 tbsp. maple syrup and 1 tsp. water. Cool before serving.

Variations:
• Add 1/2 cup roasted chopped walnuts.
• Substitute 2 cups of peaches or pears for 2 cups apples.

Pumpkin Spice Pie

Pumpkin pies are so good, they deserve to be made before and after Thanksgiving. My dad's squash patch keeps us supplied with pie filling from October to March.

Servings: 2 9-inch (single
  crust) pies
Time: 2 hours

Equipment:
  pan or pressure cooker,
  bowl, blender, pie pans

Ingredients:
  1 recipe pie crust
  6 to 8 cups pumpkin purée
    (or buttercup or
    butternut squash)
  2 eggs (or 4 oz. soft tofu)
  1/4 cup arrowroot or
    3 tbsp. kuzu
  1/2 to 1 cup apple juice
  1/3 cup maple syrup
    (optional)

Procedure: Wash 1 medium-sized pumpkin, cut in half and remove seeds. Oil baking dish and add water to cover bottom of pan. Place pumpkin into dish; cut side down; cover with aluminum foil and bake at 375°F. 1 to 1 1/2 hours until a fork easily pierces skin. Dissolve arrowroot in 1/2 cup juice. Blend with eggs (or tofu), maple syrup, sea salt and spices. Pour into cup. Cube pumpkin; place in blender with above mixture and purée in batches. Add more juice if needed to make thick purée. Fill 2 pie shells. Bake at 350°F. for 45 minutes. Garnish with chopped walnuts. Cool and serve. You will find that the flavor improves and the pie is easier to slice after the first day.

Variations:
• Pumpkin can be pressure-cooked with 3 cups of apple juice for 20 to 30 minutes; then purée with remaining ingredients.

pinch of sea salt
2 tsp. cinnamon
1/2 tsp. each: nutmeg,
　cloves, ginger

Garnish:
1/2 cup chopped walnuts
　(optional)

Estella's Pecan Pie

This pie was an inspiration, created to satisfy my love of rich desserts with one that is dairy- and maple syrup-free.

Servings: 1 pie
Time:　　1 hour

Equipment:
　sauce pan, blender, mixing
　bowl, pie plate, rolling
　pin

Ingredients:

Filling:
1/2 cup dried apricots
1/2 cup dates, pitted
2 cups apple juice
2 tbsp. agar flakes
pinch of sea salt
1 1/2 tbsp. kuzu dissolved
　in 1/4 cup water
1 tsp. vanilla
2 cups roasted pecans

Crust:
1 cup unbleached white
　flour
1/2 cup whole wheat
　pastry flour
pinch of sea salt
1/4 cup oil (corn or
　safflower)
3 to 4 tbsp. cold apple
　juice
pinch of coriander or
　cardamon for extra
　flavor (optional)

Procedure: Rinse dried fruits; combine with juice, agar and sea salt in a saucepan. Bring to a boil; lower flame and simmer 20 minutes. Make crust following directions from Pie-in-the-Sky recipe and prebake. Crust must be pricked with a fork several times to prevent warping. Bake crust in 350°F. oven for 15 minutes or until light gold. Pecans can be roasted at the same time, but watch them carefully—pecans burn easily after 10 minutes. When the dried fruit is plump and agar is dissolved, add kuzu and stir until clear. Add vanilla. Purée fruit mixture in a blender or food processor until creamy smooth. Save 1/2 cup of whole pecans to garnish top of pie. Chop the rest. Mix the remaining pecans with the fruit purée. Spoon mixture into baked pie crust. Arrange 1/2 cup pecans in design on top of pie. Allow to cool. This pie should slice neatly and still be creamy.

Variations: This basic recipe can be adapted to your own tastes.
- Other types of dried fruit can be substituted.
- Filberts, walnuts or almonds can be used instead of pecans.
- Lemon or orange zest and juice can be used for lighter flavor.

Mom's Apple Crisp

Mom's choice for dessert because it's easier than apple pie. Sweet crunchy apple crisp and its variants, pear, blueberry-apple or peach crisp, are desserts we never resist.

Servings: **6 or more**
Time: **1 hour**

Equipment:
  baking dish or pie pan

Ingredients:
  **1 1/2 to 2 lbs. apples,
    sliced
  pinch of sea salt
  pinch of cinnamon
  1/2 cup apple juice or
    cider**

Crisp:
  **2 cups rolled oats
  1/2 cup whole wheat
    pastry flour
  1/4 cup oil
  2 tbsp. maple syrup
  pinch of sea salt
  pinch of cinnamon**

Procedure: Rinse apples (peeling is optional). Quarter them; remove seeds and slice across. Place apples in baking dish. Sprinkle with sea salt and cinnamon and pour juice over fruit. Apples should come to the top of the baking dish or above it. Mix crisp ingredients and crumble over apples evenly. Press down gently; bake at 350°F. for 30 to 45 minutes, until crust is crunchy and golden, and apples are soft.

Variations:
- Pear Crisp: mix pears and apples together.
- Peach or Blueberry Crisp: mix with apples or pears.
- Oat-Nut Crisp: add 1/2 to 1 cup chopped nuts.
- Omit pastry flour; add oatmeal flour.
- Reduce sweetener or try your own favorite.

Lorrie's Date-Nut Bars

Here's a superlative dessert: creamy date filling with a hint of orange between crunchy oat-nut layers. A treat for tea time, or after meals, it takes less time to make than cookies.

Servings: **12 to 14 2-inch
    squares**
Time: **30 to 40 minutes**

Equipment:
  **pot, 2 mixing bowls,
  baking dish, spatula**

Ingredients:

For Filling:
  **1 cup dates, pitted or
    pieces
  1/2 cup water
  juice and grated rind of
    1 orange
  pinch of sea salt**

Procedure: Simmer the dates in 1/2 cup water until soft. Add the orange juice, rind and a pinch of sea salt. Mash the date mixture to a spreadable paste; set aside. In a separate bowl, blend crust ingredients: maple syrup, corn oil and water. Mix the dry crust ingredients and combine with liquid. Divide dough in half. Oil the baking dish and press half the dough in the bottom. Spread the date mixture over the dough evenly. Crumble the remaining half of the dough evenly over the dates. Press gently. Bake at 350°F. for 20 minutes, until crisp and golden. Cut while still warm.

Variations:
- Use apricots instead of dates.
- Try 1/2 cup raisins and 1/2 cup dried apples, cooked and puréed in place of dates.

For Crust:
Liquid Ingredients:
  1/4 cups maple syrup
  1/4 cup corn oil
  1/4 cup water

Dry Ingredients:
  2 cups oatmeal
  1 cup chopped nuts
    (almonds, walnuts or
    pecans)
  1 cup whole wheat pastry
    flour
  1/2 tsp. cinnamon
  pinch of sea salt

- Vanilla extract can be used instead of orange juice and rind.

Coconut-Orange Jewels

The natural palatability of dates and coconut will satisfy any sweet tooth. If you like this cookie, you'll love the Outrageous Coconut-Date Cake (page 231).

Servings: 14 to 16 cookies
Time: 30 minutes

Equipment: mixing bowl,
  blender or processor,
  cookie sheet

Dry Ingredients:
  1 cup walnuts, finely
    chopped or ground
  1 cup coconut, grated
  1 cup unbleached white
    flour
  1/8 tsp. sea salt

Liquid Ingredients:
  1/2 cup dates, pitted and
    chopped
  1 tsp. orange rind
  1/2 cup fresh orange juice
  1/4 cup corn oil

Filling:
  orange marmalade or
    walnut halves

Procedure: Chop walnuts very fine or grind to coarse flour. Add coconut, flour and sea salt. Chop dates. If dates are hard, heat orange juice and pour over them. Soak until soft; then chop. Mix liquid ingredients by hand, blender or food processor until smooth. Add liquid to dry ingredients. Preheat oven to 350° F. and oil cookie sheet; form walnut-sized balls; flatten slightly; make a thumb print and fill print with orange marmalade. Bake at 350°F. for 10 minutes until golden.

Variations:
- Substitute cashews or pecans for walnuts.
- Garnish cookies with walnut halves instead of orange marmalade.
- Use apricot or date purée in place of marmalade.

Michael's Peanut Butter Cookies

Michael Vitti, the marvelous baker at The Rising Tide Natural Food Store in Long Island, New York, shares this crowd-pleasing cookie recipe.

Servings: 30 cookies
Time: 30 minutes

Equipment:
  2 mixing bowls, blender,
  2 cookie sheets

Dry Ingredients:
  3 cups whole wheat
    pastry flour
  1/2 tsp. sea salt

Liquid Ingredients:
  1 lb. peanut butter
  2/3 cup corn oil
  3/4 cup maple syrup
  1 tsp. vanilla

Procedure: Sift flour into mixing bowl; add sea salt. Cream peanut butter, oil, maple syrup and vanilla together in a separate bowl or blender until smooth. Add peanut mixture to flour and stir gently to mix evenly. Preheat oven to 350°F. Lightly oil cookie sheets. Form dough into walnut-sized balls and press down with fork. Bake 10 to 15 minutes until light brown. Cookies will be crumbly while hot; allow to cool 10 minutes; then remove to cooling rack or platter.

Variations:
- Avoid using freshly ground peanut butter: cookies will crumble.
- Substitute cashew or almond butter for peanut butter.
- Use half white flour, half pastry flour.
- Add one of the following: 1/2 cup chopped peanuts, 1/2 cup carob chips, 1/2 cup oatmeal or 1/4 cup bran.

Raspberry-Almond "Torte" Cookies

Linzer Tortes were the inspiration for these scrumptious cookies.

Servings: 16 to 18 cookies
Time: 30 minutes

Equipment:
  blender, mixing bowl, wire
  whisk or mixer, cookie
  sheet

Dry Ingredients:
  1 cup almonds, ground in
    blender
  1 cup rolled oats, ground
    in blender
  1 cup whole wheat
    pastry flour
  1/4 tsp. cinnamon
  pinch of sea salt

Procedure: Chop almonds very fine or grind in blender or food processor into coarse nut flour. Buzz oats into coarse flour. Combine dry ingredients in bowl. Whip corn oil and maple syrup together. Add wet to dry ingredients. Mix until well coated. Form walnut-sized balls and place on oiled cookie sheet. Press thumb gently in center, creating space for filling. Fill each cookie with 1/2 tsp. raspberry jam or purée. Bake at 350°F. for 10 to 15 minutes, or until golden brown.

Variations:
- Substitute filberts, walnuts or cashews for almonds.
- Apricot jam, purée or apple cider jelly can replace raspberry jam.
- Use rice syrup instead of maple syrup, for a crispy light cookie.

Liquid Ingredients:
  1/2 cup maple syrup
  1/2 cup corn oil

Filling:
  4 oz. raspberry jam or
    purée

Peanut Butter Cookies with Good 'Ole Granola─────

A cross between Michael's Peanut Butter Cookie recipe and good 'ole granola, for a crunchier treat in the lunchbox or a snack.

Servings: 20 cookies
Time: 30 minutes

Equipment:
  mixing bowl, cookie sheets

Liquid Ingredients:
  1 cup peanut butter
  1/2 cup maple syrup
  1/2 cup corn or safflower
    oil
  1/4 cup water
  1 tsp. vanilla

Dry Ingredients:
  1 1/2 cups granola
  2 1/2 çups pastry flour
  pinch of sea salt
  1 tsp. baking powder
    (optional)

Procedure: Blend liquid ingredients together until smooth. In separate bowl combine granola with sifted flour, sea salt and baking powder. Add to liquid ingredients; mix thoroughly. Spoon or roll into walnut-sized balls. Place on an oiled cookie sheet. Press down with fork that has been dipped in cold water (to prevent sticking). Another option is to make jelly drop cookies by pressing thumb into cookie and filling with jam or jelly. Bake at 350°F. till golden brown.

Variations:
- These cookies are a combination of 2 recipes. Create your own variations. Try adding orange or lemon peel for a tart flavor, or cinnamon or powdered ginger for spice.

Crispy Lemon-Walnut Cookies────────────

This recipe makes a large batch of light, crispy cookies, sweetened with raisins and apple juice. A good choice for snacks without maple syrup.

Servings: 30 cookies
Time: 30 minutes

Equipment:
  blender, bowl, cookie
    sheet

Dry Ingredients:
  2 cups walnuts, ground in
    blender or food
    processor

Procedure: Buzz walnuts in blender to rough meal. (They may need to be chopped first.) Buzz oatmeal to coarse flour. Mix with remaining dry ingredients in bowl. Purée raisins with apple juice until almost smooth. Add oil and blend again. Combine liquid to dry ingredients. Form into balls and gently press to make 2-inch circles. Garnish each cookie with a walnut half, if you wish. Bake at 350°F. for 10 to 15 minutes.

2 cups oatmeal, buzzed in
 blender to a coarse
 "flour"
1 1/2 cups whole wheat or
 unbleached white flour
pinch of sea salt
1/2 tsp. allspice
1/4 tsp. ginger
grated peel of one lemon
 and juice

Liquid Ingredients:
 1 cup raisins
 1 cup apple juice or cider
 1/2 cup oil
 1/4 cup rice syrup or
  other sweetener

Variations:
- If raisins are "dry," bring to a boil in apple juice to soften; then purée.
- Substitute almonds, pecans or filberts for walnuts.
- Try orange juice instead of lemon.
- Make "jelly-drop" cookies by pressing thumb print into cookie and fill with jam or jelly.
- Add pinch of ground cinnamon, cloves.
- Add 1 tsp. orange rind.
- Add 1/2 cup chopped dates.

Basic Great Cake Recipe

This recipe makes two 10-inch layers, enough for a party. Try some of its variations below—or improvise your own. It's a favorite at the Five Season's Restaurant in Boston.

**Servings: 10 to 12: 2 9-inch
 rounds or one large 10-
 inch × 14-inch cake**
Time: 1 hour

Equipment:
 mixing bowl, blender,
 2 10-inch cake pans

Dry Ingredients:
 3 cups whole wheat
  pastry flour
 2 cups unbleached white
  flour
 1/2 tsp. sea salt
 2 tbsp. baking powder

Liquid Ingredients:
 1 1/4 cups corn oil
 1 1/2 cups maple syrup
 1 tsp. vanilla extract
 1 cup apple juice
 8 oz. (1/2 block) soft tofu

Procedure: Sift dry ingredients. Combine liquid ingredients in a blender, until creamy; stir into dry. Whip until smooth. Batter should be thick but pourable. Oil pans and fill equally with batter. Bake at 375°F. for 45 minutes or longer—until cake tests done. Cool on rack. Frost with The Glaze (page 213) or Raisin (Fruit) Purée (page 213), or with Fruit Kanten.

Variations:
- Orange-Poppyseed: substitute fresh orange juice for apple juice; add 1 tbsp. orange rind and 1/3 cup poppyseeds.
- Lemon-Walnut: substitute 1/4 cup lemon juice for 1/4 cup apple juice; add 1 tbsp. lemon rind and 1/2 to 1 cup toasted, chopped walnuts.
- Almond Spice: substitute 2 tsp. almond extract for vanilla; add 1/2 tsp. cinnamon, 1 tsp. ginger and 1 tsp. cloves.

Outrageous Coconut-Date Cake

This moist and rich cake, sweetened with coconut milk, dates and orange, receives raves from family and friends. The recipe makes two small layers or one large (10-inch × 14-inch) cake.

Servings: 6 to 8
Time: 1 hour

Equipment:
saucepan, mixing bowl,
blender, 2 10-inch cake
pans or 1 10-inch × 14-inch
cake pan

Liquid Ingredients:
2 cups coconut milk
(bottled or fresh)
1 1/2 cups dates, pitted
1/2 cup oil (corn or
safflower)
1 orange, grated and
juiced

Dry Ingredients:
1 cup unbleached flour,
sifted
2 cups whole wheat
pastry flour, sifted
1 tbsp. baking powder
1 tsp. baking soda
pinch of sea salt
1/2 cup coconut, toasted

Procedure: Combine coconut milk and dates in saucepan. Simmer until dates are very soft. Place dates and coconut mixture in blender; add oil, grated orange and juice; purée until smooth. Sift dry ingredients into bowl. Pour liquid ingredients into dry; mix until well coated. The batter will be thick. Spoon batter into oiled baking dish. (Line with baker's paper, if available.) Bake at 350°F. for 35 to 45 minutes, until firm and golden. This cake can be made in a mixer.

Variations:
- Mixed Fruit Cake: use a mixture of dried fruits—prunes, raisins, apples, etc. with dates.
- Nutty-Coconut-Date Cake: add 1/2 cup roasted, chopped nuts.

Menu Suggestions: Spread cake with orange or other fruit glaze. Garnish with extra toasted coconut, roasted almonds or walnuts, or orange slices.

Estella's Corn Bread

Orange-flavored corn bread can be served with the meal or as dessert. It's a tasty breakfast bread or snack. I also use this recipe to make "strawberry shortcake." Try it with any fruit sauce—blueberry, peach or cherry—for an instant hit.

Servings: 6 or more
Time: 45 minutes

Equipment:
grater, mixing bowl,
blender, mixer or pro-
cessor, cake or bread pan
or cast-iron skillet

Procedure: Mix liquid ingredients together until creamy smooth (if using tofu, it must be puréed in blender). Add grated orange rind and juice. Liquid ingredients may also be combined in mixer, processor, or by hand. Sift dry ingredients in separate bowl. The bran can be added back to sifted flour if you wish, or saved for muffins. Combine wet ingredients with dry. Mix until there are no lumps. The batter should be pourable, not thick like muffin batter. Add more water if needed. Bake at 375°F. for 10 to 15 minutes.

Liquid Ingredients:
  3/4 cup oil (corn or
    safflower)
  3/4 cup maple syrup
  4 oz. tofu (or 2 eggs)
  1 1/2 to 2 tsp. grated
    orange rind
  1 orange, juiced and
    grated (optional)
  1 1/2 cups water

Dry Ingredients:
  2 cups cornmeal, sifted
  1 cup unbleached white
    flour, sifted
  1 cup whole wheat
    pastry flour, sifted
  4 tsp. baking powder
  pinch of sea salt

The bread should crack slightly and turn golden. Bake in a cake or bread pan. A cast-iron skillet works great, too, and has that country look when fresh corn bread is served hot out of it, at the table.

Variations:
- Omit orange flavor and add 1/2 cup water or juice instead.
- Reduce maple syrup and add juice for less sweet bread.

Menu Suggestions:

Breakfast:	*Dinner:*
Corn bread	Chili or Black Bean Soup
Stewed Fruit or	Corn Bread
Cranberry Relish	Green Salad with Oil and
	Vinegar Dressing
Creamy Oatmeal	Mocha Pudding
with Raisins	
Corn Bread	*Dessert:*
	Slices of Corn Bread
	covered with Strawberry
	Kanten or Cherries
	Jubilee

Angie's Banana Bread

Angie Malerba ingeniously adapted this popular dessert. One loaf is never enough. Grated zucchini can be used instead of bananas.

Servings: 6 to 8
Time: 1 hour

Equipment:
  flour sifter, blender, 2
  bowls, bread pan

Dry Ingredients:
  1 cup whole wheat
    pastry flour
  1 cup unbleached white
    flour
  1 1/2 tsp. baking powder
  1/2 tsp. baking soda
  1/2 tsp. sea salt

Procedure: Sift dry ingredients in large bowl. Mash bananas with fork on plate or in small bowl; set aside. Whip liquid ingredients together. (If using tofu, purée in blender with Cafix and water.) Add liquid ingredients to dry and mix; add bananas and mix to smooth consistency. Oil bread pan; fill 2/3 full and bake at 375°F. for 45 minutes or until toothpick comes out dry.

Variations: Try 1 of the following:
- Add 1/2 cup roasted, chopped walnuts or pecans.
- Zucchini Bread: substitute 1 cup grated zucchini for mashed banana.

Liquid Ingredients:
  2 ripe bananas, mashed
  1/3 cup oil
  2/3 cup maple syrup
  1 tsp. vanilla
  1 tsp. Cafix (grain coffee)
     dissolved in 1/2 cup
     water
  1 egg or 4 oz. tofu

Stuffed Dates

My Aunt Millie always sent us a box of dried fruit from Arizona for Christmas. We particularly loved the stuffed dates. Here is a new version with miso and tahini.

Servings: 12 to 18 dates
Time: 10 minutes

Equipment:
  bowl, wooden spoon

Ingredients:
  1 lb. large dates, pitted
  1 tbsp. miso (red or kome)
  1 tbsp. barley malt
  1 tbsp. tahini
  cinnamon to taste
  1 lemon, juiced and rind
     grated
  1 cup walnuts, roasted
     and finely chopped

Procedure: Mix all stuffing ingredients except walnuts until smoothly blended; add walnuts. Slit and stuff dates.

Variations:
 • Vary nuts. Whole nuts can be used as garnish.
 • Vary spices; try ginger, allspice or cardamom.

Distributors and Manufacturers of Natural Foods

Applegate Natural Foods, Inc., 7805 SW Hunziker Rd., Portland, OR 97223
(503–684–0030)

Arrowhead Mills, P.O. Box 2059, Hereford, Texas 79045
(806–364–0730)

Balanced Foods Inc., 2501 71st St., No. Bergen, NJ 07047
(800–634–3663; 201–662–7200)

Chico-San, Inc., 1062 Progress St., Pittsburgh, PA 15212
(412–237–3900)

Collegedale Distributors, P.O. Box 626, Collegedale, TN 37315
(800–251–6258; 615–238–4121)

Earthly Organics, Inc., 850 East Luzerne St., Philadelphia, PA 19124
(800–523–3161; 215–423–3113)

Eden Foods, Inc., 701 Tecumseh Rd., Clinton, MI 49236
(517–456–7424; 313–973–9400)

Edwards and Sons, Trading Company, Box 271, Union, N.J. 07083

Erewhon Inc., Watham St. Wilmington, MA
(617–657–8120)

Grainaissance Inc., 800 Heinz Ave., Berkeley, CA 94710
(415–849–2866)

Granum, 2901 N.E. Blakeley St., Seattle, WA 98105
(206–525–0051)

Erewhon Natural Foods, 236 Washington St., Brookline, MA 02146
(617–738–4516)

Food For Health, Inc., 3839 W. Indian School Rd., Box 23152, Phoenix, AZ 85019
(602–269–2371)

Granum, P.O. Box 14075, Seattle, WA 98114
(206–323–0892)

Great Divide Exchange, Box 5512, Missoula, MT 59806
(406–543–6480)

Great Eastern Sun, 92 Macintosh Rd., Asheville, NC 28206
(704–252–3090)

Hatch Natural Products, Ltd., 745 Germanna Highway, Culpeper, VA 22701
(703–825–4302)

Landau Co., 19 Heyward St., Brooklyn, NY 11211
(212–875–5702)

Lundberg Rice, P.O. Box 369, Richvale, CA 95974
(916–882–4551)

Mountain Ark Trading Company, 120 S. East St., Fayetteville, AR 72701
(501–442–7191)

Nature's Best, 19801 S. Vermont, Torrance, CA 90502
  (800–262–1783)
Neshaminy Valley Natural Foods Distributor, Ltd., 421–E Pike Rd., Huntington Valley,
  PA 19006
  (215–364–8440)
New England Organic, 24 Jytek Park, Leominster, MA 01453
  (617–537–6523)
Northcoast Co-op, 86 E St., Eureka, CA 95501
  (707–445–3185)
Oak Feed Store, 3030 Grand Ave., Coconut Grove, FL 33133
  (305–448–7595)
The Pavo Co., Inc., 7041 Boone Ave., N., Minneapolis, MN 55428
  (612–533–4525)
Premier Japan, P.O. Box 3150, Union, NJ 07083
Rainbow Natural Foods Dist., 4613 Monaco Pkwy., Denver, CO 80216
  (303–320–5441)
Rainbow Natural Foods, 3121 N. Rockwell, Chicago, IL 60618
  (312–539–2700)
Rainbow Wholesale, 1330 Fitzgerald, San Francisco, CA 94124
  (415–822–6000)
Shojin Natural, Ltd., P.O. Box 669, Captain Cook, HI 96704
  (808–322–3651)
Stow-Mills, Quinn Road, P.O. Box 816, Brattleboro, VT 05301
  (802–257–4666)
Tochi Products Distributing, 1107 2nd Ave., North, P.O. Box 2215, Fargo, ND 58108
  (701–232–7717)
Tree of Life, Inc., 315 Industrial Dr., P.O. Box 410, St. Augustine, FL 32085–0410
  (904–824–8181)
Walnut Acres, Penns Creek, PA 17862
  (717–837–0601)
Wheat Berries/Commodities, 117 Hudson St., New York, NY 10013
  (212–334–8330)

Bibliography

Abehsera, Michel. *Cooking for Life*. New York: Avon Books, 1971

Aihara, Cornellia. *Macrobiotic Kitchen: Key to Good Health*. Japan: Japan Publications, 1982

Arasaki, Seibin & Teruko. *Vegetables from the Sea: To Help You Look and Feel Better*. Japan: Japan Publications, 1983

Ballentine, Martha. *Himalayan Mountain Cookery*. Honesdale, Pa: Himalayan International Institute, 1976.

Brown, Edward Espe. *The Tassajara Bread Book*. Berkeley, Ca: Shambala Publications, 1970

Calella, John R. *Cooking Naturally*. Berkeley, Ca.: And/Or Press, 1978

Colbin, Annemarie. *The Book of Whole Meals*. New York: Ballantine, 1983

Esko, Edward & Wendy. *Macrobiotic Cooking for Everyone*. Japan: Japan Publications, 1980

Esko, Wendy. *Introducing Macrobiotic Cooking*. Japan: Japan Publications, 1979

Farwagi, Peta Lyn. *Full of Beans*. New York: Harper & Row Publishers, 1978

Haydock, Yukio and Bob. *Japanese Garnishes*. New York: Holt, Rinehart and Winston, 1980

Kushi, Aveline Tomoko. *How to Cook with Miso*. Japan: Japan Publications, 1978

Kushi, Michio & Aveline with Jack, Alex. *Macrobiotic Diet*. Japan: Japan Publications, 1985

Levitt, Jo Ann; Smith, Linda; and Warren, Christine. *Kripalu Kitchen*. Kripalu Publication, 1980

Morash, Marion. *The Victory Garden Cookbook*. New York: Alfred Knopf, 1982

Nearing, Helen. *Simple Food for the Good Life*. New York: Delacorte Press, 1980

Ohsawa, Lima. *Macrobiotic Cuisine*. Japan: Japan Publications, 1984

Shandler, Nia and Michael, *How to Make All the Meat You Eat Out of Wheat*. Rawson, Wade Publishers, 1980

Shurtleff, William, and Aoyagi, Akiko. *The Book of Tofu*. Brookline, Mass.: Autumn Press, 1975

Tudge, Colin. *Future Food*. New York: Harmony Books, 1980

Watanabe, Tokuji & Kishi, Asako. *The Book of Soybeans: Nature's Miracle Protein*. Japan: Japan Publications, 1984

Weber, Marcea. *The Sweet Life*. Japan: Japan Publications, 1981

Recipe Index

240

Index

244